Lessons from History of Education

In the **World Library of Educationalists**, international experts themselves compile career-long collections of what they judge to be their finest pieces – extracts from books, key articles, salient research findings, major theoretical and practical contributions – so the world can read them in a single manageable volume. Readers will be able to follow themes and strands of the topic and see how their work contributes to the development of the field.

Richard Aldrich has spent the last 30 years researching, thinking and writing about some of the key and enduring issues in History of Education. He has contributed over 15 books and 75 articles to the field.

In *Lessons from History of Education*, Richard Aldrich brings together 14 of his key writings in one place. Starting with a specially written Introduction, which gives an overview of his career and contextualises his selection, the chapters cover:

- understanding history of education
- the politics of education
- educational reformers
- curriculum and standards
- the teaching of history
- education otherwise.

This book not only shows how Richard Aldrich's thinking developed during his long and distinguished career, it also gives an insight into the development of the fields to which he contributed.

Richard Aldrich is Emeritus Professor of History of Education at the Institute of Education, University of London.

Contributors to the series include: Richard Aldrich, Stephen J. Ball, Jerome Bruner, John Elliott, Elliot W. Eisner, Howard Gardner, John K. Gilbert, Ivor F. Goodson, David Labaree, John White, E.C. Wragg.

World Library of Educationalists series

Lessons from History of Education

The selected works of Richard Aldrich

Richard Aldrich

Routledge
Taylor & Francis Group

LONDON AND NEW YORK

First published 2006
by Routledge
2 Park Square, Milton Park, Abingdon, Oxon OX14 4RN

Simultaneously published in the USA and Canada
by Routledge
270 Madison Ave, New York, NY 10016

Routledge is an imprint of the Taylor & Francis Group

© 2006 Richard Aldrich

Typeset in Sabon by
Newgen Imaging Systems (P) Ltd, Chennai, India
Printed and bound in Great Britain by
Cromwell Press, Trowbridge, Wiltshire

British Library Cataloguing in Publication Data
A catalogue record for this book is available
from the British Library

Library of Congress Cataloging in Publication Data
Aldrich, Richard.
   Lessons from history of education: the selected works of
Richard Aldrich / Richard Aldrich.
      p. cm.
      1. Education–Great Britain–History. I. Title.

LA631.A46 2005
370'.941'09–dc22   2005007378

ISBN 0–415–35891–4 (hbk)
ISBN 0–415–35892–2 (pbk)

For Averil

CONTENTS

ACKNOWLEDGEMENTS

I should like to express my sincere appreciation to Anna Clarkson who commissioned this book and to her colleagues at Routledge who have seen it into print. For some 30 years, I have benefited from the example and encouragement of colleagues and students at the Institute of Education, University of London. I thank them all. I am particularly indebted to Susan Williams, Ruth Watts, William J. Reese and Dennis Dean for their supportive and incisive comments on an earlier draft of the Introduction.

I am most grateful to the following institutions for permission to reproduce the listed pieces.

British Academy

'Educational standards in historical perspective', in H. Goldstein and A. Heath (eds), *Educational Standards*, Oxford: Oxford University Press, 2000 (*Proceedings of the British Academy*, 102), pp. 39–56.

College of Teachers (formerly the College of Preceptors)

'Learning by playing', *Education Today*, MCB University Press, 1985, 35(2): 28–36.

Professor Anja Heikkinen and the University of Tampere

'Apprenticeship in England: an historical perspective', in A. Heikkinen and R. Sultana (eds), *Vocational Education and Apprenticeships in Europe – Challenges for Practice and Research*, Tampere: Tampereen Yliopisto, 1997, pp. 71–97.

Heinemann Educational Books

'New History: an historical perspective', in A.K. Dickinson, P.J. Lee and P.J. Rogers (eds), *Learning History*, London: Heinemann Educational Books, 1984, pp. 210–24.

Institute of Education, University of London

The End of History and the Beginning of Education, London: Institute of Education, 1997.

'A curriculum for the nation', in R. Aldrich and J. White (eds), *The National Curriculum beyond 2000: The QCA and the Aims of Education*, London: Institute of Education, 1998, pp. 41–63.

Manchester University Press

'Imperialism in the study and teaching of history', in J.A. Mangan (ed.), *'Benefits Bestowed'? Education and British Imperialism*, Manchester: Manchester University Press, 1988, pp. 23–38.

Routledge/Taylor & Francis Books

'Joseph Payne: critic and reformer', in R. Aldrich (ed.), *School and Society in Victorian Britain: Joseph Payne and the New World of Education*, New York: Garland, 1995, pp. 161–94.
'Family history and the history of the family', in R. Aldrich (ed.), *Public or Private Education? Lessons from History*, London: Woburn Press, 2004, pp. 127–43.
'Sir John Pakington and the Newcastle Commission', *History of Education*, Taylor and Francis, 1979, 8(1): 21–31.
'The three duties of the historian of education', *History of Education*, Taylor and Francis, 2003, 32(2): 133–43.
'From Board of Education to Department for Education and Employment', *Journal of Educational Administration and History*, University of Leeds, 2000, 32(1): 8–22.
'The role of the individual in educational reform', in C. Majorek, E. Johanningmeier, F. Simon and W. Bruneau (eds), *Schooling in Changing Societies: Historical and Comparative Perspectives*, Gent: CSHP, 1998 (*Paedagogica Historica* Supplementary Series IV), pp. 345–57.

These pieces are generally reproduced as they were published except for the elimination of repetitions, the correction of minor errors and the standardization of references.

INTRODUCTION

Starting points

'As nothing teaches, so nothing delights more than history. The first of these recommends it to the study of grown men, the latter makes me think it fittest for a young lad.'[1] So wrote John Locke in 1693. My delight in history was acquired as a young lad and has remained to this day. My belief that there are lessons to be drawn from history, and not least from history of education, has developed over many years as a student and teacher of the subject.

History – a term variously used to describe the occurrence, study, recording and interpretation of human and other events with particular reference to the dimension of time – is all embracing. Other subjects – from art to zoology – have their devotees, and rightly so, but nothing can be compared to history. For history encompasses everything that has happened, is happening and will happen. All knowledge is its province. The study of history is not merely informative; it is also potentially instructive for it enlarges our range of human experience.

Education has also been variously defined: as preparation for knowledge, as initiation into and development in worthwhile activities, as social control, as a country's biggest business. My own working definition has been that education is concerned with the promotion of knowledge over ignorance, of truth over falsehood, of concern for others over selfishness, of mental and physical well-being over despair and debility. While education may be variously defined, however, its centrality to human existence is not in doubt. 'Education will not supply all the answers to the problems that beset us, either as individuals or as a nation, but it is the best means of promoting intellectual, moral, physical and economic well-being.'[2]

Two important acknowledgements must be made at this point. The first is that some historians, including historians of education, would deny that it is possible to draw any lessons from history. The second is that different lessons may be drawn from consideration of the same events. Each of us brings her or his own assumptions, predispositions and frames of analysis to bear. These are shaped by a variety of factors, including individual and societal histories, experiences, beliefs and principles. Factors in my case include a wartime childhood in a heavily bombed part of south-east London and for two years as an evacuee in Wales, a host of defining adult moments in terms of personal and professional commitments, a never-ending spiritual and intellectual journey across the borderlands of religious belief and unbelief, and principles (though sadly less frequently practices) drawn from sources ranging from the Sermon on the Mount to Rudyard Kipling's poem, 'If'.[3]

My approach to education has been construed in the most fortunate circumstances. Six years of school teaching and eight in a college of education were followed by 30 years at the Institute of Education of the University of London, an institution with a metropolitan and international culture and characterized by 'brave leadership, challenging students, intellectual daring, wit, incandescent teaching, and fierce dedication to matters of the mind'.[4] This experience has been complemented by visiting professorships, lectures and consultancies in more than 20 countries.

What lessons can be drawn from history of education? Specific examples are to be found in this Introduction and in the conclusions to the several pieces included in the collection, but four basic lessons are drawn here.

The first is a response to the general question of what can be learned from history overall:

> My personal answer would be couched in terms of: an acquaintance with a much greater range of human experience than would be possible simply by reference to the contemporary world; an enlarged understanding of that experience which may promote an enlarged understanding of one's own potential and possibilities; opportunities for creating interpretations of human experience which may be of interest in themselves and which, though not directly transferable from one situation to another, may promote the capacity better to interpret other situations – both historical and contemporary; a more sophisticated awareness of the nature of knowledge and of truth.[5]

The second lesson is that the historian of education has a particular responsibility to draw conclusions from her or his study because the subject of education is not neutral but includes a concept of value or merit. For example, to teach someone to be a liar or a thief would be described not as education but as mis-education. A study of the history of education, therefore, has the potential to demonstrate not only how people have lived their lives in the past, but also how we may live better in the present and future. Such study is all-embracing. The site of struggle is not simply the school or the formal educational system; it is life itself. During the twentieth century, millions of lives were sacrificed and millions more blighted in pursuit of such creeds as nationalism, imperialism, fascism and communism. The twenty-first century has already seen the rise of elements of Christian neo-conservative and Islamic extremism. Of course the history of education may also be seen as 'a history of conflict, contest and grudging accommodation'. Nevertheless, 'There has been a broad consensus that education is a prime agent in increasing culture and civilization and in diminishing anarchy and barbarism.'[6]

The third lesson is that our journeys in the present and the future may be enhanced by having as accurate a map of the past as possible. Informed decision-making depends upon locating ourselves and our society accurately in time. For example, it is salutary to remember the extreme brevity, in historical perspective, of civilized human existence as we know it, and the miniscule span of time of those economic and social (including educational) contexts that are often taken for granted today. Although the Earth is millions of years old, 20,000 years ago most of what now constitutes the United Kingdom was under ice, while even 10,000 years later the entire population of the British Isles was 'possibly no more than a few hundred people'.[7] Less than 200 years ago the only means of land transport, apart from walking, was still by horse power. Elementary schooling for all was a product of the second half of the nineteenth century; secondary schooling for all of the second half of the twentieth. In 1900, university education in the United Kingdom was experienced by less than one per cent of the population. Even by 1962 this had only risen to four per cent.[8] Little wonder that the widely proclaimed target of 50 per cent participation in the first decade of the twenty-first century raises fundamental questions about the nature, provision and financing of higher education.

Two examples of the value of such a map of the past are provided here.

On the one hand, it is clear that the lack of an historical perspective can lead to avoidable errors, not least in the re-invention of the wheel (a potentially flawed wheel) by educational reformers ignorant of the fate of previous similar schemes. One instance is the fate of Education Action Zones, apparently established with little regard to the experience of the Educational Priority Areas, introduced some 30 years before following the report of the Plowden Committee of 1967. Indeed, the recent history of educational reform in the United Kingdom shows the limitations of quick fixes of a political or administrative kind. Structures are important, as are broader economic and social contexts, but successful education depends essentially upon the long-term commitment of good teachers and motivated students. Ravitch and Vinovskis and Semel and Sadovnik have provided substantial studies of lessons to be drawn from history of education in respect of school reform in the United States.[9] The first of these volumes provides a variety of examples – from the value of early childhood education for poor children to the application of business methods to school administration – in support of its general thesis that contemporary policy-makers in the United States who propose school reforms 'need the knowledge, experience and wisdom that history provides'.[10] Similarly, in their historical study of American progressive education Semel and Sadovnik argue that 'educational reformers would do well to study the child-centred progressive schools for models of what worked, what failed, and why'. They rightly conclude that 'It is time that educational reformers and practitioners stop reinventing the wheel. It is also time for historians of education to assume active roles in policy conversations.'[11]

An accurate historical map may serve not only in a cautionary capacity but also as a means of providing answers to what may otherwise appear to be baffling contemporary questions. For example, in 1993 the Secretary of State for Education, John Patten, was reported as asking 'Why don't people in this country feel they own state education?' An answer to this question, which demonstrates how during the nineteenth and twentieth centuries the ownership of education was removed from English people, is provided in *Education for the Nation*.[12] While conducting research for this book it became clear that this and many other key questions about education today can only be understood, and in some cases answered, by reference to history.

The final lesson is that historical study shows the complexity of human events, including the co-existence of continuities and changes. Continuities are represented by values, practices and institutions that have stood the test of time. Thus the fundamental attributes of a good teacher were much the same in the seventeenth century as they are in the twenty-first. So, too, were some of the basic pedagogical principles – for example, John Locke's advice to 'Praise in public; blame in private'.[13] Significant general and specific changes over time include the rise of a literate culture from the medieval period onwards and the increased participation of girls in formal schooling and of women in higher education over the last 150 years. Even changes, however, may exhibit some continuity in the shape of cycles or patterns. For example, the school curriculum has been a contested site between advocates of religious, child-centred, subject-based and vocational schemes, as exemplified by the Education Act of 1944, the Plowden Report of 1967, the Education Reform Act of 1988 and the establishment of the Department for Education and Employment (DfEE) in 1995.[14] In October 2004, the government introduced the first national framework for religious education in England.

One example of the co-existence of continuity and change is to be found in the history of the Institute of Education of the University of London. Soon after its foundation in 1902, a combination of location, size, singular purpose and quality of staff and students, coupled with the reluctance of the universities of Oxford and Cambridge to champion the subject of education, ensured its pre-eminent role in the training of teachers and educational research. Nevertheless, during the first century it experienced different identities – as the London Day Training College until 1932, thereafter as the University of London's Institute of Education with an additional role as the 'Central Institute' of a wider Institute of Education of some 30 associated colleges and departments of education between 1949 and 1975, and as a self-governing college of the University of London from 1987. It also occupied three different buildings – in Southampton Row from 1907, the north wing of the Senate House from 1938, and in Bedford Way from 1976.[15]

A second example of the co-existence of continuity and change is provided by *A Century of Education*. In this edited volume ten authors employ quite different approaches to such elements as chronology, primary and secondary sources and methodology in examining ten topics in the history of British education in the twentieth century. Nevertheless an explanatory framework of continuity and change lies at the heart of each chapter and of the book's overall conclusion.[16]

An understanding of the complexities of continuity and change is important in guarding against the assumption that the past has existed merely to lead to the present and that educational progress is similar to that in science or technology. As Elliot Eisner, one of the contemporary educational reformers included in this volume, has commented:

> Education will not have permanent solutions to its problems, we will have no 'breakthroughs', no enduring discoveries that will work for ever...What works here may not work there. What works now may not work then. We are not trying to invent radar or measure the rate of free fall in a vacuum. Our tasks are impacted by context, riddled with unpredictable contingencies, responsive to local conditions, and shaped by those we teach and not only by those we teach.[17]

The pieces in this collection have been selected to cover major themes from writings that span more than 20 years.[18] They are set principally within a British or English context. Limitations of space and format mean that some important themes, for example, those of the education of girls and women, schooling and social class and teacher education and training, do not appear as separate sections.[19] All, however, receive some coverage elsewhere, especially in the longest piece, 'Joseph Payne: critic and reformer'. This was originally published as a book chapter.[20] One piece was written as half of a monograph,[21] seven as journal articles or chapters in edited collections,[22] while four were originally delivered as lectures and subsequently published.[23] The eight examples of contemporary reformers are taken from speeches delivered in the capacity of Public Orator when presenting these distinguished figures for honorary awards at the Institute of Education, University of London.

The six parts into which this volume is divided, and the pieces within them, are arranged in thematic rather than chronological order. The first provides an exploration and explanation of my current understanding of history of education; the second is concerned with the politics of education, the theme which first brought me into the field and which has remained a continuing interest. Another fundamental and enduring theme – that of educational reformers – constitutes the third part. The next two deal with elements of the formal education system: curriculum and standards, and the teaching of history. The final part provides examples of learning and teaching outside of school under the heading of 'Education otherwise'.

Understanding history of education

'The three duties of the historian of education' – the duty to the people of the past, to the people of the present and to truth – was published in 2003 and represents my current understanding of history of education and of the role of the historian of education. The title and the theme were suggested by an article on family history by Peter Laslett, whose lectures on the history of political thought I attended as a Cambridge undergraduate in the 1950s. The approach is wide-ranging, not least because my own work has covered a variety of topics and addressed a broad range of audiences – historians and educationists, prospective and practising teachers, policy-makers and general public. The second piece, 'The end of history and the beginning of education', is based upon an inaugural lecture, somewhat belatedly delivered on 12 March 1997. The first half of the title is taken from Francis Fukuyama's concept of 'The end of history', which first appeared in an article of 1989. The second is derived from the increased importance of education, both as a subject of study and upon the political agenda, an importance confirmed by the Labour Party's 'Education, education, education' mantra in the general election of May 1997.

The pieces in this part represent an attempt to position my work along two lines (or between two gaps) – those that exist between historians and educationists and between modernist and postmodernist historians. In 1999, William Richardson sought to emphasize the distinction between the practice of 'academic historians who reconstruct the past in ways influenced by present concerns and of educationists who invoke the past in order to apply its lessons to present concerns'. He also characterized 'The end of history and the beginning of education' as 'the most recent manifestation of the latter'.[24] This may well be an apposite description of a lecture delivered to an audience composed primarily of educationists rather than historians but I believe that the historian of education can – indeed must – be both an historian and an educationist. Much depends upon context and audience. The selection of pieces for this collection has been influenced by its title and place in a series of works by 'key educationalists', but that choice does not diminish my continuing commitment as an 'academic historian'.

As for modernism and postmodernism, the broadening of discussions about the nature of history beyond those of such historians as E.H. Carr, Geoffrey Elton and Arthur Marwick to include perspectives drawn from the work of Jacques Derrida, Michel Foucault, Richard Rorty and Hayden White is to be welcomed.[25] Keith Jenkins has played a leading role in such discussions in the United Kingdom but his argument as put forward in *Why History? Ethics and Postmodernity?* (1999) that 'we now have enough intellectual power to begin to work for an individual and social emancipatory future *without* it [history]',[26] seems to me to be incorrect. The fundamental tenets which pervade the pieces in *Lessons from History of Education* are that the teaching and writing of history will exist for the foreseeable future, that such history should be as good as possible and that a major test of good history is that it approximates most closely to the truth. Jenkins dismisses truths as 'useful fictions',[27] and is at great pains to emphasize the gulf between 'postmodern' and 'modernist' histories, but eschews any answer 'to the frequently asked question of "what would a postmodern history look like?" . . . that would be too modernistic, too prefigurative for words'.[28] Few, if any, 'modernist' historians of today are guilty of the postmodern charge that they believe that historical writing equates exactly with historical events. They may, however, be sceptical about the credibility as historians of those who condemn their work as 'under-theorized' or maintain that history is 'as much invented as found'.

The politics of education

This part contains two strongly contrasting pieces. The first is based upon detailed research in primary sources, concerned with a relatively obscure political figure, and firmly located in the middle of the nineteenth century. The second provides an overview of politics and education throughout the twentieth century.[29] One of the great delights of being an historian (and indeed an educationist) is to engage in the two roles of 'splitter': a scholar who engages in the minutiae of research and produces the detailed monograph; and 'lumper': one who synthesizes the findings from such research and presents them in accessible form to a wider audience.

Educational politics have been a continuing interest and my belief, along with Semel and Sadovnik, that historians of education can 'assume active roles in policy conversations' has recently been strengthened as a member of the Institute of Education's School of Educational Foundations and Policy Studies. Clearly the relationship between historical writing and contemporary reformism can be a complex one, as Deborah Thom has recently shown with her account of Brian Simon 'as a successful but bashful political activist'.[30]

Any claims to objectivity on my part when working in this area are based upon a tripartite background. My maternal grandfather, Albert Edward Barnes, was a Labour Councillor and Mayor of Southwark and also worked for a time as caretaker at Transport House. My mother attended West Square School, Southwark in the same class as George Brown, the future Labour Foreign Secretary. My nineteenth-century political heroes were the Conservative Prime Ministers, Peel and Disraeli, while Sir John Pakington, the subject of my doctoral research, was a minister in three Conservative governments. For many years, I have been a member of the National Liberal Club.

The first piece, 'Sir John Pakington and the Newcastle Commission', had a long gestation. My initial research and writing in history of education was for an MPhil thesis entitled 'Education and the political parties, 1830–1870', completed in 1970. This topic was 'assigned' by my supervisor and former Postgraduate Certificate in Education (PGCE) tutor, A.C.F. Beales of King's College, London, and was one in a trio of theses designed to cover the politics of education from 1830 to 1944.[31] The topic proved to be of considerable interest to me and provided the material for a first publication,[32] but it also threw up a neglected figure, a person who had played a significant part in the educational politics of these years but hitherto had been hidden from history. One of the major lessons to be drawn from this process is that it may be necessary to conduct substantial preliminary research in order to identify some key historical figures and questions. Historical study (in common with other research) involves a perpetual interaction between questions and evidence. Sir John Pakington (1799–1880) thus became the topic of my PhD thesis[33] and the subject of a first monograph.[34] This piece not only examines one episode in Pakington's previously neglected contribution to the story of mid-nineteenth-century politics and education, but also shows that an appreciation of the man and his motives is essential to an understanding of the origins, nature and outcomes of that most important and misunderstood of the major Royal Commissions on education, the Newcastle Commission.

The second piece, 'From Board of Education to Department for Education and Employment', a survey of the central authority for education throughout the twentieth century, was commissioned for the millennium number of the *Journal of Educational Administration and History*. In constructing this article reference was naturally made to primary sources and to the published work of other scholars as well as to my own previous research into twentieth-century politics and education, two examples of which are mentioned here. One lesson, presented as the article's final conclusion – that the DfEE would not long survive – soon came to pass.[35] This judgement was based upon a substantial piece of research, funded by the Nuffield Foundation, which demonstrated the department's uniqueness in historical and comparative perspectives and the contrasting cultures of the two merged departments in terms of size and sphere of activity.[36] Moreover, the Education department had already experienced three reformulations and the Employment department no fewer than five.[37] Nevertheless, similarities and continuities were also apparent. For example, between 1900 and 1994 all but five of the 46 political heads of the Education department were men while between 1916 and 1994 there were 37 ministers for Employment of whom only three were women. Ministers in the two departments served for an average of two years, permanent secretaries for five years at Employment and six at Education.[38]

A second major piece of research that also provided material to draw lessons from the past with reference to current and future policy-making, concerned the Education Act of 1944. In the early 1980s historical discussions of this legislation frequently centred upon the relative roles of politicians and administrators in its generation, construction and ownership.[39] In November 1983, however, following an excellent paper on this theme by Kevin Jefferys at the Institute of Historical Research,[40] Patricia Leighton, then Principal Lecturer in Law at the Polytechnic of North London, and I repaired to the Theatre Bar of the Russell Hotel where we proceeded to draw up a different list of questions to ask about the 1944 Act. These included the identification of flaws in the original legislation and of problems of implementation. The resulting publication, *Education: Time for a New Act?*, which appeared in 1985, included four major proposals or lessons: that the roles of the several parties concerned in education needed much clearer definition; that the general direction of formal curricula and examinations should be kept under constant review by a body composed of representatives from a wide range of backgrounds; that the schooling, training and work experience of those in the 16–19 age range should be co-ordinated and rationalized; that the 1944 Act had outlived its usefulness and a major new Education Act was required.[41]

Educational reformers

The history of educational reform has long been situated within a context of broader social change.[42] The pieces in this part, however, are principally concerned with specific educational reformers and with the origins, processes and outcomes of their work. The first, 'The role of the individual in educational reform', draws upon research undertaken for two co-authored biographical dictionaries – the *Dictionary of British Educationists* (1989) and *Biographical Dictionary of North American and European Educationists* (1997) – with a total of some 1,000 entries.[43] Production of these works was made possible by adherence to a strict regime. Peter Gordon and I would meet every six weeks, choose names from our substantial lists of potential subjects and return in six weeks' time each with a minimum of ten completed brief biographies. Marc Depaepe has warned against the misuse of the great educators and the 'mystification and even prostitution of history to hagiographical, pedagogical hero worship'.[44] My experience of researching these individuals, however, led not to hero worship but rather to a greater understanding of their lives and work and of the economic, intellectual, political and social contexts within which they were construed, and in many instances to a profound respect for their achievements. Classification and analysis of the subjects contained in these and two other volumes of educational biography also enabled conclusions to be drawn here about the construction of history, universality, continuity, competition and change and consumers of education. One notable difference between the two volumes was the much higher percentage of female subjects in the latter. This reflected both the authors' enlarged perception of the term 'educationist' and the increased number of relevant secondary sources.

The second piece examines elements in the reform agenda of Joseph Payne (1808–76), the first professor of education in England. In contrast to the scholarly process that led to my identification of Sir John Pakington as a subject worthy of study, this interest was sparked by a moment of acute embarrassment at a College of Preceptors' reception when I failed to remember Payne's name.[45] Preliminary research produced some surprising coincidences. Payne's first teaching post had been at the Rodney House Academy in the New Kent Road in Southwark, almost opposite a block of flats named for my maternal grandfather. For many years I lived in Leatherhead, Surrey and regularly used the local library without realizing that it was the very building, The Mansion, in which Payne had lived and carried on a school for 19 years. Like Payne I began working for the College of Preceptors in connection with examinations for teachers, and like Payne I became interested in the historical study of education and the enhancement of the professional status of teachers.[46] A growing sense of identity with the subject led me to write a book about Joseph Payne.[47] Clearly such identification brings dangers; biography may all too easily become autobiography.

My particular affection for this book stemmed not only from this identification, but was also enhanced by the excitement of discovering hitherto unused primary sources. For example, in the summer of 1991 I rescued a considerable amount of material relating to the College of Preceptors from the loft of its premises in Theydon Bois, where it had long been subject to the depredations of assorted birds and rodents.[48] Two years later I purchased a collection of Payne's manuscript materials, including three of his boyhood journals and more than 50 letters. The first two parts of the book provide personal and institutional frames of reference through which to address the overall topic of school and society in Victorian Britain. 'Joseph Payne: critic and reformer', the piece included here, is one of three chapters relating to intellectual and pedagogical issues.[49] Most of the conclusions to the book are located within the nineteenth century. Payne's educational ideas and contributions to a variety of educational institutions and associations are summarized and classified, and his life and work interpreted in terms of his position as a social, religious and political outsider in Victorian Britain. But some attempt is also made to place Payne and his work within twentieth century and historiographical contexts. For example, it is suggested that although many of the educational reforms he advocated were achieved, Payne would no doubt have deplored other features – including the poverty of much of late-twentieth-century educational debate and ill-considered schemes for national curricula and testing. He might also have been dismayed that the contribution of private educational ventures such as his own had found so little place in historical accounts.

In 1993 the Institute of Education, University of London was accorded the right to present its own awards, including honorary fellowships and degrees. Since then, as Public Orator, I have made many speeches in presenting the honorary recipients. The Institute's Logan Hall has a capacity of a thousand and presentation ceremonies are packed to overflowing with former students receiving degrees, their guests and staff. The speeches have two main purposes. The first is to do justice to the work and achievements of the honorary fellow or graduate. The second is to interest, to inspire and to entertain the audience as a whole. The eight pieces included here have been chosen to represent a wide range of contemporary educational reformers and reforms: Marie Clay's battle against gender stereotyping and professional orthodoxy; Elliot Eisner's championing of a broad interpretation of education and intelligence; Beryl Gilroy's educational and literary achievements in the face of racial prejudice; Charles Handy's search for the meaning of life while explaining the complexities of the modern business world; Michael Marland's flamboyant mixture of classroom management and cultural excellence; Koïchiro Matsuura's leadership in the cause of peace through education; Donald Woods's bravery in the face of bigotry and tyranny; Ted Wragg's unique combination of professional expertise and humour. The pieces have been edited to remove references to links with the Institute of Education and jokes that seemed (to me at least) more humorous at the time. They are arranged in alphabetical order.

Curriculum and standards

Two issues are addressed in this part. The topic of the curriculum raises the enduring question of 'What knowledge is of most worth?' This piece has been chosen for two reasons. First, it provides a practical example of how lessons may be drawn from history and applied to current policies. In response to this publication of 1998, representatives from the Qualifications and Curriculum Authority (QCA) came to the Institute to discuss with John White, Professor of Philosophy of Education, and myself, the revision of aims for the National Curriculum after 2000.[50] Second, it takes a longer historical perspective than many other writings in this volume, with its analysis of the seventeenth-century (although arguably largely universal) curricular aims of the greatest educational and political thinker in English history, John Locke.[51] Locke's treatise on education was written for the son of a gentleman but its basic principles are widely applicable. Locke's belief that nine tenths or even ninety-nine hundredths of a person's qualities were the result of education has recently been mirrored by genetic tests that show that all human beings share more than 99.9 per cent of their DNA with everyone else. Thus even 'Ethnicity is almost entirely, socially and culturally constructed.'[52]

Locke lived in a turbulent age, riven by wars between Catholics and Protestants, King and Parliament. His political writings, most notably the *Two Treatises of Government* and *Letters Concerning Toleration*, with their championship of liberal principles with regard to the nature and degree of governmental authority and of civil and religious freedom, are as appropriate to the twenty-first century as to the seventeenth. The major lesson to be drawn from Locke's *Some Thoughts Concerning Education* and from this piece is the enduring importance of Lockeian values – civility, courage, humanity, industry, justice, liberality, self-denial and truthfulness – in education.

The second issue is that of standards. What light can the historian bring to bear upon the vexed question of whether educational standards are improving or declining? This piece was originally delivered to a British Academy symposium on educational standards held on 9 October 1998. Each paper was subject to formal responses and then opened to general discussion.[53] Several points emerged from this exercise. These included identification of variations and confusions in the use of the term 'standards' – for example, in respect of specified yardsticks and actual levels of attainment, or between excellence and adequacy. It is also clear that educational and broader societal changes mean that it is difficult to try to maintain the same yardstick (or indeed metre length) of measurement over time. The historian of education can demonstrate a steady improvement in standards of literacy in the United Kingdom over the last five hundred years, but there is a conflicting evidence as to whether such improvement was maintained in the second half of the twentieth century. Some goals – for example, the universal attainment of a high degree of literacy – may be unattainable.

The teaching of history

The two pieces in this section – the first concerned with historical skills and the second with values and bias – bring historical perspectives to bear upon the school subject of history. Historians of education in the United Kingdom have frequently also been responsible (as I was for many years) for tutoring groups of PGCE students preparing to teach history in secondary schools. History was the most contentious subject in the National Curriculum of 1988. My involvement in these debates included participation in the Ruskin College history conferences organized by Raphael Samuel and the production of an edited book entitled *History in the National Curriculum*.[54]

The first piece, published in 1984 as the last of nine chapters in an edited book entitled *Learning History*,[55] was pioneering in its challenge to the ahistorical and unhistorical contexts in which contemporary discussions about teaching history – the so-called 'New History' – were taking place. Previous debates about the relative merits of the intellectual and moral purposes of history and how best to teach the subject, were being ignored. Former history teachers and history teaching were simply dismissed as content-dominated and boring. Lessons drawn from the research undertaken for this piece show that the place of history in the school curriculum depends upon a variety of social and political factors, and that the 'New History' of the 1970s and 1980s was but the latest in a series of new histories that had enriched the teaching and study of the subject.

The second piece is concerned with the teaching of a particular historical theme – the British Empire – and the effect upon it of changing circumstances and values.[56] The method adopted is that of revisiting an issue after a gap of 100 years – in this case from the 1880s to the 1980s.[57] Radical changes in the teaching of imperialism occurred. At the start of the period many university and school historians saw their role as being to glorify the growth of empire; at the end the task was rather to explain its demise. This piece demonstrates the potential role of the historian as educator of the nation and ways in which history, especially as taught in schools, has reflected the institutions and values of dominant groups in society.[58]

Education otherwise

Section 36 of the 1944 Education Act stated that 'it shall be the duty of the parent of every child of compulsory school age to cause him [sic] to receive efficient full-time education suitable to his age, ability and aptitude, either by regular attendance at school, or otherwise'. In this book, however, the concept of 'Education otherwise' is not simply a minor adjunct to schooling but a recognition that most education has taken place, and probably will continue to take place, outside of the formal school system. The street, the club, the workplace and above all the family, are prime sites of learning.[59] Increased participation in higher education may be seen as yet a further element in the rise of the schooled society that has occurred in the United Kingdom and many other countries over the last two centuries. Nevertheless, the development of modern communications, including the internet which in the last 20 years has revolutionized access to knowledge, means that the educational future is not what it was. Thus the placement of this section does not indicate that it is the least important of the six, but rather that it is forward looking in that the historical perspectives included here may help to illumine the substantial changes in the relationship between education and formal schooling that will surely occur in the twenty-first century.

'Learning by playing', the shortest piece in the whole collection, is nevertheless one of the most wide-ranging. It shows the fundamental role of play as preparation for adult life in humans and other higher mammals, and the continuities of some children's games across centuries and cultures. Johan Huizinga argued that play was an essential cultural element which reached a peak in Western European society in the eighteenth century. Children had always worked, but their role in the industrial revolution, so memorably portrayed in the poems of William Blake or the novels of Charles Dickens, left little time for traditional games. In the second half of the nineteenth century, England was to the fore in developing and codifying the rules of new types of play. Lessons drawn include the importance of providing adequate play facilities for children and adults in the modern urban environment.

Medieval education was essentially vocational. Apprenticeship was a means of preparing for one group of skilled occupations, and schooling for another. Ideally the master or mistress was responsible for the health, literacy, morals and religious observance, as well as the occupational competence, of the apprentice. The second piece in this part charts how over the succeeding centuries apprenticeship took on many forms. From the early nineteenth century its rationale and role were fundamentally changed as the increasing division of labour in education meant that in future some skills would be learned at home, others at school and others again in employment. In the twentieth century, apprenticeship forms of training for entry to some professions – school teaching is but one example – gave way to degree-level qualifications awarded by an institution of higher education. Vocational education acquired a pejorative connotation – as second-rate preparation for low-skilled jobs. In the 1980s, government initiatives such as the Youth Training Scheme (YTS) were widely interpreted as temporary means of eliminating juvenile unemployment rather than of supplying genuine vocational education. The relationship between apprenticeship and the modern schooled society remains contentious. In October 2004, the Tomlinson Report sought to modify existing hierarchies of knowledge, educational institutions and occupations with its proposals to incorporate academic qualifications and modern apprenticeships into a single framework of diplomas for 14–19 year olds.[60]

The final piece, a chapter from my most recent edited book, *Public or Private Education? Lessons from History* (2004),[61] has been chosen for three reasons. The first is to reiterate the broad nature of education and its public and private dimensions. 'Family history and the history of the family' brings together two forms of knowledge construction and identity which may be taken as representative of the 'informal' and 'formal' spheres of education. Family history is probably the oldest form of human history. It has been a largely private and amateur form – in respect of its historians, subject matter and readers. On the other hand, the historian of the family is generally a public professional – interested not in a particular family but in the role of the family, or groups of families, as an historical phenomenon.

The second ground for inclusion is the importance of family education. Throughout history the family has been the first site of education. Indeed it predates schooling and may well outlast it. Most children still learn their basic skills, including speech – the most important means of communication – and acquire many of their values and attitudes in a domestic setting.

The final justification is personal. This piece contains the briefest summary of my father's unpublished autobiography. His father was killed in the First World War and for many years a photograph of my widowed grandmother and her three young sons has stood on my study desk – a reminder of the sacrifices and struggles they endured and a perpetual source of inspiration in my search for lessons from history, and especially from the history of education.[62]

Notes

1 J.L. Axtell (ed.), *The Educational Writings of John Locke*, Cambridge: Cambridge University Press, 1968, p. 293. *Some Thoughts Concerning Education*, first published in 1693, was based upon letters written by Locke to Edward Clarke, advising him on the education of his eldest son.

2 R. Aldrich, *Education for the Nation*, London: Cassell, 1996, p. 1.

3 See R. Aldrich, *An Introduction to the History of Education*, London: Hodder and Stoughton, 1982, pp. 22–40 for a discussion of educational ideas and ideals.

4 R.J.W. Selleck, *The Shop: The University of Melbourne, 1850–1939*, Melbourne: Melbourne University Press, p. 1.

5 R. Aldrich, 'History in education', in J. Sturm, J. Dekker, R. Aldrich and F. Simon (eds), *Education and Cultural Transmission*, Gent: CSHP, 1996 (*Paedagogica Historica* Supplementary Series II), p. 63.

6 R. Aldrich, *An Introduction to the History of Education*, London: Hodder and Stoughton, 1982, p. 37.

7 P. Crawford, *The Living Isles: A Natural History of Britain and Ireland*, London: BBC Publications, 1985, p. 31.

8 A.H. Halsey with J. Webb (eds), *Twentieth-Century British Social Trends*, London: Macmillan, 2000, p. 226.

9 D. Ravitch and M.A. Vinovskis (eds), *Learning from the Past: What History Teaches Us about School Reform*, Baltimore, MD: The Johns Hopkins University Press, 1995; S.F. Semel and A.R. Sadovnik (eds), *'Schools of Tomorrow,' Schools of Today: What Happened to Progressive Education*, New York: Peter Lang, 1999.

10 Ravitch and Vinovskis, op. cit., p. ix.

11 Semel and Sadovnik, op. cit., pp. 373, 376.

12 R. Aldrich, *Education for the Nation*, London: Cassell, 1996, especially pp. 2, 129–37. The research on which this volume is based was funded by the Leverhulme Trust.

13 See R. Aldrich, *Education for the Nation*, London: Cassell, 1996, pp. 62–3 for a development of this point.

14 See, for example, R. Aldrich, 'The National Curriculum: an historical perspective', in D. Lawton and C. Chitty (eds), *The National Curriculum*, London: Institute of Education, 1988; R. Aldrich, 'Vocational education in Britain: an historical and cultural perspective', in A. Heikkinen (ed.), *Vocational Education and Culture – European Prospects from History and*

Life History, Tampere: Tampereen Yliopisto, 1995; R. Aldrich, 'Educational reform and curriculum implementation in England: an historical interpretation', in D.S.G. Carter and M.H. O'Neill (eds), *International Perspectives on Educational Reform and Policy Implementation*, London: Falmer Press, 1995.

15 See R. Aldrich, *The Institute of Education 1902–2002: A Centenary History*, London: Institute of Education, 2002.

16 R. Aldrich (ed.), *A Century of Education*, London: RoutledgeFalmer, 2002. The 10 topics are: primary education, secondary education, further education, higher education, central and local government, teachers, pupils and students, special educational needs, curriculum, qualifications and assessment.

17 E.W. Eisner, *The Kind of Schools WE NEED: Personal Essays*, Portsmouth, NH: Heinemann, 1998, p. 5.

18 See the list of publications at the end of this book.

19 For example, on this last theme see, R. Aldrich, 'The evolution of teacher education', in N. Graves (ed.), *Initial Teacher Education: Policies and Progress*, London: Kogan Page, 1990; R. Aldrich, 'Teacher training in London', in R. Floud and S. Glynn (eds), *London Higher: The Establishment of Higher Education in London*, London: Athlone Press, 1998; R. Aldrich, *The Institute of Education 1902–2002: A Centenary History*, London: Institute of Education, 2002.

20 This chapter, the longest piece in the collection, has been included because of its treatment of several topics, but otherwise issues of length and context have led to the decision to exclude chapters in authored (as opposed to edited) books.

21 No. 8.

22 Nos. 1, 3, 4, 10, 11, 12, 14.

23 Nos. 2, 5, 9, 13.

24 W. Richardson, 'Historians and educationists: the history of education as a field of study in post-war England. Part II: 1972–96', *History of Education*, 1999, 28(2): 138.

25 K. Jenkins, *On 'What is History?' From Carr and Elton to Rorty and White*, London: Routledge, 1995.

26 K. Jenkins, *Refiguring History: New Thoughts on an Old Discipline*, London: Routledge, 2003, pp. 1–2.

27 K. Jenkins, *Re-thinking History*, London: Routledge, 1991, p. 32.

28 Jenkins, op. cit., 2003, p. 6. The conclusion to this volume, p. 70, declares that 'All histories always have been and always will be aesthetic, figurative discourses . . . epistemological histories just ought never to have existed; histories ought never have been modern'. The conclusion to Jenkins, op. cit., 1991, p. 70, states that 'In the post-modern world, then, arguably the content and context of history should be a generous series of methodologically reflexive studies on the makings of the histories of modernity itself'.

29 For an overview of nineteenth-century politics and education see my introductory chapter, 'The nineteenth-century legacy', in P. Gordon, R. Aldrich and D. Dean, *Education and Policy in England in the Twentieth Century*, London: Woburn Press, pp. 3–15.

30 D. Thom, 'Politics and the people: Brian Simon and the campaign against intelligence tests in British schools', *History of Education*, 2004, 33(5): 515.

31 The others were D.W. Dean, 'The political parties and the development of their attitudes to educational problems, 1918–1942', London, MPhil, 1968; and L.O. Ward, 'An investigation into the educational ideas and contributions of the British political parties (1870–1918)', London, PhD, 1970.

32 R. Aldrich, 'Radicalism, national education and the grant of 1833', *Journal of Educational Administration and History*, 1973, 5(1): 1–6.

33 R. Aldrich, 'Sir John Pakington and National Education', London, PhD, 1977. The MPhil thesis was registered in History, the PhD in Education. Both theses were undertaken when I was in full-time employment, initially at Southlands College and from 1973 at the Institute of Education, University of London.

34 R. Aldrich, *Sir John Pakington and National Education*, Leeds: University of Leeds, 1979.

35 R. Aldrich, 'From Board of Education to Department for Education and Employment', *Journal of Educational Administration and History*, 2000, 32(1): 21.

36 R. Aldrich, D. Crook and D. Watson, *Education and Employment: The DfEE and its Place in History*, London: Institute of Education, 2000.

37 Board of Education, Ministry of Education, Department of Education and Science, Department for Education; Ministry of Labour, Ministry of Labour and National Service, Ministry of Labour, Department of Employment and Productivity, Department of Employment, Employment Department.

38 R. Aldrich, D. Crook and D. Watson, *Education and Employment: The DfEE and its Place in History*, London: Institute of Education, 2000, p. 13.

39 See, for example, R.G. Wallace, 'The origins and authorship of the 1944 Education Act', *History of Education*, 1981, 10(4): 283–90; and K. Jefferys, 'R.A. Butler, the Board of Education and the 1944 Education Act', *History*, 1984, 69: 415–31.

40 K. Jefferys, 'R.A. Butler, the Board of Education and the 1944 Education Act', 10 November 1983.

41 R. Aldrich and P. Leighton, *Education: Time for a New Act?*, London: Institute of Education, 1985, pp. 76–8.

42 See, for example, F. Clarke, *Education and Social Change: An English Interpretation*, London: Sheldon Press, 1940; H. Silver, *Education and the Social Condition*, London: Methuen, 1980; and B. Simon, *Education and the Social Order, 1940–1990*, London: Lawrence and Wishart, 1991.

43 R. Aldrich and P. Gordon, *Dictionary of British Educationists*, London: Woburn Press, 1989; and P. Gordon and R. Aldrich, *Biographical Dictionary of North American and European Educationists*, London: Woburn Press, 1997. This research also led to a role as an associate editor for the *Oxford Dictionary of National Biography*.

44 M. Depaepe, 'A professionally relevant history of education: does it exist?', *Paedagogica Historica*, 2001, XXXVII(3): 634.

45 When talking to Roy Jenkins at a College of Preceptors' Charter Ceremony.

46 As a Director of the General Teaching Council Company (England and Wales) established in 1990. A General Teaching Council for England was established in 2000.

47 R. Aldrich, *School and Society in Victorian Britain: Joseph Payne and the New World of Education*, New York: Garland, 1995.

48 These materials are now in the archive collection of the Institute of Education, University of London.

49 The others are entitled 'The science and art of education' and 'Historical and comparative dimensions'.

50 R. Aldrich and J. White, *The National Curriculum beyond 2000: The QCA and the Aims of Education*, London: Institute of Education, 1998 consists of two sections: 'New aims for a new National Curriculum' by John White and 'A curriculum for the nation' by Richard Aldrich.

51 For an extended treatment see R. Aldrich, 'John Locke', *Prospects*, 1994, XXIV(1–2): 61–76.

52 Mark Henderson, 'Gene tests prove that we are all the same under the skin', *The Times*, 27 October 2004.

53 R. Aldrich, 'Educational standards in historical perspective', in H. Goldstein and A. Heath (eds), *Educational Standards*, Oxford: Oxford University Press, 2000 (*Proceedings of the British Academy*, 102), pp. 39–56. The responses of Gillian Sutherland, Anthony Heath and Sig Prais are in pp. 56–67. The three other papers were by Alison Wolf on the comparative perspective, Mike Cresswell on the role of public examinations and David J. Bartholomew on the measurement of standards.

54 R. Aldrich (ed.), *History in the National Curriculum*, London: Kogan Page, 1991.

55 R. Aldrich, 'New History: an historical perspective', in A.K. Dickinson, P.J. Lee and P.J. Rogers (eds), *Learning History*, London: Heinemann Educational Books, 1984. The historical perspective was not always welcome and one of the editors was less than enthusiastic about the inclusion of this chapter.

56 R. Aldrich, 'Imperialism in the study and teaching of history', in J.A. Mangan (ed.), *'Benefits Bestowed'? Education and British Imperialism*, Manchester: Manchester University Press, 1988. Unfortunately shortly before going to press it was necessary to reduce the length of this chapter so that the final two sections are somewhat truncated. See, however, R. Aldrich, 'History in education', in J. Sturm, J. Dekker, R. Aldrich and F. Simon (eds), *Education and Cultural Transmission*, Gent: CSHP, 1996 (*Paedagogica Historica* Supplementary Series II); and R. Aldrich, 'Education as nationbuilding: lessons from British history', in S. Vaage (ed.), *Education and Nationbuilding*, Volda: Volda University College, 2001.

57 For a development of this method, where a starting point of 2000 is used before returning to 1900 to trace changes and continuities, see R. Aldrich (ed.), *A Century of Education*, London: RoutledgeFalmer, 2002, especially p. 3 which quotes from a leading article in *The Times* of 1 January 1901 on the prospects for the coming century.

58 On this point see V. Chancellor, *History for Their Masters: Opinion in the English History Textbook, 1800–1914*, Bath: Adams and Dart, 1970; and R. Gilbert, *The Impotent Image: Reflections of Ideology in the Secondary School Curriculum*, London: Falmer Press, 1984.

59 For an examination of some of the basic social and economic dimensions within which to locate a broad history of education see R. Aldrich, *An Introduction to the History of Education*, London: Hodder and Stoughton, 1982, pp. 9–21.

60 www.14-19reform.gov.uk (accessed on 10.5.2005).

61 R. Aldrich (ed.), *Public or Private Education? Lessons from History*, London: Woburn Press, 2004. This book is divided into three parts. The first provides three examples of key issues and turning points in the relationship between public and private education in the eighteenth, nineteenth and twentieth centuries; the second examines four areas of education and knowledge that have remained largely in private hands; the third provides three comparative perspectives.

62 This photograph is reproduced on the back cover of the *Public or Private Education?* book.

PART 1

UNDERSTANDING HISTORY
OF EDUCATION

CHAPTER 1

THE THREE DUTIES OF THE HISTORIAN OF EDUCATION

History of Education, Taylor and Francis, 2003, 32(2): 133–43

Introduction

This article is located within two main contexts: current debates about the nature and state of history of education and of history itself. The approach is personal and may be interpreted to some extent as a professional *apologia pro vita sua*. The tone is positive. The overall theme is not that 'things ain't what they used to be', but rather that things are still more like what they used to be than is often realized. The title is taken from an article by Peter Laslett, who in 1987 argued that the historian of the family, in common with all investigators of society and of its history, must recognize three duties.

> The first is a duty to his [*sic*] own generation and the second to people in the past. The third is shared not only with other historians and social scientists but with all scholars and scientists. This is the duty to search after the truth to the utmost of his capacity, or of hers, recognizing that it may be impossible to avoid some degree of bias but doing all that can be done to avoid it.[1]

The purpose of this article is to consider Laslett's three duties as they apply to the work of historians of education.[2]

Two preliminary points of definition may be made in respect of the terms 'duty' and of 'the historian of education'. The word duty is rarely employed in historiographical debate and is here taken to mean 'a task, service, or function that is assigned or that arises from one's position or job'.[3] It must be acknowledged, however, that no simple or universal definition of the historian of education's duties can be supplied. No doubt the several tasks, services and functions of historians of education have varied, and will continue to vary, across cultures and ages. Differences in duty may even be found within a single institution at a particular moment in time. Thus the job description of an historian of education within the history department of a particular university may differ from that of a colleague in the education department. There may also be differences within a department. The main task of the senior professor may be to profess, principally in print and in public debate. The major function of the lecturer may be to teach undergraduates and to fulfil a range of pastoral duties.

Is it possible, therefore, to talk or write about 'the historian of education'? In 1999 in two substantial and important articles in this journal,[4] William Richardson emphasized (overemphasized?) a distinction between the work of 'historians' and 'educationists' in the field of history of education, a distinction resting in part upon a perceived difference between the attitudes of the two groups towards past and present. Thus he identified 'a long-standing and defining difference between the practice in England (and overseas) of academic historians who reconstruct the past in ways influenced by present concerns and of education-ists who invoke the past in order to apply its lessons to present concerns'.[5] It is impossible here to consider in detail the many issues raised by Richardson's work but, as I have argued elsewhere, such distinctions are not absolute.[6] All historians of education have a duty to history and to education. The duty of the historian of education to the discipline of history is as great as that of the historian of politics or of foreign affairs or indeed, as Laslett argued, of the historian of the family. The relative strengths of these commitments to history and education, however, may vary according to circumstance. Two examples may be given in respect of audience and location. On one occasion, an historian of education may be addressing a lec-ture or publication to historians whose prime interest is in seeking a better under-standing of the people of the past. On another, the same historian of education may be engaged with an audience whose major interests lie in an enhanced aware-ness not only of the people of the past but also of themselves and their own gener-ation. As for location, experience at the Institute of Education, University of London is instructive. During the last 30 years, historians of education have been successively located within five different 'departments'.[7] Each re-location has reflected and been accompanied by subtle changes in their roles.

In an article of this length, there is clearly insufficient space to enter into the many issues raised by the terms 'duty' and 'the historian of education'. Nor is there room to explore the meanings of other key words, except to acknowledge that the word, 'history', is variously used, for example, to mean the past and the study of the past. The treatment here is necessarily brief. Although located within an inter-national context, and engaging with debates featured in the pages of *Paedagogica Historica* and at the American History of Education Society meeting at Yale University, New Haven in October 2001, examples are drawn mainly from English history and historiography. Personal instances of teaching and publication are cited. The article is organized into three main sections, corresponding to Laslett's three duties. Nevertheless, there are no absolute distinctions between them, for all three sections, in common with the duties of the historian, are inextricably intertwined.

The duty to the people of the past

The historian's prime duty is to record and interpret the events of the past for contemporaries and for future generations. The duty to the people of the past may be simply stated. It is to record and interpret those events as fully and as accurately as possible. Issues of truth and accuracy will be considered in detail in the third section of this article. Two points may be made in terms of 'fully'.

The most obvious interpretation of the word, 'fully', lies in remedying the vast gaps that exist in historical knowledge. The duty of the historian of education is to rescue from oblivion those whose voices have not yet been heard and whose stories have not yet been told. 'Women and childhood first' has been an appropriate rally-ing cry in recent years, and the popularity of these two subjects in terms of courses, conferences and publications is eloquent testimony to their long-standing neglect and to the vitality of current work. Many people of the past, including women and children, have been neglected because their lives have been held to be of little inter-est and account. This dismissal has been further justified in terms of problems of evidence. The historian's duty to the people of the past is best fulfilled by employing a wide variety of sources, both public and private. Late-twentieth-century technological developments have revolutionized the availability of sources, both primary and secondary. In addition to traditional written and archaeological sources, the historian of education can utilize the many opportunities provided by the internet, while those studying the people of the immediate past can create and draw upon oral history and sound and film archives.

The invisibility of some groups of people has been complemented by the neglect of some dimensions of education. While issues of formal education, for example, schools and colleges, legislation and administration (the acts and facts approach) have received substantial attention, others have been manifestly ignored. A very considerable amount of teaching and learning takes place outside of formal educational institutions – via the media, through friendships, in the home, the family, the workplace, the club, the street. There is a duty to record and interpret such education and, where necessary, to reconceptualize the historian's very nature and role. For example, in recent years 'family history has become England's fastest-growing hobby'.[8] Family historians are fulfilling their duties to the people of the past in a most immediate and personal way. Their findings have enormous potential for a new era of historical research and writing, based upon an alliance between amateur and professional historians, and with particular implications for the work of historians of education.[9]

The duty to our own generation

The first element in the historian of education's duty to the present generation is the same as the duty to the people of the past – to research, record and interpret past events as fully and as accurately as possible. This duty is of a general nature but is frequently applied within specific contexts, for example, departments of education and of history within institutions of higher education.

In 1999, in an important article entitled 'The history of education: state of the art at the turn of the century in Europe and North America', Jurgen Herbst provided a survey of history of education during the last four decades of the twentieth century. His basic thesis was that the enthusiasm of the 1970s had evaporated and 'that the discipline lacks a sense of direction and purpose'.[10] His solutions were twofold:

1) that historians of education consider anew their presence as academics in programs of professional education, and 2) that, concentrating their attention on teaching and learning in schools, they pay as much attention to the history of private as they have to the history of the public schools and education.[11]

The first of these calls provoked a riposte from Marc Depaepe who cited the misuse of 'the great educators' and of 'historical pedagogy' in Europe, China, South Africa and the United States in justification of his warning against the 'mystification and even the prostitution of history to hagiographical, pedagogical hero worship and a partisan and presentistic reading of history'.[12] Depaepe concluded that:

The relevance of the history of education for educators of the 21st century can in my view only be the relevance of an intrinsic nature, i.e., one that is critical and inevitably uncomfortable...For what can the professional competence of the practical educator consist other than in critical reflection on his [sic] activities past and present, certainly now that the ideological coverage of normative philosophy has fallen away?[13]

The historian of education's duty not to abuse or misuse the record of the past to advance contemporary causes is clear. Critical reflection is to be generally encouraged and is in accord with the contemporary culture of the Western world. On the other hand, Depaepe's argument that duty to the current generation is to be expressed only in intrinsic or methodological terms is too restrictive.[14] Of course it can be argued that it is not necessary to know our past in order to know ourselves. Indeed, there have been many instances, for example, via emigration, where individuals or members of a community have deliberately chosen to forget their histories and start afresh. Nevertheless, our journeys in the present and future may benefit from the possession and understanding of an accurate map of the past. History provides the memory and the curriculum vitae of the human race. Past deeds are no guarantee of future performance, but the historian's role in recording and interpreting what has gone before has the potential to enlarge our understanding of the human condition with reference to particular public activities, including education. It may also be important in the promotion of informed discussion and decision-making. As Simon Jenkins has argued:

> I cannot debate the Middle East with anyone who knows nothing of the story of Palestine. Nobody can fathom the depths of America's current paranoia who has not read of Pearl Harbor. An analysis of an economic downturn is worthless without an analysis of previous ones. Any event is part of a continuum. Without history we are infants. All good news becomes ecstasy and all bad news disaster.[15]

The 'continuum' dimension referred to by Jenkins has two important implications. The first is that some historical study may be of particular interest and value for our own generation if it places recent and contemporary events in historical perspective. The second is that such events must be located within a variety of contexts and perspectives. Two examples of teaching and publication are provided here to demonstrate the potential contributions of historians of education to professional education and to contemporary educational debate.

The first lecture to the 750 students who take the one-year Postgraduate Certificate in Education (PGCE) course at the Institute of Education, University of London in preparation for teaching in secondary schools is an historical one.[16] In contrast to the 1970s and early 1980s when studies in the educational foundations of history, philosophy, psychology and sociology were distinctive elements in the Institute's PGCE courses, most of the students' work is now school-based and focused on the classroom. The purpose of the lecture is to provide students with a series of contexts – in terms of the Institute, secondary schools and teachers and teaching – within which to locate changes and continuities in education.

The first context is the history of the Institute of Education itself. It is important for students (and staff) to be informed about the history of the institution to which they belong. Founded in 1902 by the London County Council (LCC) as the London Day Training College to supply teachers for the capital's elementary schools, in 1932 its growing national and international status as a centre for educational enquiry led to its transference to the University of London with a new title of the Institute of Education. After the Second World War the Institute assumed a dual role at the centre of an Area Training Organization composed of more than 30 colleges. These arrangements were dismantled in the 1970s, and by the end of the century the Institute was a chartered college of the University. Some continuity is indicated by the Institute's long-standing pre-eminence amongst British institutions of teacher education in terms of size and prestige. No simple celebratory message, however, is conveyed. Weaknesses are identified as well as strengths. The reputation of any institution has constantly to be earned and re-earned through the quality and commitment of its staff and students.[17]

A longer historical perspective is needed to demonstrate changes and continuities in the concept and nature of secondary schooling. Some awareness of the variety of schools can be provided by illustrations of buildings in use today – Winchester College founded in the fourteenth century, grammar schools from the Tudor and Stuart eras, endowed schools of the eighteenth century, public schools and board schools from the nineteenth, comprehensives from the twentieth. Some 90 per cent of British children of secondary age attend comprehensive schools, but since their proliferation from the 1960s even these schools have experienced a variety of iden-tities. Further perspectives on secondary schools are provided by a comparative analysis over time of the changing purposes and organizational cultures of primary and secondary schools and of institutions of higher education.

Teachers and teaching are considered under three heads: training, profession and pedagogy. Training of teachers for secondary schools in England has been informed by different models: for example, apprenticeship, theory before practice and the reflective practitioner. Professional status has been sought through qualifi-cations and associations. Principles of pedagogy have been defined and redefined across the centuries. Changes in the principles and practice of teaching and learn-ing are manifest, but continuities are also indicated by the wisdom enshrined in *The Christian Schoolmaster* of James Talbott in 1707 or the method manuals of nineteenth-century training college lecturers.

In a single introductory lecture it is impossible to do more than to supply some initial insights into the potential of historical perspectives and provide suggestions for reading. One example from the reading list of 2002 is an edited volume that employs contemporary starting points and the concepts of change and continuity to provide an examination of education in England during the past century.[18] The intention behind this volume is to fulfil duties both to the people of the past and to the present generation. Past events are considered in their own terms, but are also examined to furnish historical perspectives upon current educational issues. The book is one entity in terms of overall subject matter and design, but each chapter is written by a separate expert.[19] Chapters begin with an assessment of the situation in the year 2000, before returning to the year 1900 and tracing change and continuity across the century.

The most obvious element of change was the expansion of the formal system. In 1900, only a small percentage of English children attended secondary school; a century later all had a minimum of five years of secondary schooling. At the start of the century less than one per cent of the population attended university, now one third of the age cohort has experience of higher education. During the twentieth-century educational expansion could be measured in terms of more pupils and students, more teachers, more schools, more universities, more exami-nations and more qualifications. Such expansion might well justify the term, 'a century of education'.

Change and continuity may go hand in hand. Although all-age schools were abolished in 1944, in the second half of the twentieth century the ideal and the reality of secondary schooling for all remained problematic. The elite origins and continuities of many secondary schools were tellingly reflected in the different resources and examination results of fee-paying as opposed to maintained schools. So, too, were the elite origins and continuities of the universities of Oxford and

Cambridge, where half of the undergraduate students were recruited from the seven per cent of pupils who attended fee-paying schools. As George Smith concluded in his chapter on schools in *Twentieth-Century British Social Trends*:

> Despite the massive expansion in all aspects of education, and the quite dramatic increases in staying-on rates and qualifications in the last two decades of the century, the relative chances of children from different social backgrounds were still apparently as unequal as they had been at the start of the century.[20]

At the end of the twentieth century more than 80 per cent of the children of professionals obtained university degrees as contrasted with only 14 per cent of those from working-class homes.[21]

Historical evidence and analysis of this type, presented in lectures, seminars and publications, can encompass a multiplicity of concepts and standpoints. For those historians of education who work in institutes or departments of education, the employment of evidence from the past to provide a greater understanding of the present is part of the duty to our own generation. While every lecture or publication is naturally positioned by the background and values of its author, the overall purpose, as Laslett enjoined, is to search after, and to enhance the capacities of others to search after, truth. Conclusions are open to challenge and procedures 'public'. These may be favourably contrasted with the more limited 'private' and 'official' views of the past represented in the following exchange.[22] In April 2002 in a farewell speech to the conference of the National Association of Schoolmasters/ Union of Women Teachers at Scarborough the General Secretary, Nigel de Gruchy, was reported as saying that:

> during 33 years as a union activist, politicians had caused the most damage to children's education. 'On my kinder days, I would describe many of them ... as a bunch of ambitious, self-seeking, self-opinionated rogues. They spend one decade pulling us one way and the next pulling us back in the opposite direction, always with inadequate resources. Unfortunately, every minister that comes along feels they have to make their mark. I would describe that as teachers' biggest marking problem'.
>
> The Department for Education and Skills said: 'We are all used to intemperate remarks at Easter conferences. The Government's record on education speaks for itself, with £540 extra per pupil and 12,000 more teachers than in 1997.'[23]

In conclusion, the historian of education's duties to the people of the past and to the current generation are not necessarily incompatible. Both require the provision of a map of the past which is as accurate as possible. On occasion, however, some historians of education have a further duty – to indicate the potential relevance of that map to current and future concerns.

The duty to search after the truth

There is no room here to examine in detail the full implications of postmodernist and postempiricist writings for the historian's duty to search after truth.[24] For those, however, who believe that 'truth is dependent on somebody having the power to make it true',[25] or that history is a narrative discourse which is as much invented or imagined as found, the duty to search after truth is meaningless.

For example, Keith Jenkins has argued that history must abandon its search for objective truth about the past and come to terms with its own processes of production. For Jenkins, 'Truth is a self-referencing figure of speech, incapable of accessing the phenomenal world: word and world, word and object, remain separate.'[26] On the other hand, most historians (by whom I mean those who research, write and/or teach history, as opposed to those who only write about the writing of history) still interpret their task as being to record and interpret events as fully and as accurately as possible. Historians continue to search after truth, even when they have come to terms with history's processes of production. They know that there were realities in the past, for once they were the realities of the present. The passage of time is a matter of (relative) certainty. Today is the tomorrow historians worried about yesterday. The realities of the past are accessed mainly through historical evidence – primary and secondary sources. Historians' (relative) success in the search for truth is confirmed by a close correspondence between historical accounts and historical facts based on evidence, and by consensus among historians when such correspondence is widely recognized. Most historians would acknowledge that their work is of a hypothetical or tentative nature, and few are unaware of the difficulties of the task. As Joyce Appleby, Lynn Hunt and Margaret Jacob have argued:

> At best, the past only dimly corresponds to what the historians say about it, but practical realists accept the tentativeness and imperfections of historians' accounts. This does not, however, cause them to give up the aim for accuracy and completeness and to judge historical accounts on the basis of those criteria.[27]

Jurgen Herbst's provocative article of 1999, referred to in the previous section, attracted a variety of responses. Milton Gaither accused him of misinterpreting pre-1960 educational historiography and the work of Bailyn and Cremin, and called for a refocusing of educational history 'through the lens of economic globalization'.[28] Kate Rousmanière questioned the accuracy of Herbst's account of the field as stagnant and lacking in innovative input. She supplied examples from the conferences of the International Standing Conference for the History of Education and the newly formed European Educational Research Association of 'the historical work of recent years that I have found to be particularly fresh, creative and innovative'.[29]

The articles of Depaepe, Gaither and Rousmanière raised questions about the accuracy of Herbst's interpretations of the state of the history of education and possible remedies. A more fundamental disagreement, however, occurred about the nature of history of education and of historical truth. Herbst's main assault was upon those 'postmodernist theorists' who regarded historical research and writing as politically inspired, and 'the practitioners of the linguistic turn' who argued that there was nothing to explain, 'only texts that can be decoded, deconstructed, and manipulated'.[30] The response from Nick Peim, a 'cultural materialist' at the University of Birmingham in England, raised questions of an ontological, phenomenological and hermeneutic nature. Writing as a member of the research group, Domus, Peim emphasized that history of education was a hybrid business. History, moreover, had no privileged status within it: 'It is not possible for DOMUS to speak of a "parent" discipline, as the home we claim for ourselves is not a space that is governed by any such patrimony.'[31] Peim rejected Herbst's assumptions about the nature and identity of history of education and the forms of enquiry appropriate to it. Having commended poststructuralist suspicions of 'ideas like truth', Peim concluded that he neither wished to, nor could, advocate any particular directions or solutions for history of education.

> What I would propose, however, would be a movement (decentred, of course) to investigate the theoretical bearings of the subject, the constitution of its objects, and a (perhaps renewed) self-awareness about the positionings of practitioners of the history of education – wheresoever they may be – and the institutions, networks and spaces they inhabit and may want to create as well as the restrictions and affordances they work with and within.[32]

This is a challenging agenda. Nevertheless, it raises the possibility of a history of education written in language which some may find impenetrable, with no particular commitment to history as historically understood, no practitioners with a claim, nor indeed wish, to be called historians of education, and no duty to search after truth.[33]

As Peim rightly argues, both postmodernism and poststructuralism are highly differentiated fields. So, too, however, is historiography. The study of history of education, like the study of history itself, has been and always will be a changing and contested terrain. One of the great problems of the 'post' approach is that historical accounts of various shapes and sizes are lumped together as 'modernist' or 'empiricist', and uniformly condemned. For example, Alun Munslow recently proclaimed that 'Post-empiricist history is for me an authored story constructed out of evidence, argumentation, language, culture and my ethical choices.'[34] The term 'Post-empiricist', here, however, seems redundant. Surely this is what history has always been, both an art and a science with different emphases according to priorities of individual historians and of different cultures and moments in time. Munslow's assault on 'the desperate modernist insistence that empirical reality will equate with truth'; and his assertion that 'the bulk of the historical mainstream are still reluctant to let go of the modernist wreckage and accept that we can not know the true meaning of the past',[35] seem wide of the mark. Munslow's claim that 'Moral argument does just as well [as documentary traces] when I want to believe things about the past',[36] appears retrogressive, with its echoes of Bolingbroke's dictum that history is 'philosophy teaching by example'.

Across the centuries historians have acknowledged the partial nature of their enterprise and the impossibility of complete capture of the past, and yet have continued to search for ways of representing segments of it as accurately or as provocatively as possible.[37] Two classic examples must suffice. In 1828, in an essay on 'History' for the *Edinburgh Review*, a youthful Macaulay wrote: 'No picture, then, and no history, can present us with the whole truth: but those are the best pictures and the best histories which exhibit such parts of the truth as most nearly produce the effects of the whole.'[38] In his preface to *Eminent Victorians*, published in 1918, Lytton Strachey mischievously declared that: 'The history of the Victorian Age will never be written: we know too much about it. For ignorance is the first requisite of the historian.' Strachey's technique was to 'row out over that great ocean of material, and lower down into it, here and there, a little bucket, which will bring up to the light of day some characteristic specimen from those far depths, to be examined with careful curiosity'.[39] Such acknowledgements that there must be a large gap between history as happened and history as written or taught, do not absolve the historian from searching for truth. Indeed, as Fritz Stern has maintained, 'the impossibility of attaining absolute truth heightens the historian's responsibility' so that 'even if the existence of Truth be problematical, truthfulness remains the measure of his [*sic*] intellectual and moral achievement'.[40] Words, whether spoken or written, will never be able to recapture the events of the past in their entirety, but the search for as accurate a representation as possible is as important for the historian in the lecture hall or journal article as for the judge and jury in the courtroom.

There are two reasons why historians of education should be in the vanguard of this duty to search after truth. The first is specific, in that education as a field of study is central to human existence and values, in a way that some other matters, for example, philately or railways are not. The second is of a more general nature. In an age of increasing commercialism, scepticism and spin, much of the trust that was formerly placed, and sometimes misplaced, in politicians, professionals (including clergy and teachers) and the media, has been lost. Information proliferates, but the motives of many of those who produce it are highly suspect. A recent discussion document on social capital produced by the Downing Street Performance and Innovation Unit found that the proportions of people willing to trust others had fallen from 50–60 per cent in the 1950s to some 30 per cent today.[41] Trust has diminished because the concept of truth is in short supply. It may, of course, be that this is an inevitable outcome of the condition of postmodernity and that trust and truth will completely disappear, not least in universities, in a welter of incredulity towards all narratives, both great and small. My own preferences, however, are for engaging in the changing and contested terrain that is history of education equipped with concepts of 'high modernity' rather than 'postmodernity', and 'enhanced empiricism' rather than 'postempiricism'. In the light of these concepts, the traditional duty of those in institutions of higher education to search after truth is rendered more problematic but even more necessary.

The final argument for the importance of historical truth (as opposed to untruth or claiming that all versions of the truth are equally valid) is provided by a recent book by Richard Evans, *Telling Lies About Hitler: The Holocaust, History and the David Irving Trial*.[42] In 2000, during the lawsuit brought by David Irving against Deborah Lipstadt and Penguin Books, Evans was called as an expert witness to challenge Irving's denial of the gas chambers at Auschwitz and the systematic murder of millions of Jews on Hitler's orders. As Evans correctly argues, during the court case not only Irving, but also history itself, was on trial. His belief that objective historical knowledge was both desirable and attainable was set out in *In Defence of History*, which concluded that:

> So when Patrick Joyce tells us that social history is dead, and Elizabeth Deeds Ermarth declares that time is a fictional construct, and Roland Barthes announces that all the world's a text, and Hans Kellner wants historians to stop behaving as if we were researching into things that actually happened, and Diane Purkiss says that we should just tell stories without bothering whether or not they are true, and Frank Ankersmit swears that we can never know anything at all about the past so we might as well confine ourselves to studying other historians, and Keith Jenkins proclaims that all history is just naked ideology designed to get historians power and money in big university institutions run by the bourgeoisie, I will look humbly at the past and say despite them all: it really happened, and we really can, if we are very scrupulous and careful and self-critical, find out how it happened and reach some tenable though always less than final conclusions about what it all meant.[43]

Notes

1 P. Laslett, 'The character of familial history, its limitations and the conditions for its proper pursuit', *Journal of Family History*, 1987, 12(1–3): 264.
2 This article is based on a paper entitled 'A century of education: whatever happened to education in England in the twentieth century?', presented on 9th May 2002 to the History of Education seminar at the Institute of Historical Research in London. I am most grateful to the editors and to the external reviewer for their comments on a previous draft.
3 *Longman Dictionary of the English Language*, 1991, p. 489.
4 W. Richardson, 'Historians and educationists: the history of education as a field of study in post-war England. Part I: 1945–72', *History of Education*, 1999, 28(1): 1–30; 'Part II: 1972–96', 1999, 28(2): 109–41.
5 Richardson, op. cit., p. 138, citing R. Aldrich, *The End of History and the Beginning of Education*, London: Institute of Education, 1997, as 'the most recent manifestation of the latter'.
6 R. Aldrich, 'A contested and changing terrain: history of education in the twenty-first century', in D. Crook and R. Aldrich (eds), *History of Education for the Twenty-First Century*, London: Institute of Education, 2000, pp. 77–8.
7 Department of History; Department of History and Humanities; Department of History, Humanities and Philosophy; History and Philosophy Group; School of Educational Foundations and Policy Studies.
8 D. Hey, *Family History and Local History in England*, London: Longman, 1987, p. xii. Examples of the continuing growth include the recent proliferation of such magazines as *Ancestors, Family History Monthly, Family Tree Magazine* and *Practical Family History*. R. Blatchford (ed.), *The Family and Local History Handbook*, York: The Genealogical Services Directory, 6th edn 2002, lists more than 300 national, local, genealogical, specialist and one-name family history societies in the United Kingdom.
9 For a full discussion of this phenomenon see R. Aldrich, 'Family history and the history of the family', in R. Aldrich (ed.), *Public or Private Education? Lessons from History*, London: Woburn Press, 2004, pp. 127–43.
10 J. Herbst, 'The history of education: state of the art at the turn of the century in Europe and North America', *Paedagogica Historica*, 1999, XXXV(3): 737.
11 Ibid., p. 747.
12 M. Depaepe, 'A professionally relevant history of education for teachers: does it exist?', *Paedagogica Historica*, 2001, XXXVII(3): 634.
13 Ibid., p. 640.
14 Depaepe's use of the words 'intrinsic' and 'extrinsic' is not entirely clear, a problem compounded by his use of the terms, 'science' and 'scientific', in respect of historical study. For example, in 'Demythologizing the educational past: an endless task in history of education', *Historical Studies in Education/Revue d'histoire de l'éducation*, 1997, 9: 208, he warned that 'A purely "extrinsic" relationship between educational history and utility, present or future, endangers the "scientific" claims of history'.
15 Simon Jenkins, 'History is not bunk, but most historians are', *The Times*, 5 July 2002.
16 The current title is 'The History of the English Education System'. The lecture receives consistently high ratings from students.
17 For further details see R. Aldrich, *The Institute of Education 1902–2002: A Centenary History*, London: Institute of Education, 2002.
18 R. Aldrich (ed.), *A Century of Education*, London: RoutledgeFalmer, 2002.
19 Primary education (Peter Cunningham), secondary education (Gary McCulloch), further education (Bill Bailey), higher education (Roy Lowe), central and local government (Paul Sharp), teachers (Philip Gardner), pupils and students (Ruth Watts), special educational needs (Ian Copeland), curriculum (Peter Gordon), qualifications and assessment (Alison Wolf).
20 G. Smith, 'Schools', in A.H. Halsey with J. Webb (eds), *Twentieth-Century British Social Trends*, London: Macmillan, 2000, p. 219.
21 *The Times*, 12 April 2002.
22 For a discussion of public, private and official views of the past see G. McCulloch, 'Publicizing the educational past', in D. Crook and R. Aldrich (eds), *History of Education for the Twenty-First Century*, London: Institute of Education, 2000, pp. 1–16.

23 Reported in *The Times*, 5 April 2002.
24 For a discussion of some of the implications of postmodernity for historians of education see 'History of Education in the Postmodern Era', a special issue of *Paedagogica Historica*, 1996, XXXII(2).
25 K. Jenkins, *Re-thinking History*, London: Routledge, 1991, p. 29.
26 Ibid., p. 30.
27 J. Appleby, L. Hunt and M. Jacob, *Telling the Truth about History*, New York: Norton, 1994, p. 248. As Oscar Wilde observed, 'Any fool can make history; it takes a genius to write it.'
28 M. Gaither, 'Globalization and history of education', *Paedagogica Historica*, 2001, XXXVII(3): 644.
29 K. Rousmanière, 'Fresh thinking: recent work in the history of education', *Paedagogica Historica*, 2001, XXXVII(3): 649.
30 J. Herbst, 'The history of education: state of the art at the turn of the century in Europe and North America', *Paedagogica Historica*, 1999, XXXV(3): 740.
31 N. Peim, 'The state of the art or the ruins of nostalgia? The problematics of subject identity, its objects, theoretical resources and practices', *Paedagogica Historica*, 2001, XXXVII(3): 655. Domus is a 'Research Centre for Histories in Education' based at the University of Birmingham. Its membership includes Ian Grosvenor, Helen Gunter, Kevin Myers, Nick Peim and Ruth Watts, and associate UK members, David Coppock, Joyce Goodman, Martin Lawn and Jane Martin. Information kindly supplied by Dr Ruth Watts. There are diverse views within the Domus group and in spite of his use of the term 'we', Peim's rejection of history as a 'parent' discipline is not necessarily shared by all of its members. The formulations 'DOMUS' and 'Domus' appear to be used interchangeably in Peim's article.
32 Ibid., p. 660.
33 But see N. Peim, 'The history of the present: towards a contemporary phenomenology of the school', *History of Education*, 2001, 30(2): 177–90.
34 A. Munslow, *The Routledge Companion to Historical Studies*, London: Routledge, 2000, p. 19.
35 Ibid.
36 Ibid.
37 Classic aphorisms include: 'History is but a pack of tricks we play upon the dead' (Voltaire); 'History is much an art as a science' (Renan); 'There will always be a connection between the way in which men contemplate the past and the way in which they contemplate the present' (Buckle); 'We get our ethics from our history and judge our history by our ethics' (Troeltsch); 'The study of history is a personal matter in which the activity is generally more valuable than the result' (Galbraith); 'A mere collector of supposed facts is as useful as a collector of matchboxes' (Febvre); 'Sociology is history with the hard work left out; history is sociology with the brains left out' (MacRae). See A. Marwick, *The Nature of History*, London: Macmillan, 1970, pp. 244–6.
38 F. Stern (ed.), *The Varieties of History: From Voltaire to the Present*, London: Macmillan, 2nd edn 1970, p. 76.
39 L. Strachey, *Eminent Victorians*, London: Chatto and Windus, 1948 edn, p. 6.
40 Stern, op. cit., p. 26.
41 *The Times*, 25 April 2002.
42 R.J. Evans, *Telling Lies about Hitler: The Holocaust, History and the David Irving Trial*, London: Verso, 2002.
43 R.J. Evans, *In Defence of History*, London: Granta, 1997, p. 253.

CHAPTER 2

THE END OF HISTORY AND THE BEGINNING OF EDUCATION

The End of History and the Beginning of Education,
London: Institute of Education, 1997

Introduction

A professorial lecture has many purposes. One is to enable the professor to pose questions in respect of scholarship throughout the chosen field and to reflect at some length upon her or his past work (one of the many reasons why I prefer attending inaugural lectures given by younger members of staff).

A second purpose, a purpose which I believe is incumbent upon all of us who are privileged to work in higher education, is to make a genuine contribution to the amounts of truth, justice, understanding and goodwill in the world. That general mission receives a particular focus in an Institute such as this, which is committed to a postgraduate, research-based, metropolitan and international approach to the promotion of truth and scholarship, understanding and goodwill within the field of education.

Sidney Webb may be counted as the founder of this Institute, or the London Day Training College as it originally was. In an article entitled 'London University: a policy and a forecast' published in June 1902, Webb declared that:

> The obvious and imperative duty of a rightly organised and adequately endowed London University is to become the foremost post-graduate centre of the intellectual world... No place provides, in each subject of study, so highly specialised a society, in which the ablest thinkers and investigators can meet, in friendly converse, not only their foreign colleagues visiting the great city, but also those who are, in the practical business of life, both needing and using the newest discoveries.[1]

Just four months later, on 6 October 1902, the Principal, Professor John Adams, delivered the first professorial lecture at the London Day. At that time the new institution had no buildings it could call its own, and Adams had to deliver his lecture at its temporary home, and another of the Webbs' creations, the London School of Economics. The title of that lecture was simply, 'The Training of Teachers'. Adams began from the premise that there was no longer any question as to whether teachers should be trained. The only point at issue was how. Adams put the matter in a pithy form which is as appropriate today as it was then: 'There are two ways in which the public can pay for the training of its teachers: it can pay in money, or it can pay in children.'[2]

This evening I am very conscious of the great traditions of this Institute, and of my own inadequacies when contemplating the work of the many eminent scholars who have occupied chairs here in the past. Any confidence that I may have at this point comes from a knowledge that this lecture draws in a general sense upon the wisdom and scholarship of countless colleagues and friends, the great majority of whom I have come to know through membership of the two societies of which I have had the honour to be President – the International Standing Conference for the History of Education and the UK History of Education Society. But it also draws more particularly upon the wisdom, scholarship and friendship of those colleagues with whom I have worked most closely within this Institute. I thank them all.

Let me begin with some basic points of definition. These have been elaborated elsewhere but, given the nature of my argument this evening, it is necessary to summarize them at this point.

History may be variously defined: for example as the past; the study and representation of the past; the study and representation of the past in accordance with a set of procedures. Other definitions might emphasize that history is not simply about the past, but about the human past; others again define history in terms of human activity with particular reference to the whole dimension of time – past, present and future. Another type of definition is that which identifies history as:

> a verbal artefact, a narrative prose discourse of which, après White, the content is as much invented as found, and which is constructed by present-minded, ideologically positioned workers (historians and those acting as if they were historians) operating at various levels of reflexivity...a rhetorical, metaphorical, textual practice governed by distinctive but never homogenous procedures...[3]

Each and every one of these definitions of history is useful. Taken together they demonstrate both the immense richness and variety of the subject, and the need to recognize the complexity and responsibility of the historian's role.

Education has also been variously interpreted and defined. No doubt from some standpoints, education and educational reform may be 'best understood as a part of the process of social regulation'.[4] An even more limited approach is to be found in the United Kingdom at present where it has been officially declared that:

> The Government's principal aim for the education service at all levels and in all forms of learning is:
>
> To support economic growth and improve the nation's competitiveness and quality of life by raising standards of educational achievement and skill and by promoting an efficient and flexible labour market.[5]

This may be sharply contrasted with Richard Peters' definition of education as initiation into worthwhile activities. Emphasis upon the concept of worthwhileness is important, because clearly the term education would not be used with respect to preparing a person to be a liar or a thief, even for the purpose of promoting economic growth. A recent definition of education which is consistent with this approach is that furnished by Willem Frijhoff of the Erasmus University, Rotterdam. In the context of a general discussion of education and cultural transmission, Frijhoff argues that 'both are two aspects of the same reality, education being the instrument of culture, and culture the goal of education'.[6]

Just as history and education are highly complex entities in themselves, so, too, is the relationship between them. To most observers, education may seem to be more important than history. Others would consider history and education as equals, inasmuch as each provides a means of understanding and enhancing the human condition. Others again would interpret history as a discipline, albeit one which lacks particularly distinctive procedures and employs everyday rather than specialist language, and education as a field of study. Whatever position is taken, however, it is clear that one of the most highly visible and important connections between history and education is the history of education.

My own personal contributions to the history of education have covered a range of topics: from biography[7] to policy,[8] from teacher education[9] to the teaching of history.[10] One methodological approach has been that of historical perspectives, and many chapters and articles have been written in this frame and borne the subtitle: 'an historical perspective'. In 1988 I founded a study group within the UK History of Education Society to promote this approach. The formula has been used by others for their publications, for example, by Paul Sharp in his recent study of school governing bodies.[11] The term has been taken up for conferences, for example, the UK History of Education Society Conference held at Cambridge in December 1996 was entitled 'Teachers' lives: training and careers in historical perspective'. That to be held in London at this Institute in May 1997 is called 'Policy-making in Education in historical perspective'. The recent remodelling of the History of Education MA at this Institute, undertaken by my colleague David Crook (who now chairs the Historical Perspectives study group of the UK History of Education Society) has produced successful modules with such titles as, 'Childhood: an historical perspective', and 'Education and employment: an historical perspective'. Between 1993 and 1995 the Leverhulme Foundation funded my project entitled 'Historical perspectives upon current educational issues in England', which led to another successful MA module, now entitled 'Understanding English education', and to a range of national and international lectures and publications, culminating in *Education for the Nation*,[12] published in November 1996.

There is no intention on this occasion to try to deconstruct my own ideological position or levels of reflexivity. These matters have been considered elsewhere.[13] But it seems appropriate to say that in common with most historians I do stand somewhere along that continuum which stretches between Carr and Elton on the one hand and Rorty and White on the other, and have drawn upon insights from them all. And, as the next section of this lecture will clearly demonstrate, I do believe that if history is regularly used in the promotion of contemporary causes it is incumbent upon the professional historian of education to ensure that such usage is as accurate as possible, both in its representation of the past and in the connections established between past, present and future.

Such a position depends upon the further belief that some history as constructed is better than other history, and that the most important criterion for making such a judgement is the extent to which history, as written or otherwise presented, reflects the past as it actually was. Some historical writing may indeed be, as Hayden White has stated, 'a narrative discourse the contents of which are as much imagined/invented as found'.[14] Most historians, however, do find more evidence about the past than they imagine or invent, and the quality of that evidence, coupled with the quality of the necessary selection, ordering and presentation of it, is one important distinction between good history and bad. A high degree of fact as opposed to fiction is also a means of distinguishing historical writing from many other branches of literature.

Of course the historical perspectives approach is but one use of the history of education, and at this point it must be acknowledged that the use of history for purposes other than to understand the past in its own right has been questioned, indeed condemned, by many. There is neither time nor space here to enter into a detailed consideration of the general issue of the uses and abuses of history,[15] but three comments may be made on the dictum that history should be studied for its own sake.

The first is that the past is connected to the present and future in various ways. The past, indeed, has an existence as itself, irrespective of the present and the future, and the historian's first duty may be to reflect that past as accurately as possible. Nevertheless, the past is connected with the present both by virtue of itself having formerly been both a future and a present, and through the medium of the historian who represents it. No historian can divest her- or himself of a life in the present, nor of its several concerns as reflected in such mundane matters as the securing of research grants or the support of publishers. The historian of education, moreover, frequently represents a particular connection between past and present. While some historians may declare themselves to be allergic to the twentieth century, and live their lives in rarefied atmospheres, many historians of education are regularly at the chalk face. Some also teach Postgraduate Certificate in Education (PGCE) History students, supervise them on school practice, and become only too familiar with the heady whiff of diesel fumes while caught in traffic jams, and the even more memorable aroma of school dinners, unmistakably pressure cooked and bottled in by the tightly closed windows which invariably accompany a wet dinner hour.

Second, we live in a society which is characterized by an orientation 'towards change rather than conservation, towards exploitation and consumption...The past becomes, therefore, a matter of curiosity, of nostalgia, of sentimentality'.[16] The task of the historian is to rescue the past from such a fate, and, in so doing, to provide a more sophisticated representation and analysis of the world we have lost, one which acknowledges continuities as well as discontinuities.

This is not to advocate a return to Whig history. Hayden White is surely correct when he argues that 'The historian serves no one well by constructing a specious continuity between the present world and that which preceded it.' But to proceed, as he does, to assert that 'On the contrary, we require a history that will educate us to discontinuity more than ever before; for discontinuity, disruption and chaos is our lot',[17] seems to me to raise two very important questions. The first is on what grounds is it to be supposed that discontinuity, disruption and chaos in the 1970s, 1980s and 1990s are any greater than during previous (or for that matter future) periods of history? The second is that if discontinuity, disruption and chaos do, indeed, characterize the lot of human beings in the last quarter of the twentieth century, why should history be employed to condition such human beings to an acceptance of that state, rather than to educate them to reject and overcome it?

My final comment is to share with you two penetrating and provocative observations on the uses of the past which I have found to be particularly enlightening. The first is from Sir John Seeley, Regius Professor of History at the University of Cambridge from 1869 until his death in 1895. In 1883 Seeley declared that 'We shall all no doubt be wise after the event; we study history that we may be wise before the event'.[18] The second is from John Maynard Keynes, who in 1926 advised that 'A study of the history of opinion is a necessary preliminary to the emancipation of the mind. I do not know which makes a man more conservative – to know nothing but the present, or nothing but the past.'[19] Some 20 years ago, on 17 May 1977, Harold Silver took these words 'Nothing but the present, or nothing but the past?' as the title of his impressive inaugural lecture at Chelsea College, London.

Historical perspectives

There are two important points to be made in this section. The first is that historical perspectives upon current educational issues are widely employed, for example, by individuals, by politicians and by the press.

Each and every one of us, whether as a private individual, or in a more public role, seeks to understand the present and to make some sense of the future, by reference to the immediate and more distant past. Let me go back, almost a year, to the day when I started to prepare this lecture. The date was Friday 31 May 1996, and the *Times Educational Supplement* carried an interview with Kenneth Baker who described the great difficulty of getting educational matters through Cabinet, 'because the one subject on which Cabinet Ministers love to digress in a very ill-formed way is reminiscing about their own school days'.[20] Baker also mentioned the particular difficulties he had encountered as Secretary of State for Education with the Prime Minister of his day. Indeed, he characterized Margaret Thatcher's approach to the national curriculum as 'Gradgrind'.[21] This was an interesting comment, because Margaret Thatcher, herself, in *The Downing Street Years*, declared that 'Ken Baker paid too much attention to the DES, the HMI and progressive educational theorists in his appointments and early decisions'.[22]

The employment of such terms as 'Gradgrind' and 'progressive educational theorists' as terms of abuse exemplifies the use and potential abuse of history of education that commonly takes place. The use of historical allusions to sharpen contemporary axes, however, does not only take place between Oxford-educated members of Conservative cabinets. In the same *TES* interview on 31 May, Kenneth Baker revealed to Michael Barber that Mrs Thatcher's hairdresser, Paul Allen, whom she saw on a more regular basis than most of her Cabinet colleagues, had had a considerable influence on educational policy. Two days later Mr Allen was reported in the *Sunday Times* as saying that when he went to school.

> We had a French teacher, and for every single mistake – even a missed accent – you would get a whack on the backside with a ruler. It hurt like hell, but you went over your homework with a fine toothcomb, and French became my best subject.

In sharp contrast Mr Allen reported to Mrs Thatcher, and now through the medium of the *Sunday Times* to a much wider audience, that the schooling of his own children had left much to be desired. For example:

> The school did not correct spelling mistakes, and so right through Lisa and Justin's school years, their spelling was terrible: there was never, ever, a correction in their work. My wife was always on about it: it was mentioned to the staff, but it never improved.[23]

Little wonder that on that weekend of 1 and 2 June 1996, teachers and others turned with more than usual relief to the back page of that same *TES* number which had carried the Baker interview, where Ted Wragg assured them that *The Times*, Mrs Thatcher and even Mrs Thatcher's hairdresser, had got it all wrong. The piece began in characteristically ebullient vein, 'I have gone right off Gillian Shephard', and proceeded to castigate her for

> repeating the interminable litany of the Right, which she knows is tosh. Back in the good old days, the story goes, there was a Golden Age. Children sat in large classes and teachers told them the facts. As a result they could all spell

every word in the dictionary, knew all their tables up to a billion times a billion, and could recite every cape and bay from Southend to Cape Squinxx on the planet Pluto.

The truth of the matter is that this 19th-century style of education produced an ignorant peasantry, unknowing about science and many other aspects of life, and hating school with a deep intensity. Even the brightest did not achieve as brilliantly as the right wing would have us believe. The D streamers in grammar schools were rubbished and like John Major often quit before A level, even though they were among the cleverest in their area. Less than 10 per cent of the population went on to higher education. Nowadays, their equivalents, alongside thousands of others who would have failed the 11-plus, are in the third of the population that goes to university.[24]

Historical perspectives upon education also frequently appear in the popular press. Here are some excerpts from the *Daily Mail*: 'the brutal truth is that standards have fallen'; 'individual acts of classroom violence that you read about – frequently you may think – do not, even so, represent the real scale of the problem'; 'most parents and many teachers believe that children are less literate and numerate than they were 20 years ago'. Similarly, from the opposite end of the political spectrum, the *Daily Mirror* assures its readers: 'literacy in Britain is marching backwards'; 'general educational standards have slipped alarmingly in the past decade or so'; and continues to applaud the 'mounting backlash against progressive methods'.[25]

Do these accounts sound familiar? In fact they are taken from 1975 and 1976. All, therefore, are more than 20 years old. Yet such judgements (or diatribes) are regularly repeated and may indicate that things have not changed much in that period. It may be true that Conservative reforms since 1979, and/or the best efforts of teachers and pupils, have been largely unsuccessful in raising standards of conduct and of academic achievement in schools. Other explanations, however, must be considered. For example, the popular (and broadsheet) press may regard teachers as easy targets, and a mixture of nostalgia, self-righteousness, horror stories and scapegoating as a standard means of attracting readers' attention and thereby of increasing circulation figures.

Of course, bad news has always sold more newspapers than good, particularly in such sure-fire areas as sex, health, wealth, sport, the Royals, and latterly, television. We live in an age of unprecedented scientific and technological development, yet these subjects do not sell newspapers. Astrology on the other hand is booming. In 1996 the *Daily Express*, *Daily Mail*, *Mail on Sunday* and *Sunday Mirror* all achieved substantial increases in sales with special promotions of annual horoscopes. Indeed, price-cutting apart, the best way to sell newspapers is to run special promotions in such areas as health, royal biographies or travel. For example, a Eurostar promotion in *The Times* and *Sunday Times* added 150,000 copies to sales of both newspapers over four weeks, and dovetailed nicely with the fire in the Channel Tunnel, which complemented the good news of free tickets with the bad news that such journeys were more hazardous than had previously been believed.[26]

My second point, therefore, is that while the use of historical perspectives is widespread, it is often dangerously deficient. Just as some history as constructed is better than other history, so are some historical perspectives better than others. Evidence about the purposes and practices, the achievements and failures of education is available, and lessons can be drawn from it. Such lessons, however, are complex and involved. They are neither easily adapted to the television sound bite, nor to the short assertive sentences of a 600-word newspaper article.

Indeed, many of the lessons to be drawn from historical perspectives upon education must be couched in terms of caution, of thorough research and planning, of emphasizing the need above all to retain that which is good while seeking to improve that which is of less worth. A clear example of this is provided by school buildings, which represent one of the most important forms of evidence from the past. Indeed, one of the greatest weaknesses of some writers *about* history, as opposed to writers *of* history, is their excessive concentration upon verbal artefacts and narrative prose discourses. School buildings represent in a most tangible way, priorities and beliefs about a variety of elements of education, including such intangibles as the nature of childhood and society, of pedagogical purposes and practices. Many of these buildings are still being used – decades, centuries even – after they were constructed. They provide a physical context for the education of the children of today and of tomorrow. Some of them are better adapted to the purposes of education than others, and it is a shame upon us all that some of the worst school buildings date from the 1960s and 1970s. In common with some of the homes constructed at that time, they were, and remain, manifestly unfit for the purposes for which they were intended.

This is, or should be, a sobering thought. The mistakes and meanness of policy makers in education may be visited not only upon the children of one generation, but even upon those of their children's children. This is not only true in respect of buildings. It also applies to curriculum and pedagogy.

In 1990, in a rare moment of public self-doubt, Margaret Thatcher acknowledged this as she began to understand the problems that her government's interventions in respect of the school history curriculum were producing:

> Now the History Report has come out. It is very detailed. There were not many secondary school teachers on the syllabus-forming committee. I think it really must be put out to great consultation and consideration. My worry is whether we should put out such a detailed one. You see, once you put out an approved curriculum, if you have got it wrong, the situation is worse afterwards than it was before. At any given time a large number of teachers are teaching a subject extremely well. But if you take them off what they know has worked for years, far better than anyone else's syllabus, then you wonder: were you doing it right?[27]

Just so, Prime Minister. Nevertheless, in spite of these doubts, Margaret Thatcher made innumerable interventions in respect of the history curriculum. Kenneth Baker has a history degree and a continuing interest in the subject, but as Margaret Thatcher explained in her memoirs:

> Though not an historian myself, I had a very clear – and I had naively imagined uncontroversial – idea of what history was. History was an account of what happened in the past. Learning History, therefore, requires knowledge of events.[28]

This is a useful definition as far as it goes, but, as indicated in the first section, it is deficient in at least two respects. First, there is no single account of what happened in the past. As the recent plethora of memoirs from retired and ousted politicians clearly demonstrates, there are many such accounts. Second, these accounts do not always agree, even when (perhaps particularly when) they are written by people who participated in the very events they are recounting. Margaret Thatcher's idea of history was a primitive one, but on the basis of that understanding she confidently proceeded, as she tells us herself, to reject Secretary of State, Kenneth Baker's original list of members of the History Working Group and the guidance to be offered to them, and subsequently to overrule the proposed responses both of Baker and of his successor, John MacGregor, to the interim and final History reports.

It is to be hoped that some lessons have been learned from the tortuous, time-consuming, expensive and irrational exercise of producing a national curriculum for schools. Unfortunately, several government interventions in the field of education have provided clear examples of the predominance of ideology over truth, examples which Michael Barber has recently characterized as 'Free-Market Stalinism'.[29]

The end of history

In 1989, a 15-page article written by Francis Fukuyama and entitled 'The end of history?' was published in the journal, *National Interest*.[30] This was to be followed in 1992 by the substantial tome entitled *The End of History and the Last Man*.[31]

Fukuyama's thesis attracted much attention. Few professional historians agreed with it fully, but the fact that his many critics felt it necessary to explain their objections, coupled with the overthrow of Communist or Socialist regimes in central and eastern Europe which seemed to endorse his interpretation, brought Fukuyama and his ideas centre stage.

Fukuyama went back to Hegel to resurrect the idea that history, as a process in human existence, had a beginning and an end. History began with the discovery that people might be free, and would end once human beings had discovered the rational way of organizing their affairs to achieve that end. The events of 1989–92 indicated that history had ended, in the sense that liberal democracy had become generally, though not universally, recognized as the best means of government. Fukuyama's thesis depended upon his particular definition of history. Of course, he did not mean that the normal process of human events would come to an end, nor that such events would become a past which historians and others would decline to study. His question was:

> Whether, at the end of the twentieth century, it makes sense for us once again to speak of a coherent and directional History of mankind that will eventually lead the greater part of humanity to liberal democracy? The answer I arrive at is yes, for two separate reasons. One has to do with economics, and the other has to do with what is termed the 'struggle for recognition'.[32]

Fukuyama argued that 'Looking around the world there remains a very strong overall correlation between advancing socio-economic modernization and the emergence of new democracies'.[33] But although the desire for a better standard of living and a market economy was a crucial factor in the revolutions which challenged or overthrew Communist regimes, equal importance in Fukuyama's analysis was to be given to an idea – the idea of recognition. In a chapter entitled 'On the possibility of writing a universal history', published in 1995, he stated that:

> people did not go into the streets of Leipzig, Prague, Timisoara, Beijing or Moscow demanding that the government give them a postindustrial economy. Their passionate anger was aroused over their perceptions of injustice which had nothing to do with economics... In the accounts of the resistance in St. Petersburg to the hardline coup in August 1991, those who rallied to the

side of the 'democrats'...demanded less a market economy than a government that recognized their elementary rights under a rule of law, a government that did not lie to them about the crimes and stupidities it had committed in the past, that would allow them freely to express their thymotic opinions about right and wrong, and that would ultimately treat them not as children but as adults capable of governing themselves.[34]

Several arguments may be advanced against Fukuyama's notion of an end of history. Many states are far from being liberal democracies. National, racial, ethnic and religious ideologies remain strong, and in the face of such ideologies liberal principles and economic well-being may count for little.

Liberal democracies, themselves, may be far from perfect. In some liberal democracies, including the United Kingdom, on occasion citizens may be deprived of their rights and treated like children, while governments frequently cover up current and past mistakes and crimes. Meanwhile the rich get richer and the poor get poorer. For example, in the United States 'in 1989 the top 1% earned more collectively than the bottom 40%'.[35] There is considerable evidence that we live in a society characterized by a breakdown in family and in family values, the emergence of an unemployed, possibly an unemployable, underclass, a rapid escalation in the use of drugs and in the incidence of violent crime. Consumerism prevails, with a new cultural imperialism based upon such universal products as Coca Cola and McDonalds.

Nevertheless, the concept of the end of history raises a number of important points for the historian of education and for the application of historical perspectives, four of which will be considered here. These relate to historiography, education, ideology and language.

The first issue is to locate Fukuyama's thesis within a historiographical context. In one sense, his argument is simply a rather grandiose comment upon the long observed bankruptcy – ideological and material – of certain political regimes. In some senses it replicates the analyses of such writers as Herbert Marcuse and Daniel Bell. Other links may be made with the writings of Karl Popper. The first volume of *The Open Society and its Enemies*, published in 1945, was inscribed 'In memory of the countless men and women...who fell victims to the Fascist and Communist belief in Inexorable Laws of Historical Destiny'. A further connection may be observed with the work of J.H. Plumb. In a volume entitled *The Death of the Past*, based upon the Saposnekow lectures given at the City College, New York in March 1968, Plumb distinguished between history and the past, arguing in support of rational, professional historians who would create 'an historical past, objective and true'.[36] In contrast, Plumb opposed that past which he depicted as having flourished in a variety of totalitarian cultures, including China across the ages, and the USSR of his own day. This he characterized as 'a created ideology with a purpose, designed to control individuals, or motivate societies, or inspire classes'.[37] He even predicted that 'Russia cannot detach itself from the West. The dogma of history, as now practised in Russia, is unlikely to remain in its present form for many more decades. Soon Russia and her satellites will be facing the problem of a past corroded by the practice of history.'[38]

Where does the concept of the end of history stand in relation to postmodernist historical interpretations? In one sense the end of history appears to be essentially modernist, insofar as it provides a logical interpretation of the development of human events, in Fukuyama's terms 'the end point of ideological evolution'. On the other hand, postmodernists may identify the end of history with the end of certaintist histories, the final demise of the great metanarratives. In the words of Jenkins, 'we have reached the end of modernist versions of what history is'.[39] Much depends upon whether the end of history is to be interpreted as the end of modernist versions of history or rather as the confirmation of such history.

A second theme is that of the place of education within this framework. Although *The End of History* contains a chapter entitled 'In the land of education',[40] Fukuyama's comments upon the relationship between education and his principal theme are both minimal and tentative. After the briefest of treatments he concludes simply that:

> It is reasonably clear that education is, if not an absolutely necessary precondition, then at least a highly desirable adjunct to democracy. It is hard to imagine democracy working properly in a largely illiterate society where the people cannot take advantage of information about the chances open to them. But it is a rather different matter to say that education *necessarily* leads to belief in democratic norms.[41]

Fukuyama's concentration upon the possible role of education in *promoting* democracy, however, should not preclude an identification of other issues concerning outcomes. Since education, as represented by such dimensions as organization, curriculum, pedagogy and assessment, both reflects values concerning society as it is, and as those who control it (and others) would wish it to be, any generalization of liberal democracy must affect the nature and purposes of provided education. More fundamentally still, if the end of history is to be accompanied by an end to some basic ideological struggles and a focus upon the nature and quality of liberal democracy, governments will have more reason and time to concentrate upon economic and social concerns, including education. Thus a Soviet regime which put a man into space has been displaced by a Russian one which places a higher priority upon getting steak and razor blades into Moscow. In the United Kingdom, the role of Secretary of State for Education and Employment may become more important than that of Secretary of State for Foreign Affairs. A more universal acceptance of liberal democracy, moreover, may diminish the nostalgia for hierarchical educational forms associated with an imperial past. Such processes will be influenced in the United Kingdom, as elsewhere, by the increased participation within liberal democracies of the members of that half of the human race who have for so long been excluded from political and professional power.

The third point concerns the ideological positions from which history, and in this context particularly history of education, is studied and written. From its modern origins in the later nineteenth century much British history of education was written in a broadly celebratory style – in which the rise of a national system of free and compulsory schooling was centre stage. This interpretation was challenged in the 1960s and 1970s by such historians as Richard Johnson, Brian Simon and Charles Webster. These writers, far from celebrating the achievements of the British educational system, characterized it as inegalitarian and heavily bureaucratized, a system specifically designed to fail the majority of children. From 1979, Conservative governments, politicians and think tanks also expressed serious criticisms of state education. Their analysis of the situation, however, was not based upon the interpretations of such historians as Johnson, Simon and Webster, but rather upon those of E.G. West, Martin Wiener and Correlli Barnett. West's delineation of the achievements of British education before the establishment of school boards in 1870, and his fundamental questioning of the role of the state, could be used to provide a rationale for the limitation of the role of local education authorities (LEAs), and for the promotion of diversity in institutions and consumer choice.[42] Wiener's study of English culture and the long decline of the industrial spirit after 1851, quoted with approval Edward Heath's warning in 1973 that:

> The alternative to expansion is not, as some occasionally seem to suppose, an England of quiet market towns linked only by trains puffing slowly and peacefully through green meadows. The alternative is slums, dangerous roads, old factories, cramped schools, stunted lives.[43]

Even more influential was the savage indictment of British industrial and educational policies and standards contained in Correlli Barnett's, *The Audit of War*. Barnett concluded that in the aftermath of the Second World War:

> the dreams of 1945 would fade one by one – the imperial and Commonwealth role, the world power role, British industrial genius, and, at the last, New Jerusalem itself, a dream turned to a dank reality of a segregated, subliterate, unskilled, unhealthy and institutionalised proletariat hanging on the nipple of state maternalism.[44]

From the mid-1980s historians of education in the United Kingdom could not but be excited, mesmerized even, by the amount of history of education that was being created before their very eyes. Such changes, however, were part of a broader pattern. Even before the revolutions in central and eastern Europe, and the emergence of the concept of the end of history, two phenomena were becoming apparent in British politics. The first was the decline in numbers of the traditional working classes, and of working-class occupations. The second was that the social and economic agenda of the Left – nationalization, high levels of taxation on the rich, an ever-increasing welfare state, a powerful trade union movement – was losing its appeal.

For historians of education, therefore, the effect upon ideological positioning produced by the concept of the end of history was compounded by the ending of the traditional (or indeed mythical) working classes. Perspectives were changing. As David Marquand noted in *The Progressive Dilemma: From Lloyd George to Kinnock* (1991), 'Conservative or predominantly Conservative governments have been in office for fifty of the seventy-odd years since the Labour Party first became the official opposition in the House of Commons, and Labour governments for only twenty'.[45] There was only one great period of Labour success and, as commentators such as Peter Clarke have noted, the victory of 1945 was the product not of a particular commitment to socialist policies, but rather of a general postwar belief that there was a need for radical social and economic change, a belief which prevailed across the boundaries of social class.[46]

Such re-examination has the widest national and international implications. The industrial proletariat of England has a particular significance in discussions about the end of history, for it was the English urban proletariat which provided evidence for the theories of Marx and Engels. The relative alienation of this proletariat from socialism, from the Labour Party and from the system of state-provided schooling, is a phenomenon which merits considerable further analysis. One starting point for such analysis is the idea that the key divisions in nineteenth- and twentieth-century British society were not only between upper, middle and working classes, but also between the religious and respectable of all classes on the one hand, and the irreligious and disreputable on the other.[47]

The final point in this section extends the implications of the concept of the end of history from the ideological positions from which history of education is written to the very language which such historians employ. Given the probability that varieties of history (including those of a postmodernist kind) are more likely to flourish in liberal democracies than in many other types of states, it is difficult to predict their nature with any certainty. The proliferation or consolidation of liberal democracies will not bring an end to disputes between conservatives and radicals, traditionalists and progressives, whether amongst historians or educationists, albeit such rivalries may be conducted within narrower parameters. Marxist and neo-Marxist positions, however, have been considerably weakened, if not rendered untenable. It may, therefore, be necessary both to abandon such historical positions and perspectives, and even to discard their very concepts and terminology. In an important recent chapter Richard Rorty has suggested that

> I think the time has come to drop the terms 'capitalism' and 'socialism' from the political vocabulary of the left. It would be a good idea to stop talking about 'the anticapitalist struggle' and to substitute something banal and untheoretical – something like 'the struggle against avoidable human misery'. More generally, I hope that we can banalize the entire vocabulary of leftist political deliberation. I suggest that we start talking about greed and selfishness rather than about bourgeois ideology, about starvation wages and layoffs rather than about the commodification of labor, and about differential per-pupil expenditure on schools and differential access to health care rather than about the division of society into classes.[48]

It is interesting to note that while such terms as capitalism and socialism may still be in use amongst academics in many countries around the world, in British politics they have been largely expunged from the vocabulary of the Labour Party under the leadership of Neil Kinnock, John Smith and Tony Blair.

The beginning of education

Education has been a supreme element in human existence since time immemorial. Education as a major subject of study in higher education in England, however, has been of brief duration and low status. Joseph Payne, the first Professor of the Science and Art of Education in Britain, appointed to that position in 1873 by the College of Preceptors, a chartered body of teachers, was a man of humble origins without a university qualification. The majority of his students were prospective or practising female teachers in girls' secondary schools.

Payne's professorial lecture courses comprised 'The science or theory of education', 'The art or practice of education' and 'The history of education'. He also conducted inspections of teaching in schools. The breadth of his interests and the esteem in which he was held are demonstrated by the roles he played in a variety of educational organizations: chairman of the Women's Education Union, chairman of the Philological Society, vice-president of the College of Preceptors, vice-president of the Scholastic Registration Association, council member of the Girls' Public Day School Company, committee member of the Froebel Society and chairman of the inaugural meeting of the Society for the Development of the Science of Education, founded in 1875. Payne believed that in his own day the science of education was in a very rudimentary condition, its basic principles scattered across a number of fields. He was also somewhat wary of a full-blown concept of a science of education, preferring the formulation 'science and art'. He believed that 'education has a basis of its own, and that basis is human nature'.[49]

A further beginning of education in England may be associated with the establishment from the 1890s of day training facilities in connection with universities and university colleges. King's College, London, was amongst the first of these. The London Day Training College, founded in 1902, soon became the largest and most important. The subject of education in the day training colleges, however, was itself largely shaped by central directives. Since 1846 the education and training of pupil teachers had been strictly controlled by governments, which from the 1850s also prescribed curricula for teacher training colleges. In May 1890, under the terms of Circular 287, central government required that in the new institutions 'a normal master or mistress must be appointed to lecture on history and theory of education, to supervise teaching and to give a course of model lessons and preside at criticism lessons'. Most of the university-trained students were destined to teach in elementary schools, a situation which continued until the Second World War. Until the 1960s, the majority of those who studied education as a subject would not attain a degree; indeed, some of those who taught them were non-graduates themselves. In the first half of the twentieth century, and beyond, where the subject of education was welcomed into universities it was frequently on practical rather than academic grounds, for intending teachers brought guaranteed funding.

Two examples of the problems associated with the status of education as a subject of study were provided by the universities of Oxford and Cambridge. Day training began in the two ancient universities in the 1890s, but Oxford refused to sanction the appointment of a single professor in the subject until 1989 (by which time this Institute had appointed 49).[50] In 1938 the first incumbent of a chair at Cambridge, G.R. Owst, accepted an appointment which he was to hold for 21 years on the understanding that he could continue with his medieval historical scholarship and not be too bothered with education.[51]

This situation may be contrasted with that in German-speaking countries where educational science (Erziehungswissenschaft) was given formal recognition in the second half of the eighteenth century, with the first chair in the subject established at the University of Halle in Prussia in 1780 and another in Vienna in 1805. Nevertheless, even in these lands where educational science had a basis in philosophy as well as in pedagogy, problems were legion. As Heinz-Elmar Tenorth has concluded, progress was pitifully slow for a discipline which was 'Caught between profession and science, between research and politics, between practice and theory'.[52]

The development of education as a university subject in England in the twentieth century has been reviewed by David Crook and myself in a chapter to be published this year in the third volume in the new ISCHE series.[53] That chapter provides some account of achievements and failures, of gains and losses. It certainly indicates the leading roles played in the development of education by such Institute staff as its first two principals, John Adams and Percy Nunn, a theme to be considered in detail in the forthcoming centenary history of the Institute.[54] But notwithstanding the contributions and international standing of such scholars, it must also be acknowledged that there have been many critics of education as an academic discipline or field of study. These include Fred Clarke, the third director of this Institute, who in 1943 declared that if other professions conducted public discussion in the same way as did educationists, then 'most patients would die, most bridges would fall down, and most manufacturing concerns would go bankrupt'.[55]

In 1994, Robert Skidelsky echoed this sentiment. In commenting on the immaturity of education with respect to disciplinary status, Skidelsky referred to 'its relative inability to generate uncontested propositions and its paucity of testable hypotheses...education is also immature in the sense that what ought to be questions of fact are too often turned into questions of interpretation'.[56]

In 1996 David Hargreaves, in a lecture entitled 'Teaching as a research-based profession: possibilities and prospects', provided an explanation for this phenomenon, arguing that:

> In medicine, as in the natural sciences, research has a broadly cumulative character...Much educational research is, by contrast, non-cumulative, in part because few researchers seek to create a body of knowledge which is then tested, extended or replaced in some systematic way.[57]

Two comments may be made at this point. The first is that since education, like history, has some of the attributes both of a science and of an art, on occasion what appear to be questions of educational fact may indeed, become questions of educational interpretation. The second, that within the United Kingdom a more coherent approach both to the development of a discipline of education and to its connections with educational policies and practices, is urgently required. History of education, which can provide many of the data for a cumulative approach, and historical perspectives, have a vital role to play in this process.

Of course, viewed as an interaction between a discipline and a field of study, history of education may appear to differ little from other thematic approaches to history: for example, those of diplomacy, female emancipation, naval warfare, politics, religion, none of which would claim to be a discipline in its own right. Nevertheless, even such comparisons from a thematic perspective, given the centrality of education in human experience across all periods and cultures, would seem to confirm the centrality of history of education among historical studies. Indeed, if, as argued in the previous section, one of the consequences of the end of history is to give a higher priority to such areas as education as opposed to other matters of state, history of education should itself assume a higher priority both in historical and in educational studies.

As yet, other factors have militated against such centrality, not least from the point of view of historians in general. Some of these reflect the purposes for which history has been studied and taught. For example, the central theme of school (and other) history has traditionally been that of high politics – monarchs, ministers, parliaments, wars, the promotion of a concept of leadership among the few and of a shared consciousness of nation and nationhood among the many. In contrast, the subject of education has been perceived to be of less interest and of lower status. The early professors of history of education in British universities, scholars such as J.W. Adamson at King's College, London and Foster Watson at Aberystwyth University College, were distinguished historians by any standards. But the institutional contexts within which they and their colleagues worked, and the specific purposes to which their work was put, meant that history of education was often taught and studied as a means of promoting the identity and sense of mission of prospective and practising members of the teaching profession, rather than as a study of the past on its own terms, or as a central contribution to the broader historical education of the population.

It would appear that the perception that history is an academic discipline, with a broadly agreed set of procedures, while education is not, is particularly strong in

England.[58] This situation may be contrasted with those in many other countries. As Marie-Madeleine Compère, in a comparative study of history of education textbooks in England, France, Germany, Ireland, Italy and Spain has shrewdly observed, in England 'education in its proper sense, however, has never enjoyed any great intellectual prestige and thus has no inertia to set against historical innovation, as might be the case if it possessed a prestigious tradition'.[59] This is a most important point, albeit the term 'inertia' has somewhat negative connotations. In the context of my argument this evening, the phrase 'inertia to set against historical innovation', may be replaced by 'broadly agreed consensus as regards educational theory and practice to set against hasty, unwarranted or ideologically based innovation'.

Conclusion

Two preliminary and four further points may be made in conclusion. The preliminary points are essentially personal, 'present-minded' and 'ideologically positioned'.

The first is to reiterate my commitment to the importance of identifying ourselves – as individuals, as groups, as nations, as a human race – as accurately as possible in historical time. Such identification is as difficult as it is important. The difficulty is inherent in the complexity of the task. The importance stems from the power provided by such identification to maximize opportunities to promote the amounts of truth, justice, understanding and goodwill in the world.

The second point is to suggest that the best means of ensuring that such power is used for good rather than for evil purposes, is to be found in a firm commitment to a broad and generous interpretation of education. Such an interpretation certainly includes a concern for economic well-being. But worthwhile education is also about the promotion of knowledge over ignorance, of truth over falsehood, of concern for others over selfishness, of effort over sloth, of mental and physical well-being over despair and debility.

The four further conclusions are drawn in respect of: the end of history, the beginning of education, the current and future agenda of historians of education, the particular role of this Institute.

The concept of the end of history is a valuable one, not least because it celebrates and strengthens the principles and practices of genuine liberal democracies, whose governments, historically, have shown themselves less likely than other regimes to commit crimes either against their own peoples or against those of other countries. Of course, neither in history nor in historiography are there absolute ends and beginnings, except, perhaps, as delimited by the lives of individuals themselves. Interpretations such as the death of the past and the end of history, which remain committed to an objective search for truth, must be set against relativist and postmodernist approaches to create a professional and public historical consciousness of the past, present and future. Such consciousness is vital to the attainment and defence of liberal democracies. For the mythologies of the present and of the future are intimately connected with the mythologies of the past. Extended analysis of the concept of the end of history, moreover, is most appropriate as the human race comes to the close of one millennium and prepares to enter another. As the annual report from the Stockholm Institute for Peace has shown, although in the past two years there have been more than 20 internal conflicts, from Afghanistan to Rwanda, perhaps for the first time since records began there have been no major wars between states. It is salutary to reflect upon the many cruelties which have been perpetrated during the present century by some human beings upon others, in the pursuit of such ideologies as Imperialism, Fascism and Communism, to name but three. The current outbreak of peace provides an opportunity both to secure such a situation, and to address other global problems in a more determined and united manner than hitherto. The concept of the end of history may be linked with another notion, that of spaceship earth, of a planet whose life support systems, threatened by such factors as overpopulation, pollution and ozone depletion, must be preserved in the interests of the several species who inhabit it.

The concept of the beginning of education is similarly useful. Of course, education has always been an important element in human existence, but at this particular point in time education as a subject of study and research in higher education in the United Kingdom has the potential for a new beginning, in the way in which other subjects, including history, probably do not. One basis for this new beginning is the enhanced profile of education upon the political agenda. Another is the increased participation rate in higher education, which has trebled in the last 20 years. Even more important is the concept of an increasing ownership of education by the whole community. In the light of such developments, Hargreaves' argument that a more productive relationship needs to be created between educational research and educational practice is a valid one, although his explanations as to the causes of the problem and the best means of solution are less convincing. Simply to castigate the educational research community (as Hargreaves does) for failing adequately to produce, co-ordinate and disseminate its findings is insufficient. It must also be acknowledged, for example, that governments, the media, teachers and parents in the United Kingdom have frequently been less receptive to such findings than similar groups in other countries. In recent years, political and economic ideology has been the mainspring for educational reform. Nevertheless, the opportunities and responsibilities for co-ordinating and disseminating the findings of research in education have never been greater. At times this may require educational researchers to stand up against governments or those agents of governments who seek to deny the truth. As the American political scientist, Alexander Meiklejohn, has written in the context of the academic freedom of professional researchers:

> those by whom we are commissioned need intellectual leadership in the thinking which a free society must do. May I state the principle bluntly and frankly? Our final responsibility, as scholars and teachers, is not to the truth. It is to the people who need the truth.[60]

The role of historians of education in the development of education as a field of study and in the promotion of educational truths is crucial. Although in recent years the contexts and means of education have changed rapidly – for example, as a result of the introduction of television and video, of computer and internet – and will no doubt continue to do so, there is a considerable corpus of knowledge about teaching and learning which does not alter. Good teachers combine a range of qualities – knowledge of their subjects, steady application of principles of management and organization, genuine concern for those whom they teach, the ability to inspire and enthuse. These qualities do not change over time. They need to be restated in every age, but their essence remains the same. Education is not susceptible to quick fixes, whether as a result of political intervention or pedagogical fashion. The role of the historian of education is to demonstrate continuities and changes, and to distinguish that which is important and long lasting from that which is shallow and transient. The privilege of working, as I do, in a History and Philosophy group whose agenda is international in scope, moreover, is that further perspectives are brought upon those elements in life which may be deemed to be worthwhile, elements which transcend both different cultures and different groups in multicultural societies. Richard Rorty wrote of banalizing discourse by using terms such as greed, selfishness, starvation wages, differential per-pupil expenditure. This is not banalizing. It is the proper language of historians of education, as of all historians and educationists.

Banality (or rather clarity) of language must be complemented by breadth of approach. Since its retreat from the 'undifferentiated mush' of the 1960s, there has been a problem in the field of education, a problem correctly identified by Hargreaves and others, of too many 'splitters' and not enough 'lumpers'. Historians of education and historical perspectives can provide solutions to this problem. Of course, as yet the historical perspectives approach in respect of education is at a relatively early stage of development. The balance between in-depth research on particular issues and general overviews has still to be struck. In a recent review of *Education for the Nation*, Tony Edwards argued that 'breadth too often defeats depth'.[61] That may be a just comment on a volume which, in seeking to explain the overall issue of ownership of education in England from an historical perspective, considered seven fundamental themes: access, curriculum, standards and assessment, teaching quality, control of education, education and economic performance and educational consumers. Nevertheless, although each of these themes merits further detailed investigation in its own right, the importance of cumulative research which contributes to an extended body of knowledge is paramount.

My final point concerns the potential role of the Institute of Education in this process. In this lecture, I have argued from the concepts of the end of history and of the beginning of education that an important opportunity now exists in this country to advance the true cause of education, both professional and public. For nearly a century, the Institute of Education of the University of London, and its predecessor until 1932 the London Day Training College, have been a central force for education, both nationally and internationally. This situation continues. In recent months such centrality has brought leading politicians, past and present – Paddy Ashdown, Kenneth Baker, Tony Blair, James Callaghan, Roy Hattersley and Gillian Shephard – to its lecture halls. The Institute's current authority and prestige rest upon a number of firm foundations. These include: the leadership of its director, Peter Mortimore; substantial library and archive collections; a top rating of five starred in yet another research assessment exercise, with no fewer than 140 scholars judged as being of international standing.

The Institute, therefore, is uniquely placed to provide leadership in education at this crucial time. Recent structural reforms, moreover, have facilitated the processes whereby specialized work in discrete areas of education may be brought into a cumulative whole. For example, my own understanding of such issues as education and employment and education and nationality have been much enhanced by the work of my colleague, John White.[62] Or again, this lecture is in one sense a discrete entity, as were those of Michael Barber and Geoff Whitty, delivered on 11 December 1996 and 9 January 1997 respectively. But it is also part of a series, and its connections with these two recent lectures are obvious, and may provide one basis for future collaboration. In 'How to do the Impossible: a guide for politicians with a passion for education', Michael Barber drew upon Fukuyama's concept of trust as expressed in his volume of that name, published in

1995.[63] Geoff Whitty, in the Karl Mannheim Memorial Lecture entitled 'Social Theory and Education Policy', showed how sociologists of education, in common with many historians of education, have turned their attention to policy studies.

An important recent study of the value and truth of historical knowledge has concluded that 'Telling the truth takes a collective effort'.[64] I believe this to be equally true of educational knowledge.

To return to the vision of Sidney Webb – 'The obvious and imperative duty of a rightly organised and adequately endowed London University is to become the foremost postgraduate centre of the intellectual world.' It is my earnest hope that this Institute will take full advantage of current opportunities to continue and to enhance its role as the foremost postgraduate centre in the intellectual world of education, and that such leadership will have a direct bearing upon educational policies and practice in the twenty-first century. I also hope that this lecture has made some contribution, however modest, towards that end.

Notes

1 E.J.T. Brennan (ed.), *Education for National Efficiency: The Contribution of Sidney and Beatrice Webb*, London: Athlone Press, 1975, pp. 143, 147.
2 P. Gordon (ed.), *The Study of Education. A Collection of Inaugural Lectures: Early and Modern*, London: Woburn Press, 1980, p. 49.
3 K. Jenkins, *On 'What is History?' From Carr and Elton to Rorty and White*, London: Routledge, 1995, pp. 178–9.
4 T.K. Popkewitz, *A Political Sociology of Educational Reform*, New York: Teachers College Press, 1991, p. 2.
5 Department for Education and Employment, *The English Education System: An Overview of Structure and Policy*, London: DfEE, 1995, p. 1.
6 W. Frijhoff, 'Education's memory', in J. Sturm, J. Dekker, R. Aldrich and F. Simon (eds), *Education and Cultural Transmission*, Gent: CSHP, 1996 (*Paedagogica Historica* Supplementary Series II), p. 340.
7 R. Aldrich, *Sir John Pakington and National Education*, Leeds: University of Leeds, 1979; R. Aldrich, *School and Society in Victorian Britain: Joseph Payne and the New World of Education*, New York: Garland, 1995; R. Aldrich and P. Gordon, *Dictionary of British Educationists*, London: Woburn Press, 1989; P. Gordon and R. Aldrich, *Biographical Dictionary of North American and European Educationists*, London: Woburn Press, 1997.
8 R. Aldrich and P. Leighton, *Education: Time for a New Act?*, London: Institute of Education, 1985; P. Gordon, R. Aldrich and D. Dean, *Education and Policy in England and Wales in the Twentieth Century*, London: Woburn Press, 1991.
9 R. Aldrich, 'The evolution of teacher education', in N. Graves (ed.), *Initial Teacher Education: Policies and Progress*, London: Kogan Page, 1990.
10 R. Aldrich, 'New history: an historical perspective', in A.K. Dickinson, P.J. Lee and P.J. Rogers (eds), *Learning History*, London: Heinemann Educational Books, 1984; R. Aldrich, 'Imperialism in the study and teaching of history', in J.A. Mangan (ed.), *'Benefits Bestowed'? Education and British Imperialism*, Manchester: Manchester University Press, 1988.
11 P. Sharp, *School Governing Bodies in the English Education System: An Historical Perspective*, Leeds: University of Leeds, 1995.
12 R. Aldrich, *Education for the Nation*, London: Cassell, 1996.
13 R. Aldrich, 'Discipline, practice and policy: a personal view of history of education', in K. Salimova and E. Johanningmeier (eds), *Why Should We Teach History of Education?*, Moscow: Rusanov, 1993.
14 Quoted in Jenkins, op. cit., p. 144.
15 M. Ferro, *The Use and Abuse of History, or, How the Past is Taught*, London: Routledge and Kegan Paul, 1984.
16 J.H. Plumb, *The Death of the Past*, London: Macmillan, 1969, p. 15.

17 Quoted in Jenkins, op. cit., pp. 144–5.
18 J.R. Seeley, *The Expansion of England*, London: Macmillan, 1883, p. 169.
19 J.M. Keynes, *The End of Laissez Faire*, London: Hogarth, 1926, p. 16.
20 *Times Educational Supplement*, 31 May 1996.
21 Ibid.
22 M. Thatcher, *The Downing Street Years*, London: Harper Collins, 1993, p. 596.
23 *Sunday Times*, 2 June 1996.
24 *Times Educational Supplement*, 31 May 1996.
25 Quoted in Centre for Contemporary Cultural Studies, *Unpopular Education: Schooling and Social Democracy in England since 1944*, London: Hutchinson, 1981, p. 212.
26 *The Times*, 1 January 1997.
27 Quoted in R. Aldrich (ed.), *History in the National Curriculum*, London: Kogan Page, 1991, p. 3.
28 Thatcher, op. cit., p. 595.
29 M. Barber, *The Learning Game: Arguments for an Education Revolution*, London: Victor Gollancz, 1996, pp. 55–60.
30 F. Fukuyama, 'The end of history?', *National Interest*, 1989, 16: 3–18.
31 F. Fukuyama, *The End of History and the Last Man*, London: Hamish Hamilton, 1992.
32 Ibid., pp. xii–xiii.
33 Ibid., p. 112.
34 F. Fukuyama, 'On the possibility of writing a universal history', in A.M. Melzer, J. Weinberger and M.R. Zinman (eds), *History and the Idea of Progress*, Ithaca, NY: Cornell University Press, 1995, p. 25.
35 C. Handy, 'What's it all for? Reinventing capitalism for the next century', *Royal Society of Arts Journal*, 1996, CXLIV(5475): 34.
36 Plumb, op. cit., p. 16.
37 Ibid., p. 17.
38 Ibid., p. 104.
39 Jenkins, op. cit., p. 35.
40 Fukuyama, op. cit., 1992, pp. 109–25.
41 Ibid., p. 122.
42 E.G. West, *Education and the State: A Study in Political Economy*, London: Institute of Economic Affairs, 1970, p. 162.
43 M.J. Wiener, *English Culture and the Decline of the Industrial Spirit, 1850–1980*, Cambridge: Cambridge University Press, 1981, p. 162.
44 C. Barnett, *The Audit of War*, London: Macmillan, 1986, p. 304.
45 Quoted in P. Clarke, 'Love's labours lost', in *History Today* (Introduction, A. Ryan), *After the End of History*, London: Collins and Brown, 1992, p. 60.
46 Ibid.
47 T.W. Laqueur, *Religion and Respectability: Sunday Schools and Working-Class Culture, 1780–1850*, New Haven: Yale University Press, 1976.
48 R. Rorty, 'The end of Leninism and history as comic frame', in A.M. Melzer, J. Weinberger and M.R. Zinman (eds), *History and the Idea of Progress*, Ithaca: Cornell University Press, 1995, p. 212.
49 Quoted in R. Aldrich, *School and Society in Victorian Britain: Joseph Payne and the New World of Education*, New York: Garland, 1995, p. 217.
50 J.B. Thomas (ed.), *British Universities and Teacher Education: A Century of Change*, London: Falmer Press, 1990, pp. 193–204.
51 P. Searby, *The Training of Teachers in Cambridge University: The First Sixty Years, 1879–1939*, Cambridge: Cambridge University Department of Education, 1982, p. 37.
52 H.-E. Tenorth, 'Geschichte der Erziehungswissenschaft: Konstruktion einer Chimäre oder Historie einer erstaunlichen Karriere?'. Paper delivered to the Seventeenth Congress of the International Standing Conference for the History of Education, Berlin, September 1995. Published in P. Drewek and C. Lüth (eds), *History of Educational Sciences, Geschichte der Erziehungswissenschaft, Histoire des Sciences de l'Education*, Gent: CSHP, 1998 (*Paedagogica Historica* Supplementary Series III), pp. 3–20.
53 R. Aldrich and D. Crook, 'Education as a university subject in England: an historical interpretation', in Drewek and Lüth, op. cit., pp. 121–38.

54 R. Aldrich, *The Institute of Education 1902–2002: A Centenary History*, London: Institute of Education, 2002. The term 'Principal' was used until 1932 and 'Director' thereafter.

55 R.A.C. Oliver, *Research in Education*, London: Allen and Unwin, 1946, p. 10.

56 *Times Educational Supplement*, 4 February 1994.

57 D.H. Hargreaves, 'Teaching as a research-based profession: possibilities and prospects', Teacher Training Agency Annual Lecture, 1996, p. 2.

58 R. Szreter, 'History and the sociological perspective in educational studies', in P. Gordon and R. Szreter (eds), *History of Education: The Making of a Discipline*, London: Woburn Press, 1989, pp. 85–9.

59 M.-M. Compère, 'Textbooks on the history of education currently in use in Europe', in Salimova and Johanningmeier, op. cit., p. 243.

60 T. Horio, *Educational Thought and Ideology in Modern Japan: State Authority and Intellectual Freedom* (edited and translated by S. Platzer), Tokyo: University of Tokyo Press, 1988, p. 393.

61 *Times Educational Supplement*, 6 December 1996.

62 J. White, 'Education and nationality', *Journal of Philosophy of Education*, 1996, 30(3): 327–43. See also J. White, *Education and the End of Work*, London: Cassell, 1997.

63 F. Fukuyama, *Trust: The Social Virtues and the Creation of Prosperity*, London: Hamish Hamilton, 1995.

64 J. Appleby, L. Hunt and M. Jacob, *Telling the Truth about History*, New York: Norton, 1994, p. 309.

PART 2

THE POLITICS OF EDUCATION

CHAPTER 3

SIR JOHN PAKINGTON AND THE NEWCASTLE COMMISSION

History of Education, Taylor and Francis, 1979, 8(1): 21–31

Sir John Pakington, first Baron Hampton (1799–1880), MP for Droitwich 1837–74 and Cabinet minister in three Conservative governments, made three significant contributions to nineteenth-century educational history. In the first place he advanced the cause of a wide variety of educational associations and institutions. Schools of every description – denominational, inter-denominational, secular, ragged, pauper, industrial, public, military, naval, trade and board, reformatories, schools of art, mechanics institutes, training colleges, schoolteachers' associations – all excited his interest and benefited from his concern. Second, he developed his own concept of national education, a national education which, while allowing free rein to denominational and private schools, also envisaged the provision of good-quality, free, rate-supported education throughout the country. Third, he championed education within Parliament, particularly in the years 1854–70. The Act of 1856, his Bills of 1855 and 1857, the Newcastle Commission of 1858, the overthrow of Lowe, the Select Committee of 1865–6 and the Act of 1870 were all important episodes in which he played a leading role.

In a sense the neglect of Pakington's contribution to national education is understandable. His parliamentary record on education was one of failure rather than success, and his Education Bills, unlike some of his other attempts at private legislation, failed to reach the Statute Book. The Newcastle Commission of which he was the originator led not to major educational reform but to the aridity of the Revised Code, whilst the draft Report from his Select Committee in 1866 was outmanoeuvred and in educational matters the Conservatives in power 1866–8 flattered only to deceive. Moreover Pakington, both as a man and as a politician, was one of nature's independents.[1] Neither he nor his concept of education fits easily into those categories which are often imposed upon the history of education in the nineteenth century.

Nevertheless an appreciation of the man and of his unique contribution, which crossed political, social and denominational boundaries in its search for a truly national basis for education, is essential to an understanding of the nineteenth-century achievement of elementary education for all. The purpose of this article is to outline Pakington's contribution to one of the many episodes in educational history in which he is often either completely ignored, or merely dismissed in a sentence or footnote – the Newcastle Commission.[2]

By the end of 1857, Pakington was 'weary of struggles and conflicts which had impeded every attempt to carry any measure through Parliament'.[3] He was still convinced of the need for legislation on the education question, but he now accepted the impossibility of achieving it without a government bill. His purpose, therefore, was to convince public opinion in general, and particularly opinion within Parliament and more especially within the Cabinet, that his interpretation of the situation was correct. He thus began to put his Bills of 1855 and 1857 into a new perspective, and declared that although they had not succeeded, indeed had stood no chance of success, 'My object was to obtain a declaration of Parliament on certain principles, and to put into shape the views which I myself entertained upon the question'.[4] Whether Pakington, as he stated in 1858, 'was always conscious of the difficulties of the question, and never supposed that hon. Members would pass those Bills into a law',[5] is more difficult to accept. If that statement is taken at its face value it renders even more remarkable his willingness to jeopardize his position within the Conservative Party in the educational cause.

Pakington's decision to move for a royal commission, therefore, should not be seen merely as stemming from the loss of the Bill of 1857. For example, in 1855 he drew attention to two areas in which there was a need for urgent inquiry. One of these was the provision of an efficient teaching force. Pakington believed that the Committee of Council had dealt with this issue in a very haphazard way: 'the masters are so overtrained that they are, in too many cases, above educational duties, and they take to other pursuits...we ought to have the means of Parliamentary inquiry into these matters'.[6] Pakington's other concern was accurately to determine the numbers of children who did and should regularly attend good schools. For example, in the 1851 Census Horace Mann had made a deduction from the possible school attendance of one million children whom he thought could or should be at work. Pakington was unwilling to allow that deduction; he believed that 'children ought not to be allowed to work before they are educated'.[7] Only such an inquiry, Pakington thought, could reveal the true dimensions of the education problem.

In the following year, 1856, during the Supply debate, Pakington asked first for a government bill, second promised that if that were not forthcoming he should himself introduce one for them and third declared that:

> If all the evidence to which I have adverted has failed to convince the House of the necessity of dealing with the question, let us have a Committee of inquiry – let us bring together gentlemen from all parts of England, who thoroughly understand the question, to state personally to us their experience and views upon it. Let the House grant such a Committee, and I am confident such a Report will be produced as will force conviction upon Parliament that this great and important subject requires to be firmly and speedily dealt with.[8]

Pakington seemed certain that once the facts were fully investigated a remedy of the type which he envisaged, namely the supplementation of the existing system by the support or outright provision of schooling in deprived areas by popularly elected local boards, based on the principles of local finance and religious toleration, would be secured by government legislation. He had already, for example, convinced Russell of the validity of his investigations, statistics and proposed remedies for securing national education, whilst Russell's party had, on Pakington's initiative and with Russell's encouragement, produced in 1856 an Education Act.

By 1857 Pakington was making, unwisely perhaps in some respects, a comparison with the Poor Law situation of the early 1830s, indeed he came to see the two cases 'as closely parallel as it is possible to conceive',[9] and it is significant that the 1857 Bill was based upon Poor Law finance. One result of this identification was that by 1857 Pakington was thinking in terms of a royal commission rather than a select committee. Thus on 31 July of that year, Pakington asked Palmerston for an opportunity to bring forward a motion for 'an Address to the Crown for the appointment of a Commission of Inquiry on the subject of Education'.[10] Some consultation with Ministers had already taken place, for Pakington was able to state that 'he believed the proposal would not be opposed by the Government'. But clearly not enough, for Palmerston, after a hurried conversation with colleagues on that evening, was unable to hold out the prospect of an early day.[11] On 13 August[12] Pakington asked again for an opportunity to proceed, but with the end of the session fast approaching and the House bogged down in the intricate details of the Divorce and Matrimonial Causes Bill, he was again refused.

When on 11 February 1858 Pakington finally moved for a commission:

> to inquire into the present state of popular education in England, and whether the present system is, or is not, sufficient for its object; and to consider and report what changes, if any, are required for the extension of sound and cheap elementary instruction to all classes of the people,[13]

the same uncertainty regarding Government attitudes still prevailed. Cowper, the Vice-President, had not resisted Pakington's initiative, and had even instructed Lingen to supply Pakington with official statistics, but the matter was far from being a *fait accompli*. Indeed the motion involved the House both in a lengthy debate[14] and ultimately in a division.

Pakington's own speech[15] makes compelling reading. He began by proving once more that existing education was deficient both in quantity and quality. He also showed that there were good grounds for concluding that the situation was worsening rather than improving, and made telling comparison with educational provision in other countries. He urged that the House devoted too much time to party struggles and not enough to matters which 'affect only the welfare and the interest of the people'.[16] He drew attention to the interest in education in the country as a whole, to the conferences and congresses, including that of the National Association for the Promotion of Social Science at Birmingham. Legislation was needed immediately, but since the Government seemed unable to act, and independent bills such as his own had achieved no success, a commission would be the next step forward. In spite of the expenditure on education from annual parliamentary grants, the army of inspectors, some 46 in 1857, the complicated system of Minutes, there was, in Pakington's view, only half a system, which still lacked effective local organization. Moreover, many years had elapsed since the last extensive inquiry into educational provision. Pakington posed the issue of a select committee or a royal commission. He would, if appointed chairman of a select committee, be able to direct the inquiry into relevant areas, and thus to influence the report.[17] But he had sufficient confidence in the justice of his cause to propose a royal commission which could be conducted in a 'more calm and dispassionate manner', and which would produce 'a Report that will carry greater weight in the country'.[18]

As an example of a successful commission Pakington returned to his Poor Law analogy:

> The Government of 1833 appointed seven of the most able and distinguished men, at the head of whom was the late lamented Bishop of London,[19] to carry out that inquiry. They sent Deputy Commissioners throughout the country to

collect facts, they put those facts together and stated their own views, and the result was, that in the following year the Government came down to this House and carried that great measure.[20]

Pakington claimed that the only difference was that whilst the Commission of 1833 had been proposed by the then government, 'In the present case the Commission is proposed by a humble Member of this House, who has not even a party support to look to on this proposal'.[21] Pakington concluded by reaffirming that his purpose in moving for a commission was to arm the government with the authority of facts and the support of public opinion so that it would 'at last legislate on this subject in such a manner as to effect that object which I have sincerely at heart, and which I hope I may live to see accomplished, solely because I believe it to be essential to the true character and welfare of the people'.[22]

There were mixed reactions to Pakington's speech. Those in support included Stanley, who seconded the motion, and Russell who saw it as likely to secure 'a very considerable object'.[23] Fox, however, wisely warned that one should not presume too much in advance on the Commission's findings or recommendations, and Edward Akroyd,[24] Liberal MP for Huddersfield, a factory owner and promoter of education both in his own works and in his local area, drew attention to the need for specific inquiry into factory education. Hadfield, Liberal member for Sheffield, went further in proposing an amendment to add to the inquiry that it should be concerned with the fundamental issue of secular or religious education.[25] Opponents included Gathorne Hardy, Conservative MP for Leominster, who argued that the situation was improving, that a commission was therefore superfluous, and that before condemning the existing system the House should consider what could be put in its place.

Cowper, too, now hesitated. He was not opposed to an inquiry as such, and he had considerable respect for Pakington, but Cowper had 'heard with some anxiety the allusion made by the right hon. Baronet to the Poor Laws',[26] and he disliked the particular wording of the motion inasmuch as it implied that the Commission itself, rather than Parliament, should determine policy. It would appear that Pakington (and he secured the support of Russell on this point) had some reason to complain of Cowper's speech, for 'It had been held out to him, that Her Majesty's Government intended to support his Motion as it stood upon the paper'.[27] Russell, indeed, urged Pakington that it would be better to withdraw the motion than to continue for the sake of a nominal success with a compromise which would effectively deprive the Commission of the power of genuine inquiry. Pakington was himself uncertain at this point, but eventually agreed to delete the words 'whether the present system is, or is not, sufficient for its object'. Cowper having accepted this amendment, and Hadfield's amendment having been withdrawn, only one more hurdle remained. Henley[28] had naturally spoken against Pakington's motion, and had urged the House to abide by the existing system. He now determined to divide the House, but Pakington carried the day with 110 votes to 49.[29]

On 19 February 1858 another important vote took place. The Radicals had their revenge when Palmerston was defeated on the Conspiracy to Murder Bill by 234 votes to 215.[30] Bright[31] and Milner Gibson[32] acted as tellers on that occasion, and they numbered amongst their majority Cardwell, Cecil, Disraeli, Ewart, Fox, Gladstone, Graham, Herbert, Pakington, Roebuck, Russell, Stanley and Walpole. Derby formed his second government, and Pakington was placed as far as possible away from educational matters in the office of First Lord of the Admiralty.[33] There had been some newspaper speculation as to whether Pakington's recent stance on education would disbar him from office, but Derby's party was not so over-endowed with men of talent that his services could be dispensed with. Pakington, for his part, graciously announced that 'after the most serious reflection I arrived at the conclusion that there was nothing in the subject of national education to prevent me from giving my humble assistance to Her Majesty's Government'.[34] Salisbury was appointed Lord President and Adderley[35] to the Vice-Presidency. There was no likelihood of Pakington's being considered for either of these posts. The Colonial Secretaryship, Pakington's former office, went to a reluctant Stanley, but only after Lytton and Manners had both refused.

Adderley, who had formerly opposed the idea of a commission, now saw it as his duty to render its labours 'efficient and useful' and he grudgingly conceded that it 'might throw some light on this great subject'.[36] Pakington's onerous duties at the Admiralty, where he was both involved in major battles with Disraeli over expenditure and faced with the delicate problem of appointing a Commission on the Manning of the Navy, did not prevent his taking an interest in the appointment of the Education Commission. He was in communication with Salisbury, whom he thought 'sincerely desirous to appoint the Commission and to appoint it fairly',[37] but lacking the experience of education which would enable him to select the best persons. This led to delay, and Pakington who hoped for a report and legislation within a year, or two at the most, in May wrote urgently to Derby to 'express my regret that the Education Commission is not yet appointed...I am apprehensive of our good faith being doubted'.[38]

Two significant points about the origins of the Newcastle Commission can conveniently be summarized at this point. First, Pakington was the true 'parent'[39] of the Commission, both in the long-term sense inasmuch as it was a logical development of his work for national education throughout the preceding five years, and in the immediate sense in that it was his persistence alone which finally persuaded the Government and the Commons to follow this course. Pakington's own account of the proceedings on the evening of 11 February gives some indication of how uncertain the matter was:

> I recently made a motion for a Royal Commission to inquire into the state of education in England, and I was told, a few days before I made it, that the Government would decidedly oppose me. When I got to the House I was told that they would decidedly support me. In the course of the evening I was informed by a friend of mine that they had changed their minds three times, and at last the Minister, when he heard everybody else speak, got up and said that he would neither support nor oppose me, but he hoped I would omit the latter half of my resolution, and he would accept the first. My answer was, 'I have a great question in hand and an important public object to attain, and I will be no party to emasculating my resolution and making it worthless because you can't make up your mind.' And I added that rather than cut it in two I would abandon it altogether. In the middle of my motion, however, there were one or two words to which a meaning different from what I had intended was attached, and when I had consented to alter these, both the first and the last half of the resolution were agreed to.[40]

Second, it is important to consider Pakington's purpose in moving for a commission. His primary aim was the achievement of an effective system of national education. The creation of the Education Department and the Vice-Presidency in 1856 had been but a first step, and Pakington had wished to see this followed by further acts. He hoped for a measure to provide good-quality schooling for all the children in the country, and having tried and failed to achieve such legislation himself, he now wanted to strengthen the hand of the Whig Government, or rather to force its hand, by bringing about the production of a report which could not be ignored. The model of the Poor Law Commission which he held up suggested the possibility of extensive yet swift report and legislation. An act could bring education under closer parliamentary control, and at the same time remove some of its superintendence from the shadowy areas of the Committee of Privy Council, 'My Lords', the administrators and the system of Minutes. Though overall a truly national system would require greater public finance, this would not necessarily result in an increase in the central government fund, indeed there could well be a diminution from this source, but might depend instead upon local finance, supervised and applied by popularly elected local bodies. Detailed and impartial inquiry, Pakington believed, would reveal the inadequacy of school provision in terms of quantity and quality. His personal experience, the witness of the Church Education Society, of the Ragged School movement, the reports of Her Majesty's Inspectors (HMIs), even the census of Mann, all pointed, in Pakington's judgement, to the inescapable conclusion that a system of education worthy of the nation – one which comprised sufficient good schools accessible to all children, dependent upon reliable sources of income, staffed by trained and dedicated teachers, offering a broad curriculum and catering for pupils into their teenage years – could not be supplied under the existing system, and necessitated a major education act. Pakington had come to that conclusion well before 1858, the Royal Commission reached it in 1861, but Parliament, the two major political parties and the country as a whole were prevented from reaching it until 1870 by the decisions of the Liberal Cabinet in 1861 and 1862, decisions which substituted in place of an act, the Revised Code.

The major conclusion of the Report of the Newcastle Commission, as the following extract indicates, was essentially that which Pakington had anticipated.

> Our attention, however, has principally been devoted to the system of aid and inspection established by Your Majesty's Government, which has now for twenty years given a powerful stimulus to the building of schools, and has created a class of schoolmasters and pupil-teachers of a superior character to any previously known in this country... We have found it stimulating voluntary subscriptions, offering many excellent models of teaching, and adapting itself to the character of the people by leaving both the general management of the schools and their religious teaching free. On the other hand we have exposed great and growing defects in its tendency to indefinite expense, in its inability to assist the poorer districts, in the partial inadequacy of its teaching, and in the complicated business which encumbers the central office of the Committee of Council; and these defects have led us to believe that any attempt to extend it unaltered into a national system would fail. We have therefore proposed, while retaining the leading principles of the present system and simplifying its working, to combine with it a supplementary and local system which may diffuse a wider interest in education, may distribute its burdens more equally, and may enable every school in the country to participate in its benefits.[41]

As Pakington had foretold, the Commissioners found the existing system to be increasingly defective in a number of ways. They concluded, as had Pakington, that no mere extension of it could be considered to be an adequate basis for national education. Instead a supplementary local system of the type envisaged by

Pakington, with local boards and local rating, was deemed by the Commissioners to be essential. Moreover, in company with Pakington, the Commissioners rejected the idea of parochial rating, and plumped instead for a system of borough and county education authorities.[42] Thus the Report recommended 'That in every county or division of a county having a separate county rate there shall be a County Board of Education', and 'That in corporate towns, which at the census last preceding contained more than 40,000 inhabitants, the town council may appoint a Borough Board of Education.'[43] Finance would thus be supplied from the proceeds of the county or borough rate. Moreover the Commissioners, fortified by the encouraging evidence as to the numbers of children whose names were entered on the school rolls, followed Pakington's recommendation of 1857 that the first step should not be the erection of new schools, but rather the improvement of those already in existence. Indeed the Report acknowledged that 'It is quite possible to support a school already in existence by a rate in aid, and yet to leave its management and its religious teaching substantially free, and proposals to this effect were made...in the Bill of Sir John Pakington.'[44] This cautious attitude towards local agency, which sought to avoid both controversies over the issues of religion and management by suggesting initially rates in aid of existing schools, and the charge of indiscriminate expense by advocating the principle of payment by results, showed that the lessons of the legislative proposals of the 1850s in general, and of Pakington's conclusions in particular, had been well learned.

Pakington had justified his scheme for a national system based upon local intervention by frequent reference to evidence which showed the deficiency of existing school provision in relation to both quality and quantity, The most important fact to be borne in mind in relation to the current controversy over educational provision in the mid-nineteenth century is that the Commissioners reached the same conclusions as Pakington in spite of the evidence collected as to the quantity of children in schools.[45]

That evidence, in brief, was that of an estimated population in mid-1858 for England and Wales of 19,523,103, the names of 2,535,462 children were on the books of weekday schools, a shortfall of only 120,305 children. This constituted a proportion of the total population of 1 in 7.7, or 12.99%, and though not as impressive a figure as that of Prussia, 1 in 6.27, where schooling was compulsory, significantly better than in Holland, 1 in 8.11, or France, 1 in 9.0. Nevertheless these figures gave the Commissioners little comfort. They observed that 'many of the schools are exceedingly bad, and the attendance is frequently so irregular as to be of little value'.[46] In spite of the progress made since the return of 1818 which had shown a proportion of only 1 in 17.25, the Newcastle Commissioners concluded 'that a very delusive estimate of the state of education must result from confining attention to the mere account of numbers under day-school instruction'.[47] The Report was at one with Pakington, therefore, on the poor quality and inappropriate nature of much of the education, and on the inability of the existing system substantially to improve that situation. The Commissioners sadly concluded that though the un-inspected schools had been shown to be far worse than the inspected, 'even with regard to the inspected, we have seen overwhelming evidence from Her Majesty's Inspectors, to the effect that not more than one-fourth of the children receive a good education'.[48]

The lengthy proceedings of the Newcastle Commission relieved Pakington of the necessity of introducing any further education bills into the Commons during the years 1858–61, but he determined to hold a watching brief over the Commission's work. Thus on 22 July 1859, he used the occasion of a Supply debate to ask Lowe whether Newcastle's appointment to the Colonial Secretaryship meant that he was no longer presiding over the Royal Commission, and that, if that were the case, would a new chairman soon be appointed? But his second and more urgent question was 'what prospect was there of the House receiving the Report of the Commission?'.[49] As 1859 and 1860 came and went without the production of a report, Pakington doubtless sensed that the existence of the Commission, in the short term, was a handicap to the national education cause. He therefore continued to press for the early presentation to Parliament of the Report,[50] though its appearance was irritatingly further delayed as a consequence of the inclusion of appendices and statistical returns.

Finally, in 1861, when the Report of the Commission had been presented to Parliament, and Granville[51] in the Lords had indicated that the Government, far from introducing a bill to implement the Commissioners' recommendation of establishing county and borough education boards, was proposing merely a Minute relating to the simplification of the business of the Council Office and the appointment of teachers, Pakington made an impassioned plea to the Liberal Government not to shirk its responsibility. In May, Pakington had taken the opportunity of a discussion initiated by Northcote's motion for a Select Committee on the Education of Neglected and Destitute Children to praise the Commissioners 'for issuing a most important compendium of the great subject of national education', and to remind Russell of the support he had given in securing the Commission's appointment. He then cordially invited Russell to 'find leisure to look into the book', and not to allow the Report 'to remain long without leading to practical results'.[52] Now on 11 July 1861, however, three days after Granville's announcement in the Lords, aware that his whole long-term strategy for securing an act to establish local education boards was about to be lost by default, Pakington used the occasion of a Commons order for Committee of Supply for an attempt to convince Palmerston and his Government that they were now perfectly poised finally to establish by legislation a worthy basis for national education.

Pakington's speech[53] had five main purposes: to place the Report of the Commission in the context of the legislative attempts of the 1850s; to appeal personally to Russell and Newcastle to exert their influence in the Cabinet to secure a bill; to show the impartial nature of the Commission and its workings; to draw attention to the findings of the Report; and to secure from the Government a promise of legislation early in the next session. In describing the origins of the Commission and its conclusions, Pakington emphasized the identification of his own and Russell's aims. Thus he stressed the links between his own Bills of 1855 and 1857 and Russell's Resolutions of 1856. He implied that Russell and he had stood shoulder to shoulder in their determination to achieve either legislation or 'inquiry with a view to legislation',[54] and advised that Russell's views 'were in entire harmony with those of the Commissioners'.[55] He also referred to Newcastle and to his chairmanship of the Commission in very flattering terms.

The impartiality of the Commission was another of Pakington's themes. His motion in 1858 had been approved during Palmerston's ministry, but the Commission had been appointed under Derby's premiership. Salisbury in nominating its members, Pakington now stated, had consulted neither Henley nor himself, but had chosen impartial and moderate men, whilst the Commission's proceedings and its voluminous Report were both characterized by a 'calm and dispassionate temper'.[56] The Report itself, Pakington justly concluded, fully upheld the five conclusions which Russell and he had earlier drawn as to the fundamental deficiencies of the existing elementary school system. These were that large numbers of the population were in a deplorable state of ignorance, that large districts of the country were supplied with very inefficient schools or no schools at all,[57] that children left school at too early an age, that local agency was indispensable and that the existing system could not be extended in its present form to meet the requirements of the whole country. Having summarized the main conclusions of the Report, Pakington addressed himself again to the Liberal front bench. With both Russell and Newcastle in the Cabinet, Pakington thought:

> it was not unreasonable to ask the Government to tell the House whether they would seriously consider the contents of the Report with a view to legislation at no distant date. The circumstances of the present moment were particularly favourable...and made him sanguine that the Government would approach the consideration of the Report with an earnest desire to found upon it some measure which might supply those deficiencies in the present system which could hardly be disputed or denied...He hoped, therefore, that he should receive from the Government an assurance that they were aware of the deep importance of the Report...and that at no distant day – he hoped in the next Session of Parliament – they would be ready to propose such legislation as after mature deliberation they might think the case required.[58]

That assurance was not forthcoming. There was no bill, but in its stead, the Revised Code.

The Revised Code was a defeat for Pakington, a defeat for his carefully laid plans for an education act, a defeat for local agency and increased public expenditure, a defeat for a genuine basis for national education. It was a victory, on the other hand, for Gladstone and Lowe, for economy, for the existing system, for the central Department and its system of Minutes. But it was only a temporary defeat and a hollow victory. The Revised Code in its conception and in its application brought condemnation from contemporaries and subsequent commentators alike. The Vice-President was hounded from office in April 1864, and a year later admitted to Pakington's Select Committee 'my idea is that education would certainly be better conducted by rates levied by local bodies, with some central inspection',[59] though he still maintained that it was impossible to do so. By 1867 even Lowe was fully convinced:

> We cannot suffer any large number of our citizens, now that they have obtained the right of influencing the destinies of the country, to remain uneducated. It was a great evil that we did so before – it was an evil and a reproach, a moral stigma upon us. But now it is a question of self-preservation – it is a question of existence.[60]

For Lowe, once that existence – of the Constitution, of the political and social order – was immediately endangered, education of the poor was essential. Pakington had for some 20 years prior to 1867 deemed education to be essential, for the true existence of the poor themselves.

Lowe's change of heart, the subsequent adoption of the national education cause by Gladstone and his Cabinet in 1869 and the success of the Acts of 1870 and 1902, show that there was nothing intrinsically wrong in Pakington's formula of private pressure, investigation, report and government legislation to achieve a basis for national education by the statutory establishment of local education agencies. Two questions must therefore be considered at this point. Why did

Palmerston's government reject the recommendation of county and borough education boards in the Report of the Newcastle Commission, and was such a rejection inevitable in 1861–2? The principal answer to the first question would seem to be that those members of the Cabinet who from their concern for education might have been expected to support a proposal for local education agencies succumbed to the arguments and to the greater resolve of the exponents of strict economy. On the second issue, although a new Minute or Code, rather than a bill, was basic Department policy from 1860, there were significant moments when that resolve faltered, and had the Revised Code been abandoned, Pakington's policy might well have come to be seen as the natural alternative.

Pakington's purpose in securing the appointment of the Royal Commission was soon forgotten by contemporaries, thus in April 1861 Kay-Shuttleworth wrote that the Commission was established 'chiefly in consequence of the questions raised by the increase of the charge on the public revenue',[61] and has subsequently been neglected by historians. In consequence, one of the major purposes and effects of the Revised Code has been overlooked. The Code has been variously interpreted: as an instrument of social control, as a natural development of a wider concern for economy and efficiency, as an exercise in secularization, as a crash course in literacy.[62] But the Code was also the means employed by the Liberal Government, and especially by such politicians within it as Gladstone, Granville and Lowe, to avoid the necessity of introducing an education bill at that time, and in particular to reject the principle of local education agencies and finance.

Pakington's commitment to the cause of national education, however, was such that he did not give up the struggle but merely adopted a new plan of campaign. He now decided to justify his drive for local education agencies by revealing the deficiencies and ineffectiveness of the Privy Council system, the Department, and the attitudes of some of its personnel. He had already found one chink in Lowe's armour, the antipathy which existed between the Vice-President and some of the inspectors. He also found allies in this cause, unexpected names, Cecil, Forster and Walter among them. An attack was launched on the credibility of Lowe, Granville and Lingen, an attack which after the resignation of Lowe in 1864 and the Reports of Pakington's Select Committee of 1865–6, showed the bankruptcy of the Privy Council system, and of the Revised Code as a policy for national education, and secured the defeat of its progenitors. With that purpose accomplished, the way was at last clear for the achievement of an education act of the type which Pakington had hoped would follow the Report of the Newcastle Commission in 1861–2.

Notes

1 The *Worcestershire Chronicle*, 17 April 1880, described Pakington as 'a consistent but Liberal Tory throughout his Parliamentary career'. Gillian Sutherland in *Elementary Education in the Nineteenth Century*, London: Historical Association, 1971, p. 27, characterized Pakington as 'the eccentric Tory radical'.

2 This article is derived from R. Aldrich, 'Sir John Pakington and National Education', London, PhD, 1977, ch. 6. See also R. Aldrich, *Sir John Pakington and National Education*, Leeds: University of Leeds, 1979.

3 Speech to the Edinburgh Philosophical Institution, reported in *The Times*, 1 November 1862. See also the account in the *Scotsman* of the same date.

4 *Hansard* CXLVIII, 1194, 11 February 1858.

5 Ibid.

6 *Hansard* CXXXVII, 645, 16 March 1855. See also on this point his exchange of letters with Derwent Coleridge. This correspondence was printed in the *Monthly Paper* of the National Society, April 1855, pp. 74–5.

7 *Hansard* CXXXVII, 648, 16 March 1855.
8 *Hansard* CXLII, 1358–9, 12 June 1856.
9 *Hansard* CXLVIII, 1198, 11 February 1858.
10 *Hansard* CXLVII, 811, 31 July 1857.
11 Pakington had hoped for the Thursday or Friday of the following week.
12 *Hansard* CXLVII, 1567, 13 August 1857.
13 *Hansard* CXLVIII, 1184–5, 11 February 1858.
14 It occupied 65 columns of *Hansard*.
15 *Hansard* CXLVIII, 1184–98, 11 February 1858.
16 Ibid., 1191.
17 It was normal practice for the proposer of such a motion, if successful, to be nominated to the chairmanship of the committee.
18 Ibid., 1197.
19 Bishop Charles James Blomfield (1786–1857). Blomfield had considerable influence in education. The Blomfield Letter Books (Fulham Papers) are deposited in the Lambeth Palace Library. See also G.E. Biber, *Bishop Blomfield and his Times*, London: Harrison, 1857; and A. Blomfield, *A Memoir of C.J. Blomfield, Bishop of London*, London: John Murray, 2 vols 1863.
20 *Hansard* CXLVIII, 1197–8, 11 February 1858.
21 Ibid., 1198. Pakington was usually at odds with his Conservative colleagues over national education, especially on the issue of rate support.
22 Ibid.
23 Ibid., 1244.
24 In 1857 Akroyd attended the Birmingham meeting of the NAPSS where Pakington presided over the Education Department.
25 Palmerston persuaded Hadfield to withdraw this amendment.
26 *Hansard* CXLVIII, 1231, 11 February 1858.
27 Ibid., 1246.
28 Ibid., 1232–7. J.W. Henley, Conservative member for Oxfordshire and father-in-law of Archdeacon Denison, another of Pakington's educational adversaries, had led the opposition to Pakington's Bills of 1855 and 1857.
29 Ibid., 1248. Unfortunately no list of the division is given in *Hansard*.
30 *Hansard* CXLVIII, 1847, 19 February 1858.
31 John Bright had only recently re-entered Parliament, having been returned for Birmingham following the death of George Muntz.
32 Though Milner Gibson found a place in Palmerston's Cabinet in July 1859 as President of the Board of Trade.
33 Though he did have responsibility for naval schools and training establishments and was in consequence a member of the Committee of Privy Council. Russell had suggested to Grey that Pakington should be invited to serve on the Royal Commission. Granville Mss, PRO 30/29/18/6/56-8, Russell to Granville, 19 February 1858.
34 Pakington's speech to his constituents on the occasion of his re-election consequent upon his accepting the office of First Lord of the Admiralty, *The Times*, 4 March 1858.
35 Adderley was not of the Cabinet, though he was also President of the Board of Health.
36 *Hansard* CLI, 138, 21 June 1858.
37 Hampton Mss, WRO 705.349. B.A. 3835/11/(iii)/19a, copy of Pakington to Derby, 25 May 1858. The Hampton Mss are deposited at St Helen's Record Office, Worcester, now part of the Hereford and Worcester Record Office.
38 Ibid.
39 He himself used this term on more than one occasion.
40 Pakington's speech to his constituents, *The Times*, 4 March 1858.
41 PP 1861, XXI, *Report of the Commissioners appointed to inquire into the State of Popular Education in England* (hereafter the *Newcastle Commission*), I, pp. 542–3.
42 Pakington had not included county boards in the Bill of 1857, but had intended the provision for cities and corporate towns to be a first step only.
43 *Report of the Newcastle Commission*, I, p. 545.
44 Ibid., I, p. 302. The Commissioners here, however, were probably referring to the Bill of 1855 rather than that of 1857.
45 Or, to be as precise as possible, the numbers of names returned as being on the school rolls.

46 *Report of the Newcastle Commission*, I, p. 86.
47 Ibid., I, p. 294.
48 Ibid., I, p. 295. The Commissioners however were probably over-pessimistic in their judgement. The subsequent controversy, which involved HMI Norris and Revd T.R. Birks, is usefully summarized in A. Tropp, *The School Teachers*, London: Heinemann, 1957, p. 73. A more fundamental critique of the Commissioners' figures is to be found in Central Committee of Schoolmasters, *Returns concerning the Assistant Commissioners of Education and Inspected Schools in the Ten Specimen Districts*, London: n.p., 1862.
49 *Hansard* CLV, 335, 22 July 1859.
50 As, for example, on 21 February 1860 when he asked Lowe point blank when the Report would be presented to Parliament. *Hansard* CLVI, 1472, 21 February 1860.
51 Lord President of the Council, in response to a question from Lyttelton. *Hansard* CLXIV, 484–90, 8 July 1861.
52 *Hansard* CLXIII, 213, 28 May 1861. Russell, Secretary of State for Foreign Affairs, was much exercised in 1861–2 by issues arising from the Civil War in the United States.
53 *Hansard* CLXIV, 699–709, 11 July 1861.
54 Ibid., 701.
55 Ibid., 708.
56 Ibid., 702.
57 Pakington henceforth wisely modified his more extreme earlier statements about deficiencies in the numbers of schools.
58 *Hansard* CLXIV, 708–9, 11 July 1861.
59 Quoted in D.W. Sylvester, *Robert Lowe and Education*, London: Cambridge University Press, 1974, p. 118.
60 R. Lowe, *Primary and Classical Education*, Edinburgh: n.p., 1867, p. 9.
61 J. Kay-Shuttleworth, *Four Periods of Popular Education*, London: Longmans, 1862, p. 555.
62 Interpretations of the Revised Code are examined in A.J. Marcham, 'The Revised Code of Education, 1862', London, PhD, 1977, ch. 8; and A.J. Marcham, 'Recent interpretations of the Revised Code of Education, 1862', *History of Education*, 1979, 8(2): 121–33.

CHAPTER 4

FROM BOARD OF EDUCATION TO DEPARTMENT FOR EDUCATION AND EMPLOYMENT

Journal of Educational Administration and History, University of Leeds, 2000, 32(1): 8–22

Introduction

> The rise of a central authority for English education had been a slow, tortuous, makeshift, muddled, unplanned, disjointed and ignoble process.[1]

So A.S. Bishop concluded his study of central government of education in England in the nineteenth century. This article begins where Bishop ended, with the creation of the Board of Education in 1900. It concludes with an analysis of the current situation, with particular reference to the formation of the Department for Education and Employment (DfEE) in 1995. Bishop's study was substantial. Four of its 14 chapters were devoted to the Education Department, three to the Science and Art Department and three to the Charity Commission. In a piece of this length it is impossible to provide more than a survey of key issues. Later this year a more detailed examination of twentieth-century developments, with particular reference to the relationship between the central departments for Education and Employment, will appear in book form.[2]

This article is divided into four sections. The first three examine changes in the title of the central authority: the amalgamation which led to the constitution of the Board in 1900; its replacement by a Ministry of Education in 1944 which is extended to include the reformulations as a Department of Education and Science (DES) in 1964 and the reversion to a Department for Education (DfE) in 1992; the amalgamation represented by the DfEE in 1995. The fourth section is concerned with the culture and status of the department across the century. Finally, some conclusions are drawn. The first of these addresses the question: has the history of the central authority for education in the twentieth century exhibited similar characteristics to those identified by Bishop for the nineteenth?

Board of Education 1900

The Board of Education, established under an Act of 1899, came into being in the following year.[3] Its origins lay in the field of secondary education. The Bryce Report of 1895 had recommended the establishment of a central authority in order to co-ordinate the development of secondary education. It noted a 'remarkable consensus' amongst the 85 witnesses who were examined:

> That in order to constitute an efficient and satisfactory Central Authority there must be a Minister of Education, the head of a Department, responsible to Parliament with a seat in the Cabinet, a Minister who, as Sir William Hart-Dyke

said, would be a Secretary of State. On this matter witnesses of all orders, Charity Commissioners, Government officials, schoolmasters, representatives of local authorities, and statesmen, were agreed.[4]

The first draft of the Bill did, indeed, propose a Secretary of State, but the measure as presented to Parliament in August 1898 specified a President of a Board instead. The original Bill received a cool reception, and a revised Bill of 1899 fared little better. Indeed, in May 1899 some MPs tabled a Bill providing for the appointment of a Secretary of State for Education. The Duke of Devonshire, Lord President of the Council, was forced to respond to critics in the House of Lords as to why a Board had been preferred to a Ministry. His statement was indicative not only of his own 'failure to grasp any complicated detail half an hour after he has listened to it',[5] but also of the spirit in which the Conservative Government of Lord Salisbury had approached the matter:

> As far as I remember, the point was mooted when the Bill was first prepared, but I quite admit that I am unable, at the present moment, to recollect the reasons which weighed in favour of a Board rather than a secretariat. It has the advantage, at all events, of numerous precedents, and it is perfectly well understood that there will be no Board at all.[6]

One argument adduced by the Assistant Parliamentary Counsel, Sir Courtenay Ilbert, was that a Board was to be preferred to a single minister, because there was no one to act for a single minister should he fall ill. The more likely explanation is that Education was seen to be commensurate with such departments as the Board of Agriculture, the Local Government Board and the Board of Trade. It was clearly not to be a principal office of state. Sir George Kekewich, Secretary to the Education Department from 1890 and the first Secretary to the new Board, was among those who would have preferred a major department headed by a Secretary of State. Nevertheless, as he noted in his autobiography, 'Treasury red-tape carried the day'. Kekewich found little change in his new role, as he was already head both of the Education Department and of the Science and Art Department. Technically promoted from the third to the second class of permanent official, however, he 'was entitled to wear a good deal more gold on my Court uniform, an expensive privilege of which I never availed myself'.[7]

The Board of Education, which commenced operations in 1900, was not a modern ministry. In some senses it was a continuation of the Education Committee of the Privy Council established in 1839 by the Whig Government of Lord Melbourne. Yet the need for a single minister and ministry of high status had been urged throughout the nineteenth century. Brougham's proposals of 1837 had envisaged placing the superintendence of education either under a Board of Education or under a minister.[8] In the middle years of the century, Pakington's draft Report from the Select Committee of 1865–6 concluded:

> That there should be a Minister of Public Instruction with a seat in the Cabinet, who should be entrusted with the care and superintendence of all matters relating to the national encouragement of science and art and popular education in every part of the country.[9]

Two outcomes of this report were Lord John Russell's resolution of 1867 for the appointment of a Minister of Public Instruction and, in the following year, an unsuccessful Bill introduced by Disraeli's Conservative Government. The main purpose of this Bill was to 'enable the Crown to appoint an additional Secretary of State for the Educational Department'.[10]

In contrast with these earlier proposals, therefore, the Bill of 1899 was pusillanimous in the extreme. Bishop noted that even after the Act no fewer than seven different Cabinet ministers had some responsibility for educational matters and that they rarely consulted together.[11] Initial attempts to provide a fusion of the three bodies were problematic, and Peter Gosden has argued that 'the senior officials of both the Science and Art Department and of the Charity Commission met with a considerable measure of success in their efforts to preserve their particular offices from that drastic upheaval with which they had seemed to be threatened by the Board of Education Act'.[12]

The Board's role was to be further complicated, and in some sense curtailed, by the achievement of another of the proposals of the Bryce Commissioners, the establishment of local education authorities (LEAs) based upon counties and county boroughs. In January 1898, the Duke of Devonshire had acknowledged that 'a central authority has become an almost indispensable preliminary to the establishment of satisfactory local authorities'.[13] In 1899, the Board had been charged with 'the superintendence of matters relating to education in England and Wales' at a time when educational provision was fragmented across a range of authorities and providers. These included more than 2,500 school boards and 14,000 managing bodies of voluntary elementary schools. The 1902 Act saw the demise of the school boards and the assumption by some 318 LEAs of jurisdiction over elementary education. It also declared that:

> The local education authority shall consider the educational needs of their area and take such steps as seem to them desirable, after consultation with the Board of Education, to supply or aid the supply of education other than elementary, and to promote the general co-ordination of all forms of education.[14]

The Board of Education soon came to be organized into three branches – Elementary, Secondary and Technical – each under the control of an Assistant Secretary, and regional organization proceeded from 1903. Nevertheless, in the years between 1902 and 1944 the Board of Education was concerned more with overseeing and monitoring rather than with control and direction. In this period, LEAs gained considerable experience of owning, providing and administering schools. Indeed, as Aldrich and Leighton have noted, the central authority's 'prestige and interventionist role was in many respects weaker in 1944 in relation to school providers than it had been in 1870'.[15] As Professor Gruffydd, MP for the University of Wales, argued in the debates on the 1944 Bill:

> It is becoming clearer, year after year, with each successive Education Bill, that we in Britain, at least in England and Wales, have not got a national system of education. Our education, as far as it is a system, is provincial in all senses of the word.[16]

A month later the *Times Educational Supplement* commented that, 'forty years of lack of effective power at the centre have amply proved the absolute necessity for central direction and control'.[17]

Ministry of Education 1944

The 1944 Act was widely hailed by contemporaries. It has since been seen as the most important piece of legislation of the war, the centrepiece of the Welfare State. H.C. Dent, editor of the *Times Educational Supplement* at the time, called it 'a very great act'.[18] Timothy Raison declared it a 'Rolls Royce among Statutes'.[19] In recent years, however, the Act has been subjected to more searching analysis.[20] For example, Gary McCulloch has identified at least five types of interpretation of the Act – celebratory, critical, conspiratorial, cultural and nostalgic.[21]

There is no space here to examine such interpretations in detail. There can be no doubt, however, that the 1944 Act was construed and constructed in an atmosphere of consensus and conciliation. It reflected a widely shared vision of a better educational future for the nation's children, with the provision of secondary schooling for all and the raising of the school-leaving age to 15. The harsh economic and social realities of postwar Britain, as experienced in shortages of school buildings and teachers and the cruel winter of 1947, however, cast an immediate blight upon on such hopes.

The 1944 Bill did not propose the establishment of a Ministry of Education. In introducing the second reading Butler announced that 'Under Clause I the Minister retains his traditional title but loses the assistance of a Board which has never met.'[22] The absurdity of this proposal, highlighted by Greenwood's riposte that Butler would thus become the 'President of no Board of Education',[23] eventually forced the government to concede. Sir Griffith Williams, who was to become Deputy Secretary in the new Ministry, 1946–53, later argued that 'In effect the change of name made little difference and those who saw in it some sinister ambitions for a greater measure of central control were no doubt relieved.'[24]

The Minister was charged with the duty:

> To promote the education of the people of England and Wales and the progressive development of institutions devoted to that purpose, and to secure the effective execution by local authorities, under his control and direction, of the national policy for providing a varied and comprehensive educational service in every area.

Such a call to action contrasted strongly with the realities of the postwar situation. In the first ten years of the new Ministry there were no fewer than five Ministers and three Permanent Secretaries. In 1951 its status reached rock bottom when the Minister, Florence Horsbrugh, was excluded from Churchill's Cabinet. Matters improved under her successor, Sir David Eccles, who unusually served on two occasions – from 1954 to 1957 and from 1959 to 1962.

In the 1960s, increasing concerns about science and technology were fuelled from various sources. C.P. Snow's Rede lecture, 'The Two Cultures and the Scientific Revolution', delivered at Cambridge University in May 1959, was one starting point. At this time Harold Macmillan, Prime Minister 1957–63, and his successor Sir Alec Douglas-Home, 1963–4, engaged in considerable reorganization of government departments. In April 1964, following the recommendations of the Trend Committee on Civil Science and the Robbins Committee on Higher Education, the Ministry of Education and the Office of the Minister of Science were merged to form a department of state, the DES. The new Department assumed responsibilities for civil science and for the financing of higher education. In 1965, further financial responsibilities were acquired – for the arts and for the public library service.[25] Harold Wilson, Prime Minister, 1964–70, whose Labour Government on coming to office in October 1964 immediately created six new departments and abolished another, endorsed the amalgamation.[26] He sought to represent Labour as the party of science, democracy and modernity, in contrast to the supposedly effete and aristocratic culture of his Conservative predecessors.

The early years of the DES were characterized by new hopes and new initiatives, as exemplified in the abolition of the 11 plus examination and the spread of comprehensive secondary schools, the Plowden Report of 1967 and the White Paper, *A Framework for Expansion*, of 1972. Such hopes, however, were in their turn overborne by the economic crises of the 1970s, and the growing belief that schools were failing to produce the goods. In 1977–8, expenditure on public education in Britain accounted for 12 per cent of public expenditure overall and represented 7 per cent of gross national product.[27] Concern was expressed that this money was not being well spent. In October 1976 in a speech at Ruskin College, Oxford, James Callaghan called for a 'Great Debate on Education'. The Labour Prime Minister expressed his support for 'a basic curriculum with universal standards' and declared that the purpose of education was to equip 'children to the best of their ability for a lively constructive place in society and also to fit them to do a job of work'.[28] This agenda was taken up by the Conservative Governments of Margaret Thatcher from 1979, albeit initially in piecemeal fashion. It found full expression in the Education Reform Act of 1988. This mammoth piece of legislation drastically reduced the power of the LEAs, and abolished the largest of them, the Inner London Education Authority. In sharp contrast, the Secretary of State for Education and Science acquired some 400 new powers. In 1992 responsibility for science was lost and the DES became the DfE.

Department for Education and Employment 1995

The creation of the DfEE in July 1995 reflected a number of factors. These included the state of Conservative Party politics at the time, following a bruising leadership election, and a concern to reduce both the size of the Cabinet and the numbers of civil servants. For example, there was a 32 per cent reduction of posts at divisional manager level. More fundamentally, the merged department represented an attempt to bridge perceived longstanding divisions between academic and vocational courses and qualifications, and between the worlds of education and employment. In the 1970s and 1980s the creation of agencies such as the Manpower Services Commission (MSC) under the aegis of the Employment Department (ED) had denoted the rise of the 'vocationalists' and the enterprise culture, particularly associated with Lord Young. Critics of such initiatives as the Youth Opportunities Programme (YOP) and Youth Training Scheme (YTS) argued that these schemes were fundamentally flawed. They were short-term solutions, designed to take young people out of the job market and reduce unemployment figures, rather than to provide a skilled workforce that would generate more jobs. Nevertheless, the extent of the ED's inroads into the traditional preserve of the DES became apparent when in November 1982 Margaret Thatcher announced the Technical and Vocational Education Initiative (TVEI) as an MSC venture. The Education Reform Act of 1988 has been interpreted in many ways: as a first step in the privatization of public education; a victory for consumers over producers; a means of drastically reducing the powers of the LEAs; a belated fulfilment of the empowerment of the central authority presaged in the 1944 Act. It must also be seen as a victory for the old humanists and the traditional academic school curriculum in the face of a burgeoning new vocationalism.

Although the 1988 Act brought Kenneth Baker and the DES to the centre stage of politics, implementation of the national curriculum and national testing proved to be highly problematic, not least when John Patten was Secretary of State, 1992–4. The relative economic decline of the United Kingdom was increasingly attributed to a shortage of skilled workers. Demands grew for an end to conflict and 'turf wars' between the Education and Employment departments, and for the establishment of a Department for Education and Training (DET). Thus the Paul Hamlyn Foundation National Commission on Education, which reported in 1993, proposed that 'the Department for Education should merge with those parts of the Employment Department which are responsible for training to form a new Department for Education and Training (DET)'.[29]

The antecedents of the ED can be traced back to the Ministry of Labour, established in 1916. Its creation may be interpreted in two ways. The first is as a response to the immediate labour requirements of the First World War; the second as a reflection of the growing power of the labour movement and a heightened concern for an improvement in the working conditions of the mass of the populace. The new Ministry was constructed on firm foundations. Since 1893 there had been a Labour Department at the Board of Trade, and the Ministry of Labour soon assumed responsibility for many of the functions previously exercised within the Board of Trade – labour exchanges, industrial relations and conciliation, elements of national insurance and the compilation of employment statistics. In the 1920s it also acquired powers in respect of youth employment, which were transferred from the Board of Education. In the inter-war period the Ministry of Labour was principally concerned with issues of unemployment, including the payment of the dole and the creation of public works schemes. At this time it became one of the largest government departments in terms of staffing and budget.

In 1939, as a result of the need to provide military training, the Ministry of Labour was transformed into a Ministry of Labour and National Service. From May 1940 with the appointment of Ernest Bevin, the Ministry was rapidly developed into a major department of state. Bevin sought to avoid the difficulties of dislocation and unemployment which had followed the ending of the First World War, and to transform his Ministry into a Department of Employment. This was ultimately achieved in 1970, the Ministry having dropped the words 'National Service' from its title in 1959 and existed as a Department of Employment and Productivity from 1968. From the later 1970s, the Department was increasingly concerned with policies designed to reduce youth unemployment.

Gillian Shephard, appointed Secretary of State for Education and Employment in 1995, was well qualified for the post. She had worked as a careers adviser, and had served as Secretary of State for Employment 1992–3, and for Education since 1994. She had also been a leading supporter of John Major's campaign for re-election as leader in June 1995. Her appointment from Education was balanced at Permanent Secretary level, where Michael Bichard from Employment was preferred to Sir Tim Lankester. An even-handed approach was adopted towards other appointments, although both sets of civil servants feared that they had been taken over by the other.

Reactions to the merger were generally positive, although some concerns were expressed that the creation of the DfEE meant the disappearance of a separate ministry whose historic role had been to champion the cause of the unemployed. For while the Employment Service and the Training, Enterprise and Education

Directorate were transferred to the DfEE, other responsibilities were lost to the Department for Trade and Industry, the Department of the Environment and the Central Statistical Office. Doug McAvoy, General Secretary of the National Union of Teachers (NUT), exemplified the reactions of many within the world of education.

> Abolition of the Employment Department is to be deplored as a panic measure. Nonetheless the transfer of training to Education has merit. The NUT has long argued that the distinction between education and training created artificial barriers and resulted in training being given lower status. Bringing education and training together should serve to promote vocational education and the development of life long education and training as an important facet of the nation's future.[30]

Lifelong learning was to become a major theme of the DfEE under the Labour Government.

From the Employment side, the creation of the DfEE was justified by reference to the United Kingdom's relative economic decline. Competitiveness was a major theme of Conservative policy documents of the 1990s. There was a widespread belief that the United Kingdom was hampered by the low levels of education and training of many of its citizens. A plentiful supply of skilled labour was seen as the best means of job creation and of promoting economic and social well being. In September 1995 the DfEE set out its overall aim as being: 'To support economic growth and improve the nation's competitiveness and quality of life by raising standards of educational achievement and skill and by promoting an efficient and flexible labour market.'[31]

Departmental culture

Sir Michael Bichard, Permanent Secretary at the DfEE, has argued that the aim of the DfEE is 'not just bringing together two cultures', but the creation of 'a different culture, a different kind of government department'.[32] What of the culture of the Education department in the twentieth century?

Throughout the twentieth century the Education department was small in respect of the numbers of its personnel. For example, Sir William Pile, Permanent Secretary 1970–6, remarked that 'Apart from the Treasury it is the smallest of the London-based departments of state.'[33] The Department had no regional or local networks. It neither maintained educational institutions nor employed teachers. For the greater part of the century it exercised minimal supervision over school curricula and examinations.

In political terms the Education department was never of the first rank. The same was often true of its ministers. Of the Department's 46 political heads between 1900 and 1995 only one, Margaret Thatcher, subsequently became prime minister or even the leader of a party. Five of the political heads but only one of the 16 permanent secretaries were women.[34] From these figures it is apparent that the average tenure of office for a minister was a mere two years. In contrast permanent secretaries served for some six years.

One consequence of the rapid turnover of ministers was that civil servants frequently held the upper hand, inasmuch as ministers needed time to become familiar with their brief. This applied not only in matters of administration but also of policy. Indeed, given that throughout the twentieth century the Department had few administrative responsibilities, some of its senior civil servants naturally turned their attention to policy making.[35]

This was certainly true of one of the most powerful and controversial civil servants, Sir Robert Morant. An influential figure in the construction of the 1902 Act, as Permanent Secretary 1903–11 Morant was also responsible for its implementation. He 'built the Board of Education into an efficient and effective department dealing in a reasonably co-ordinated and coherent manner with the various areas of education'.[36] Much of this prestige and energy was forfeited under his successor, Sir Lewis Selby-Bigge. Indeed in the inter-war period torpor, rather than initiative, seemed to characterize the Board of Education. Some of its senior civil servants, including Selby-Bigge, were scholars as well as gentlemen. For example, both E.K. Chambers, who served from 1910 until 1926 as Assistant and Second Secretary, and John Dover Wilson, one of Her Majesty's Inspectors (HMIs) of Schools, 1912–24, were Shakespearean scholars. Wilson, indeed, ended his career as Regius Professor of Rhetoric and English Literature at the University of Edinburgh. Williams noted that some of the early staff, like Chambers, had already 'followed an academic career as lecturers or teachers at universities'.[37] Little wonder that at this time the Board acquired something of the style and reputation of an Oxford college.

Some civil servants laid the blame for decline at the door of their political masters. For example, in 1940 R.S. Wood, then Deputy Secretary, pointed the finger at Lord Eustace Percy, President 1924–9, whose 'general policy was to belittle the powers and position of the department and to circumscribe their control. I do not think that we have ever fully recovered from the damage of that period'.[38]

R.S. Wood, together with S.H. Wood, William Cleary, Griffith Williams and the Permanent Secretary, Maurice Holmes, were among the senior civil servants at the Board who recognized the need for educational reform in the context of wartime concerns. Thus, in respect of the legislation of 1944, R.G. Wallace has argued that 'The principal authors of the Act were a group of civil servants', and concluded that 'At the Board of Education in the early 1940s the balance of power was strongly in favour of the officials and against the politicians'.[39]

Although both the authorship and the nature of the 1944 Act have remained contentious, there is no doubt that the new Ministry acquired a higher profile and greater powers. One tangible sign of this increased role was the establishment of an Architects and Buildings Branch in 1949. In the postwar period, however, the new powers were exercised in a spirit of co-operation with both LEAs and teacher unions.

Thirty-five years after the 1944 Act, Pile emphasized the growing role of the civil servants and the extent to which DES officials had the duty to advise ministers on policy. In 1979 he noted that:

> The Department's permanent staff has in recent years become increasingly equipped, through the departmental planning organization, to undertake systematic thinking about national policy objectives and their resource implications, and to identify longer term issues that may require policy decisions by ministers.[40]

Pile was aware of critics who questioned the Department's efficiency and effectiveness. Nevertheless, he concluded that 'The main testimonial to the present system, however, is simply that it has worked well. Over thirty years it has got done those things that had to be done and could be done.'[41] Many politicians of the 1980s and 1990s rejected this interpretation. Challenge and confrontation replaced co-operation and acquiescence. In his Ruskin College speech of 1976 James Callaghan signalled Labour's disquiet with the products of state education. Margaret Thatcher's hostility towards the Department over which she presided 1970–4 was well known. Policy initiatives in education became the province of ministers, even of prime ministers, who turned for inspiration to think tanks that operated outside of the confines of Westminster. Political advisers such as Stuart Sexton and Michael Barber were brought into the rarefied portals of Whitehall. As James Christoph has concluded, 'a largely self-recruiting and self-governing mandarinate is a thing of the past'.[42]

Until the end of the First World War the Board of Education appointed its civil servants by nomination. This practice of patronage, according to Ministry of Education's own review of the first half of the twentieth century, 'enriched the work of administration with a leaven of scholarship and humanity which was in the best tradition of public life'.[43] Looking back from the vantage point of 1955 Sir Griffith Williams similarly commended the nomination system which brought in 'experienced amateurs' and 'made it possible to draw this staff from a wide field'. He noted the loss of men of the calibre of Spencer Leeson and Charles Douie which occurred as a result of the contraction of staffing following the Geddes 'axe' of 1922, and the recruitment of new and younger candidates from the 1930s.[44] Williams also remembered that from time to time the question had been raised as to:

> whether it would not be sensible for successful candidates for the Ministry's staff to spend some time before their confirmation outside the office studying at first hand the lay-out of education and the problems which arise in practice ... and that paper work gains in reality if it is done in the light of an actual experience of schools and institutions.[45]

Such questions went unanswered. Throughout the twentieth century senior staff at the Education department, the great majority of whom had been educated in independent schools, presided over a public education system of which they had no personal experience. Michael Bichard, Permanent Secretary at the DfEE from 1995, reported that 'When I came here the department was very strong on administration and very strong on the law of education ... but actually knew absolutely nothing about teaching in the classroom.'[46]

In some respects the culture of the ED resembled that of Education. Between 1916 and 1994 there were 37 Ministers for Employment of whom three were women. Their average length of tenure, as at Education, was a mere two years. All of the 16 permanent secretaries were male, their average period of office being five years. All received knighthoods, as did their counterparts at Education, where the one woman, Mary Smieton, became a Dame. Yet, there were also significant differences. Throughout the twentieth century, the ED was a 'hands on' institution. It was responsible for the organization of the labour market and for the promotion of good industrial relations. Its regional and local staff saw themselves as providing an important service to both sides of industry. It had a large complement of staff, commonly some ten times as great as that of Education. In 1939, indeed, there were some 30,000 employees.[47] By the 1980s, this figure had swollen to nearly 60,000. Such numbers were required to maintain a substantial local presence in the shape of employment exchanges and benefit offices. Many of the staff were temporary clerks, whose numbers fluctuated in line with the numbers of unemployed. The ED was at its strongest in times of national crisis, including those of war, recession and high unemployment. In contrast, the Education department was at its weakest in such periods. In the 1980s, the ED's identity as a 'labour ministry' was challenged by the development of Conservative doctrines of competitiveness and a return to Victorian values.

Conclusion

Four conclusions may be drawn from this overview.

First, it is clear that many of the characteristics identified by Bishop in respect of the rise of the central authority during the nineteenth century are applicable to the twentieth. Once again the process has been 'slow, tortuous, makeshift, muddled, unplanned, disjointed'. Even periods of apparently fundamental and rapid change have often proved to be illusory. This was true of 1944. Similarly, the Education Reform Act of 1988 signalled a massive development in the role of the central authority. This was stifled, however, by a simultaneous commitment to the application of market forces and parental choice, and a failure to assume direct responsibility for schools and teachers. In consequence, despite the best efforts of Conservative governments, many elements in the reform package were unfulfilled. Grant maintained schools remained in a minority; city technology colleges were few and far between. The National Curriculum was subjected to incessant change until it was decided that the only sensible way forward was to have a moratorium on further revision. Standards of attainment did not rise in dramatic fashion.

The second conclusion is that since 1995, and particularly since the advent of a Labour Government in May 1997, the DfEE has enjoyed a higher profile and acquired more powers than those exercised by the two separate ministries. In April 1998, in an assessment of his first year of office, David Blunkett maintained that 'a big department with an economic and an education brief actually does have some clout and Balkanized departments don't. Neither the DES nor latterly the Department of Employment had much clout separately. This department does have clout'.[48] Similarly, Sir Michael Bichard has argued that 'the Department has got an economic arm which actually means that the new department has got a place at Cabinet Committee which Education never had access to. There is no department in Whitehall that is taken seriously unless it has got an economic dimension to it'.[49]

Two comments may be made upon such statements. The first is that although the DfEE may be more powerful than either of the two separate departments, it is still not comparable with such departments as the Exchequer, the Foreign Office or the Home Office. The second is that while the DfEE may promote itself as the best means of investing in human capital to produce guaranteed economic and social rewards, frequent ministerial assertions that the economic and employment future belongs to those nations with the best educated and skilled workforces have yet to be proven. Viewed from the Treasury, economic and social success may be seen to depend upon a range of other factors, for example, free market policies, unregulated labour markets and low wages.

The third conclusion concerns the relationship between central and local government in education. Has this fundamentally changed across the twentieth century? The system of education in England and Wales has traditionally been referred to as a 'partnership', 'a national service locally administered' and 'an all-embracing network of dispersed responsibility'.[50] Nevertheless, as Selby-Bigge observed in 1927, it is a service 'conducted by representative local bodies which are not the agents of the central authority'.[51] During the second half of the twentieth century, there have been several modifications of the relationship between central and local – for example, under the 1944 Education Act and under the provisions of the Local Government Acts of 1958, 1962, 1972 and 1974. Although the Education Reform Act of 1988 seriously weakened the LEAs, and marked the determined re-entry of the government into the secret garden of the curriculum, since that date other local agencies have been created. For example, in December 1988, a mere five months later, a White Paper entitled *Employment in the 1990s* proposed the establishment of local Training and Enterprise Councils (TECs). These local bodies were to make contracts for the provision of training with various institutions and groups, including private employers. Although currently consuming some £1.5 billion per year, the TECs have had a chequered history, not least as a result of financial scandals and actual collapse. Since 1997, the Labour Government has sought to redraw the relationship between central and local once more. Some powers have been restored to LEAs; league tables to measure the performance of LEAs and TECs have been introduced. Merger at the centre, however, has not been accompanied by similar rationalization in the localities. Indeed, the plethora of local initiatives, Education Action Zones, National Training Organizations and Regional Development Agencies, coupled with competition between TECs, further education and sixth form colleges, suggests the opposite. In the year 2000, as in 1900, in a direct sense the central authority for education still 'maintains no schools or colleges; it employs no teachers'.[52]

Finally, it is clear that the formation of the DfEE in 1995 was a most significant event in the history of the central authority for education, as indeed for that of employment. It may, indeed, prove to have been the most significant event in this regard, not only of the twentieth century, but also since the formation of the Education Committee of the Privy Council in 1839. Nevertheless, there can be no certainty that the merged department will continue in its present form. The DfEE is almost unique in international terms. Elsewhere, mergers between employment and welfare structures and policies have been more common than those between employment and education. Indeed, as indicated in this article, previous reformulation of the two departments in the twentieth century suggests that further change is almost certain to occur. One possible trigger for such a process might be an increase in levels of unemployment, or in problems in the industrial relations sphere. This could promote yet another redistribution of responsibilities. For example, the creation of a merged Department of Trade, Industry and Employment might pave the way for a DET – or even a Department for Lifelong Learning.

Notes

1 A.S. Bishop, *The Rise of a Central Authority for English Education*, Cambridge: Cambridge University Press, 1971, p. 276.
2 R. Aldrich, D. Crook and D. Watson, *Education and Employment: The DfEE and its Place in History*, London: Institute of Education, 2000. The authors are most grateful to the Nuffield Foundation for the grant to carry out the research upon which the book and this article are based. Other publications arising from this project include D. Crook and R. Aldrich, 'Education and employment in England: historical perspectives, research and teaching', in A. Heikkinen, T. Lein and L. Mjelde (eds), *Work of Hands and Work of Minds in Times of Change*, Jyväskylä: University of Jyväskylä, 1999; and D. Watson, 'Relations between the education and employment departments, 1921–45: an anti-industrial culture versus industrial efficiency?', *History of Education*, 1998, 27(3): 333–43. I am most grateful to my colleagues, David Crook and David Watson for their comments on an earlier draft of this article.

3   For details of the Act see Bishop, op. cit., ch. 13; and P.H.J.H. Gosden, 'The Board of Education Act, 1899', *British Journal of Educational Studies*, 1962, XI(1): 44–60.
4   PP 1895, XLIII, *Report of the Commissioners on Secondary Education*, p. 86.
5   B. Webb, *Our Partnership*, 1948, p. 239, quoted in Bishop, op. cit., p. 269.
6   *Hansard*, H. of L. LXX, 353, 24 April 1899.
7   G.W. Kekewich, *The Education Department and After*, London: Constable, 1920, p. 107. The President of a Board commanded a salary of £2,000 per annum, while that of a Secretary of State 'had to be fixed independently of tradition'. Ibid., p. 108.
8   On this point see Bishop, op. cit., p. 14, and D.G. Paz, 'The composition of the Education Committee of the Privy Council, 1839–1856', *Journal of Educational Administration and History*, 1976, 8(2): 1.
9   PP 1866, VII, *Second Report of the Select Committee on the Constitution of the Committee of Council on Education*, p. xvi.
10 *Hansard*, H. of C. CXCI, 120, 24 March 1868. For Pakington see R. Aldrich, *Sir John Pakington and National Education*, Leeds: University of Leeds, 1979. For the 1868 Bill see A. Bishop and W. Jones, 'The Act that never was: the Conservative Education Bill of 1868', *History of Education*, 1972, 1(2): 160–73.
11 Bishop, op. cit., p. 267.
12 Gosden, op. cit., 1962, p. 57.
13 PRO ED 24/8, quoted in Bishop, op. cit., p. 260.
14 2 Edw. 7 c. 42, *An Act to make further provision with respect to Education in England and Wales*, section 2(1).
15 R. Aldrich and P. Leighton, *Education: Time for a New Act?*, London: Institute of Education, 1985, p. 21.
16 *Hansard*, H. of C. 396, 419–20, 20 January 1944.
17 *Times Educational Supplement*, 12 February 1944.
18 H.C. Dent, *The Education Act 1944*, London: University of London Press, 11th edn 1966, p. 3.
19 T. Raison, *The Act and the Partnership*, London: Bedford Square Press for the Centre for Studies in Social Policy, 1976, p. 76.
20 See, for example, Aldrich and Leighton, op. cit.; C.H. Batteson, 'The 1944 Education Act reconsidered', *Educational Review*, 1999, 51(1): 5–15; G. McCulloch, *Education Reconstruction: The 1944 Act and the Twenty-First Century*, London: Woburn Press 1994; B. Simon, 'The 1944 Education Act: a Conservative measure?', *History of Education*, 1986, 15(1): 31–43.
21 McCulloch, op. cit., pp. 45–68.
22 *Hansard*, H. of C. 396, 210, 19 January 1944.
23 *Hansard*, H. of C. 396, 1675, 8 February 1944.
24 Sir G. Williams, 'The first ten years of the Ministry of Education', *British Journal of Educational Studies*, 1955, III(2): 101.
25 Sir W. Pile, *The Department of Education and Science*, London: Allen and Unwin, 1979, p. 6.
26 G. Davis, P. Weller, E. Craswell and S. Eggins, 'What drives machinery of government change? Australia, Canada and the United Kingdom, 1950–1997', *Public Administration*, 1999, 77(1): 21–6.
27 Pile, op. cit., p. 7.
28 P. Gordon, R. Aldrich and D. Dean, *Education and Policy in England in the Twentieth Century*, London: Woburn Press, 1991, pp. 94–7.
29 National Commission on Education, *Learning to Succeed*, London: Heinemann, 1993, p. 344.
30 NUT press release, 5 July 1995.
31 DfEE, *The English Education System: An Overview of Structure and Policy*, London: DfEE, 1995, p. 1.
32 Interview with Michael Bichard, 8 January 1998.
33 Pile, op. cit., p. 7. In 1979 the entire headquarters staff numbered some 2,500.
34 Dame Mary Smieton was Permanent Secretary at the Ministry of Education, 1959–63.
35 Indeed, Sir George Kekewich, the first Permanent Secretary, 1900–3, was Liberal MP for Exeter, 1906–10.

36 P. Gosden, *Public Education in England 1839–1989: The Department and the Governance of the System*, London: DES, 1989, p. 10. This is a printed version of a lecture given on 10 April 1989, being the 150th anniversary of the establishment of the Committee of Council for Education.
37 Williams, op. cit., p. 110.
38 PRO 136/212. R.S. Wood to M. Holmes, 8 November 1940, quoted in Gosden, op. cit., 1989, p. 13.
39 R.G. Wallace, 'The origins and authorship of the 1944 Education Act', *History of Education*, 1981, 10(4): 283, 290.
40 Pile, op. cit., p. 36.
41 Ibid., p. 238.
42 J.B. Christoph, 'The remaking of British administrative culture: why Whitehall can't go home again', *Administration and Society*, 1992, 24(2): 179.
43 Ministry of Education, *Education 1900–1950. The Report of the Ministry of Education for the Year 1950*, London: HMSO, 1950, p. 2.
44 Williams, op. cit., p. 110.
45 Ibid., p. 112.
46 Interview with Michael Bichard, 8 January 1998.
47 R. Lowe, *Adjusting to Democracy: The Role of the Ministry of Labour in British Politics, 1916–1939*, Oxford: Clarendon Press, 1986, p. 11.
48 Interview with David Blunkett, 23 April 1998.
49 Interview with Michael Bichard, 8 January 1998.
50 See, for example, Pile, op. cit., pp. 23–4, 237.
51 Sir L. Selby-Bigge, *The Board of Education*, London: Putnam, 1927, p. 15, quoted in Pile, op. cit., p. 33.
52 Pile, op. cit., p. 23.

PART 3

EDUCATIONAL REFORMERS

CHAPTER 5

THE ROLE OF THE INDIVIDUAL IN EDUCATIONAL REFORM

C. Majorek, E. Johanningmeier, F. Simon and W. Bruneau (eds), *Schooling in Changing Societies: Historical and Comparative Perspectives*, Gent: CSHP, 1998 (*Paedagogica Historica* Supplementary Series IV), pp. 345–57

Introduction

This article is divided into four parts. It begins with an introduction which identifies key themes in respect of the two elements of educational reform and the role of the individual. The second and third sections provide quantitative and qualitative analyses taken from four recent studies of educational reformers. Finally conclusions are drawn in respect of universality, continuity, competition and change, historical construction and consumers of education.[1]

The article has a thousand starting points, or to be more accurate, 993. That is the number of subjects contained in two biographical dictionaries of educationists: the first British; the second North American and European.[2] These volumes provide short biographical and bibliographical entries in respect of 465 and 528 subjects respectively, all deceased, the vast majority of whom lived and worked during the last two hundred years. They are intended as works of reference, and insofar as the information contained therein is taken from secondary rather than from primary sources, represent established – even traditional – patterns of selection and scholarship. But though the volumes and their brief entries may appear prosaic in the extreme, the experience of more then ten years of researching the lives of these men and women has been one of great challenge, excitement and inspiration. This article has two large, and in some senses naive and over-ambitious purposes. The first is to attempt to convey some sense of that challenge, excitement and inspiration. The second to suggest that it is possible to draw upon these studies, and others, to re-visit the role of the individual in educational reform from an international perspective.

At this point two basic acknowledgements must be made. The first is that although the aspirations of this paper are international, its antecedents and assumptions, in common with those of its author, are essentially western European. The second is that the re-visitation contained herein is neither particularly novel, nor particularly profound. As Harold Silver has shown, the theme of 'Where have all the people gone?', with which Barbara Finkelstein began her presidential address to the American Educational Studies Association in 1982,[3] was raised both in the United States and in the United Kingdom from the 1970s,[4] and included a search for real people engaged at every stage of the educational process. With respect to profundity, although at first sight reference books of this type may appear to be less subject to the type of theorizing about history to be found in the works of such writers as Dominick La Capra, Hans Kellner and

Hayden White which Sol Cohen has sought, somewhat unavailingly, to apply to studies in educational history,[5] that is not necessarily the case. Though biographical dictionaries may raise fewer questions about literary and rhetorical devices than more narrative works, any major selection and presentation of subjects impinges heavily upon issues concerning history as a mode of construction and emplotment. Other important theoretical issues which are not considered here in any depth include those that arise from Marxist interpretations in which the role of the individual is minimized or even negated. In an article of this length it is difficult to do more than acknowledge such dimensions. The remainder of this introduction is devoted to providing brief developments of the themes of educational reform and of the role of the individual in education.

Educational reform has been a central theme in history of education. 'Educational' (following Richard Peters) may be defined as pertaining to initiation into and development in worthwhile activities; 'reform' as deliberately induced change for the better. Of course concepts of 'worthwhile' and 'better' are not, and have not, been universally agreed, not even within a particular group or nation. Nevertheless, two assumptions are made at this point. The first is that some values and conditions are widely, if not universally, approved: knowledge as opposed to ignorance; respect for others as opposed to disrespect; physical well-being as opposed to ill-health; personal well-being as opposed to despair; material well-being as opposed to destitution. The second is that education, and educational reformers, are concerned to promote such values and conditions.

Educational reformers do not exist in a vacuum. Whether as individuals or as groups their work is located within a variety of social, economic, political and administrative contexts. One of the most obvious features of twentieth-century history has been the rise of the schooled society. At the end of the twentieth century, some states like Brazil, through the work of such reformers as Darcy Ribeiro, still strive to bring universal schooling to their people. In other countries, where universal schooling dates from the nineteenth century, there is a renewed emphasis upon increasing the efficiency of school systems – particularly with reference to securing success in an increasingly competitive global economy. Many historical and contemporary educational reforms may be located within this broad explanatory frame. Thus, for example, in England the major Education Acts of 1870, 1902 and 1944 were fundamentally aimed at the provision of universal elementary (subsequently primary) and secondary schooling. In contrast, the prime purpose of the Education Reform Act of 1988 was not so much to increase the supply of education as to ensure the efficiency and cost-effectiveness of that which already existed. This was to be accomplished by the establishment of a national curriculum and national testing under the direct control of central government, by the abolition of the Inner London Education Authority on the grounds of its perceived extravagance, inefficiency and radicalism, and by a severe reduction in the powers of other local education authorities (LEAs). In November 1995, the newly created Department for Education and Employment (DfEE) – a merger of two previously distinct ministries – declared that:

> The Government's principal aim for the education service at all levels and in all forms of learning is:
>
> To support economic growth and improve the nation's competitiveness and quality of life by raising standards of educational achievement and skill and by promoting an efficient and flexible labour market.[6]

One recent comparative analysis of the historical relationship between the rise of the schooled society and the state in England, France and the United States has been provided by Andy Green in *Education and State Formation*.[7] Green, who is currently extending his analysis to include twentieth-century developments in countries of the Far East – notably Japan, Singapore and Taiwan – attributes differences between national education systems to varying trajectories in the creation of national states. Other interpretations of the schooled society include those of the human capital variety, which suggest that the interests of the state, and of the individual, are both best served by investment in education, and those which see universal schooling essentially as a means of social control. One recent collection of essays provides a combination of these approaches while arguing that in the countries of sub-Saharan Africa there is a need to incorporate appropriate personality characteristics in the education and training of the labour force.[8]

Although in most contemporary societies, children and young people are initiated into the acquisition of such properties and qualities as knowledge, respect for others and physical well-being in formal school systems, such systems are neither necessarily the most important source of education nor the most effective. Throughout human history the main site of education has been the family, frequently complemented by the workplace and the place of worship. One important new educational dimension of the late twentieth century is that of television, a medium which has considerable capacity not only for education but also for mis-education. For example, it has been reported that the average American child sees 8,000 killings and 100,000 other acts of violence on film and television by the age of 12.[9]

There is an extensive literature on educational reform – both historical and contemporary. Recent comparative studies of English-speaking countries include those edited by Carter and O'Neill.[10] General studies of educational reform, however, including those of a comparative nature, tend to minimize the roles of individuals.

Biographical and autobiographical studies have been a major means of bringing individuals into history, including the history of education, but the process has not been unproblematic. It has been suggested that biography differs from history in that the one has a definite ending while the other does not, yet truly definitive biographies are few and far between, and the lives of subjects and the significance of their work, in common with other historical events, may be reinterpreted again and again in the light of new evidence or new perspectives. For example, Frank Smith's study of James Kay-Shuttleworth, the traditional 'hero' of English education, which had held the stage since 1923, has recently been completely overturned by what now seems to be another incomparable study, by R.J.W. Selleck.[11]

Within the western European tradition the hagiographical approach, exemplified in the medieval period in lives of the saints, gave way at the time of the Renaissance to a reappraisal of the relationship between truth and fiction in biographical studies. Of course sanitized, if not saintly, biographies have continued to be produced from that day to this, although in the second half of the twentieth century the demands of some publishers, and readers, have led to a concentration upon sinning rather than upon saintliness, while sanitization has been replaced by dishing the dirt.

Individuals, however, come not only singly but in groups, and official biographical collections exist in several countries. In the United Kingdom, for example, a completely new edition of the multi-volume *Dictionary of National Biography*, which originated in the late nineteenth century, and was thereafter updated by decennial additions, will be published in 2004. Two significant areas of inclusion in this new version will be much larger numbers of women, and of teachers. Single-volume biographical dictionaries abound. Those in English include national collections – Archie Brown (ed.), *The Soviet Union: A Biographical Dictionary* (London, 1990), John A. Garraty (ed.), *Encyclopedia of American Biography* (New York, 1974), Ernst Kay (ed.), *Dictionary of Scandinavian Biography* (London, 1976) – and international compilations such as the *Chambers Biographical Dictionary* (Edinburgh, 1990) and the *Macmillan Dictionary of Biography* (London, 1981).

Older specialist educational works include P. Monroe (ed.), *A Cyclopaedia of Education* (New York, 5 vols 1911–13), J.E. Roscoe, *The Dictionary of Educationists* (London, 1914) and Foster Watson (ed.), *The Encyclopaedia and Dictionary of Education* (London, 4 vols 1921–2). More recent studies are represented by John F. Ohles (ed.), *Biographical Dictionary of American Educators* (Westport, CT, 3 vols 1978), L. Glenn Smith and Joan K. Smith *et al.*, *Lives in Education: A Narrative of People and Ideas* (New York, 1993)[12] and the four-volume *Prospects* collection of *Thinkers on Education* (Paris, 1993–4).[13] There is an International Society of Educational Biography and an international journal, *Vitae Scholasticae: The Bulletin of Educational Biography*, published by Caddo Gap Press. In 1980, the UK History of Education Society produced an occasional publication, *Biography and Education: Some Eighteenth- and Nineteenth-Century Studies* (Leicester, 1980), while its Annual Conference of 1990, 'Biographical and Autobiographical Approaches to the History of Education', attracted papers from Denmark, the Netherlands, New Zealand and the United States. Joan K. Smith, who was president of the International Society of Educational Biography in 1987, reported on methodological and other issues in respect of educational biography in 'Biography as an educational history form in research and teaching' in Kadriya Salimova and Erwin V. Johanningmeier (eds), *Why Should We Teach History of Education?* (Moscow, 1993). The Society's annual conference, held in Chicago in April 1996, suggested the following possible topics to intending presenters: ethical issues in life-writing, the role of biography in educational history, oral history, use of life narratives in the classroom, narrative research, experimental approaches to life-writing, listening to silent voices, examining 'invisible' lives, feminist approaches to life-writing.

Historical studies which move beyond the contribution of an individual to groups of reformers include those by Peter Gordon and John White, *Philosophers as Educational Reformers* (London, 1979), Jean Houssaye *et al.*, *Quinze Pédagogues: Leur Influence Aujourd'hui* (Paris, 1994), and an important recent article in *Paedagogica Historica* entitled 'Break and continuity: observations on the modernization effects and traditionalization in international reform pedagogy' by Jürgen Oelkers.[14]

Facts and figures

Which individuals have been chosen to represent the several elements of educational reform, particularly during the era of the rise of the schooled society? This section provides some facts and figures from four recent studies.

The first of these is the *Prospects* collection of 100 *Thinkers on Education* (Paris, 4 vols 1993–4). Coverage is global, with a time span of some 2,500 years – from Confucius to the present day. Indeed, it is claimed that the work is 'the first systematic attempt to present, in three widely used languages, a comprehensive and first-hand view of the thought of the great educators, of every age and culture'.[15] Nevertheless, at least two thirds of the entries are European, with eleven from France, and a further eight apiece from Germany and the United Kingdom.

The second collection, by L. Glenn Smith, Joan K. Smith *et al.*, entitled *Lives in Education: A Narrative of People and Ideas* (New York, 1993), covers 73 subjects. This volume is advertised in the publisher's promotional literature as one in which, 'The history of Western education is told through the biographies of individuals, past and present, who exemplify the education of their times or have made important contributions to the developments of educational theory or practice.' The two final volumes are those by Aldrich and Gordon to which reference has already been made: the *Dictionary of British Educationists* (London, 1989) and the *Biographical Dictionary of North American and European Educationists* (London, 1997).

Data in Table 5.1 are taken from the first two collections and indicate the centuries in which these subjects were born. Table 5.1 shows that both collections are heavily weighted towards the modern period. This is particularly true of the *Prospects* selection.

Table 5.1 Subjects by centuries of birth

Centuries of birth	Thinkers on education	Lives in education
600	—	1
500	1	—
400	1	3
300	2	1
200	—	—
100	—	1
0 BC	—	—
AD 0	—	1
100	—	—
200	—	—
300	—	2
400	—	3
500	—	—
600	—	—
700	—	2
800	1	—
900	2	—
1000	1	2
1100	—	2
1200	—	1
1300	1	4
1400	3	7
1500	2	1
1600	2	3
1700	16	13
1800	58	18
1900	10	8
Totals	100	73

Table 5.2 presents a further breakdown of those born in the eighteenth, nineteenth and twentieth centuries across the four volumes. All subjects in the *Dictionary of British Educationists* and all but one in the *Biographical Dictionary of North American and European Educationists* were born in this period. One interesting feature, although admittedly the Aldrich and Gordon volumes begin with the 'modern' period and exclude living educationists, is the distribution across centuries. Some 184 subjects were born in the eighteenth century, 871 in the

Table 5.2 Subjects by decades of birth, 1700–1969

Decades	Thinkers on education	Lives in education	British educationists	North American and European educationists
1700	—	—	—	2
1710	1	1	—	3
1720	1	—	—	3
1730	1	—	2	—
1740	3	2	5	14
1750	—	2	7	5
1760	1	—	5	10
1770	4	1	11	19
1780	3	3	15	10
1790	2	4	24	20
1800	1	—	42	21
1810	5	—	50	33
1820	3	2	38	39
1830	2	3	44	44
1840	4	3	36	33
1850	7	2	52	55
1860	9	2	42	65
1870	7	2	29	59
1880	13	2	31	47
1890	7	2	12	23
1900	5	1	15	13
1910	2	—	2	7
1920	3	6	3	2
1930	—	—	—	—
1940	—	1	—	—
1950	—	—	—	—
1960	—	—	—	—
Totals	84	39	465	527

Table 5.3 Subjects by sex

	Male	Female
Thinkers on education	97	3
Lives in education	56	17
British educationists	410	55
North American and European educationists	370	158

nineteenth and only 60 in the twentieth. Even the two volumes which include extant educationists contain 29 subjects born in the eighteenth century and only 18 from the twentieth. Another, and even more interesting, fact to emerge is that of distribution across the sexes (see Table 5.3).

Classification

Though the grouping of individuals by such factors as sex, location and date presents few problems, classification in terms of role with particular reference to educational reform is more problematic.

All four volumes interpret their brief – whether 'Thinkers', 'Lives' or 'Educationists' – in a broad sense. Subjects are not confined to those whose lives were exclusively or even primarily devoted to education. Thus in his introduction to the *Prospects* collection Zaghloul Morsy comments that:

> Philosophers, politicians, sociologists, scientists, theologians, novelists, historians, poets and essayists of every period and culture have had much to say on the subject of education...Examples? Kant, al-Fārābī, Bello, Nyerere, Ibn Khaldūn, Grundtvig, Tolstoy, Tagore, to name but a few.[16]

Aldrich and Gordon, in the briefest of introductions, similarly declare that their volumes are 'representative of many of the different categories which can be subsumed under the term "educationists"', while the first entry in *Lives in Education* is that of Sappho.

Although, Morsy, in common with Aldrich and Gordon, arranges his subjects in alphabetical order, he nevertheless conjures at some length both with the issues of order and of categorization. Having rejected periodization as inappropriate for an international and transcultural collection, Morsy then acknowledges the possibility of:

> Other categorizations, classifying the thinkers according to the educative model on which their work is based...reformist, conservative, domesticating, liberating, directivist/non-directivist, secularized-humanist, religious-authoritarian, Prussian, maieutic, abolitionist, libertarian, politico-ideological, centred on culture or on pedagogy, centred on the teacher or on the pupil, on the rights of the child, on the authority of the adult, on the demands of society, democratic-republican, feudal, monarchist, Marxist-Leninist, etc.[17]

In contrast, *Lives in Education* does embrace periodization, being divided into twelve chronological chapters with between five and eight educators for each. The first six chapters progress from Greeks and Romans through Monastics and Humanists to the Reformers and the Enlightenment; the latter six are focused on Americans and particularly upon the United States. Of these the final three are concerned with 'The Outsiders', as represented by women, Native Americans and Hispanic Americans; 'The Critics' who include such names as Montessori, Maritain and Counts; 'The Paradigm Shifters', from Kuhn through Freire to Malcolm X.

Classification of the subjects contained in the second of the Aldrich and Gordon volumes is currently being undertaken. Analysis of the *Dictionary of British Educationists* was carried out in a highly perceptive review by Phillip McCann.[18]

Some 80 per cent of the entries were English, with Irish, Scots and Welsh distributed roughly in proportion to their populations. McCann placed some 15 per cent of the subjects in the aristocratic class, slightly more than 10 per cent in the plebeian or working class, with the great majority in the middle. More than half of the subjects, some 56 per cent, attended the universities of Oxford and Cambridge, with a further 15 per cent attending other universities, mainly London and those of Scotland. Similarly a majority attended public (37 per cent) or grammar (21 per cent) schools. Only a small minority were educated in elementary or other schools for the working classes.

Although, as McCann rightly suggests, this volume does not adequately represent all elements of education and educational reformers – for example, there are few classroom teachers – it does reflect education as publicly perceived during the two centuries characterized by the rise of the schooled society. Some 55 per cent of the entries found a career within the sphere of educational administration. These included such well-known figures as James Kay-Shuttleworth and Robert Morant from the nineteenth century, and Henry Morris and Alec Clegg from the twentieth. Politicians constituted another significant group of some 13 per cent. Prominent among these were W.E. Forster, A.J. Mundella, Arthur Balfour, H.A.L. Fisher and R.A. Butler, whose names are inextricably associated with the educational legislation of 1870, 1880, 1902, 1918 and 1944 respectively. Some 14 per cent spent their lives wholly or mainly within the classroom, while a further 14 per cent, in McCann's judgement, could be classed as educational theorists 'in the sense that their theories were influential in changing practice'.[19] Of the eight British entries in the *Prospects* collection of *Thinkers on Education* – John Locke, Thomas More, A.S. Neill, Robert Owen, Joseph Priestley, Herbert Read, Michael Sadler and Herbert Spencer – five are included. More and Locke are from an earlier period, only Read is missing.

Two major conclusions can be indicated at this point. The first is that the *Dictionary of British Educationists* mirrors, albeit perhaps in distorted fashion, the dominance of British society and of the educational system constructed for the poor, by male, Protestant, Oxbridge-educated figures who had very little concern for educational theory and whose own studies were classical and humanistic rather than scientific or technical. Nevertheless, while the educational ideas and works of such theorists as Joseph Payne, Herbert Spencer and A.S. Neill might find more acceptance outside Britain than within, individual reformers did profoundly influence many dimensions of formal education and culture in an institutional sense, especially during the nineteenth and early twentieth centuries. Examples include:

Robert Baden-Powell (1857–1941), founder of the Boy Scout and Girl Guide movements;

Henrietta Barnett (1851–1936), founder of the Children's Country Holidays Fund, the London Pupil Teachers' Association and co-founder of Toynbee Hall;

Andrew Bell (1753–1832) and Joseph Lancaster (1778–1838), founders of the monitorial school system;

George Birkbeck (1776–1841), founder of the mechanics' institutes;

Mary Carpenter (1807–77), founder of ragged and reformatory schools;

Maria Grey (1816–1906), founder of the Women's Educational Union, Girls' Public Day School Company and Teachers' Training and Registration Society;

Albert Mansbridge (1876–1952), founder of the Workers' Educational Association.

Conclusion

Five brief, and preliminary, conclusions may be drawn.

Thinkers on Education, though published initially in three European languages (English, French and Spanish) and concerned predominantly with European subjects, nevertheless was justified principally in terms of its international dimensions and universality – 'all these thinkers always have something to offer, over and above particular values and cultures'.[20] This concern for universality is consistent with the contention in the first section of this article that some values and conditions, and the reform of education to promote such ends, are widely approved.

A second and related issue is that of continuity. *Lives in Education* may be compared with the classic work of Robert Rusk whose *Doctrines of the Great Educators* (London, 1918) went through no fewer than four editions and 15 reprints between 1918 and 1972. Of the 14 subjects in Rusk's fourth edition, 10 (Plato, Quintilian, Loyola, Comenius, Locke, Rousseau, Pestalozzi, Froebel, Dewey and Montessori) are included in the Smiths' collection. Montessori, the only woman in the 14 subjects in the Rusk volume and in the collection of 15 pedagogues edited by Jean Houssaye, is one of the 3 female subjects amongst the 100 *Thinkers on Education*.

But while there are universals and continuities, it is also possible to discern the effects of competing and changing contemporary concerns, both in choice of subjects and of reform priorities. In the *Prospects* collection concentration upon universals produces a 'galaxy' of educational thinkers and reformers of whom only 3 per cent are female, while a coverage of 26 centuries includes a continuous period of 11 centuries which produced no subjects at all. Tables 5.1 and 5.3 show that Smith and Smith, within the narrower parameters of 'Western' education, have a much stronger concern for a more equitable distribution both across centuries and across the sexes. Nine subjects are included for the 11 barren *Prospects* centuries, while the 17 female entries constitute some 23 per cent of the whole. This is substantially higher than the 12 per cent of female subjects in Aldrich and Gordon's British volume, but rather less than the 30 per cent of their North American and European collection. The considerable increase in the percentage of female subjects between these two latter volumes reflects several phenomena, three of which may be identified here. One is a firmer resolve by the authors to achieve a more equitable balance between the sexes in selected subjects; the second, an enlarged emphasis upon the non-administrative dimensions of educational reform; the third, the greater availability of secondary material in respect of North American women as opposed to some other parts of the world, an availability exemplified by such publications as *Notable American Women* (Cambridge, MA, 4 vols 1971–80).

A fourth conclusion concerns the relationship between individuals and past, current and future educational reform. Historical studies such as those considered in this article necessitate the recognition of at least three individuals in the process – the writer, the subject and the reader. Rusk's volume retained its popularity over several decades because it was perceived to be the distillation of the best that had been thought and taught about education within Western culture. Its very title, *Doctrines of the Great Educators*, indicated a concern for cultural transmission, not least to prospective and practising teachers. *Thinkers on Education* and *Lives in Education*, though conceived and presented in a less didactic manner, are similarly designed to transmit educational ideas, ideals and practice across the centuries. The two Aldrich and Gordon volumes, on the other hand, by their very nature invite a greater control and ownership by the reader.

Finally, it is important to draw attention to the relationship between the individual and educational reform in respect of a person's own education. The rise of formal educational systems at national and local levels has tended to restrict the role of the individual as an educational reformer in terms of the production of education for others, a tendency reflected in the distribution across time of subjects in the four volumes examined here. Nevertheless, in spite of the proliferation of formal educational systems, the role of the educational consumer has recently received considerable emphasis – not least in the United Kingdom. Once formal education for all becomes the norm in any society, a greater interest may develop in the different ways in which individuals make use of that educational system than in the contributions of those who have structured and continue to restructure it. Current work by Ari Antikainen and his colleagues at the University of Joensuu in Finland, based on a research project entitled 'In Search of the Meaning of Education', shows how individuals have made, and continue to make, highly selective use of formal educational facilities in the construction of their own life patterns and identities.[21] In this late modern or postmodernist world, each person has a history, and a potential role, as a reformer of education.

Notes

1 I acknowledge with gratitude the co-operation of Peter Gordon, my co-author in the two biographical volumes referred to in this article; of my wife, Averil Aldrich, who has undertaken much of the statistical analysis; and of my colleague, David Crook, who has commented with his customary wisdom and eye for detail upon the several drafts.

2 R. Aldrich and P. Gordon, *Dictionary of British Educationists*, London: Woburn Press, 1989; P. Gordon and R. Aldrich, *Biographical Dictionary of North American and European Educationists*, London: Woburn Press, 1997.

3 H. Silver, 'Zeal as a historical process: the American view from the 1980s', *History of Education*, 1986, 15(4): 300.

4 H. Silver, *Education as History*, London: Methuen, 1983, pp. 17–34.

5 S. Cohen, 'Representations of history', *History of Education*, 1991, 20(2): 131–41.

6 Department for Education and Employment, *The English Education System: An Overview of Structure and Policy*, London: DfEE, 1995, p. 1.

7 A. Green, *Education and State Formation*, London: Macmillan, 1990.

8 S.B.-S.K. Adjibolosoo, *The Significance of the Human Factor in African Economic Development*, Westport, CT: Praeger, 1995.

9 A. Neil, 'Shots straight to the heart of our sick society', *Sunday Times*, 17 August 1996.

10 D.S.G. Carter and M.H. O'Neill (eds), *International Perspectives on Educational Reform and Policy Implementation*, London: Falmer Press, 1995; D.S.G. Carter and M.H. O'Neill (eds), *Case Studies in Educational Change: An International Perspective*, London: Falmer Press, 1995.

11 F. Smith, *The Life and Work of Sir James Kay-Shuttleworth*, London: John Murray, 1923; R.J.W. Selleck, *James Kay-Shuttleworth: Journey of an Outsider*, London: Woburn Press, 1994.

12 L.G. Smith *et al.*, *Lives in Education: A Narrative of People and Ideas*, New York: St. Martin's Press, 1993.

13 Z. Morsy *et al.*, 'Thinkers on education', *Prospects*, 1993–4, XXIII(1–2)–XXIV(3–4).

14 J. Oelkers, 'Break and continuity: observations on the modernization effects and traditionalization in international reform pedagogy', *Paedagogica Historica*, 1995, XXXI(3): 675–713.

15 Z. Morsy, 'Thinkers on education', *Prospects*, 1993, XXIII(1–2): 12.

16 Ibid., p. 8.

17 Ibid., p. 13.
18 P. McCann, Review of *Dictionary of British Educationists*, in *Historical Studies in Education/Revue d'histoire de l'éducation*, 1990, 2(1): 165–6.
19 Ibid.
20 Z. Morsy, 'Thinkers on education', *Prospects*, 1993, XXIII(1–2): 12.
21 A. Antikainen *et al.*, *Living in a Learning Society: Life-histories, Identities and Education*, London: Falmer Press, 1996.

CHAPTER 6

JOSEPH PAYNE
Critic and reformer

R. Aldrich (ed.), *School and Society in Victorian Britain: Joseph Payne and the New World of Education*, New York: Garland, 1995, pp. 161–94

Introduction

Joseph Payne (1808–76) was England's first professor of education, appointed to that position by the College of Preceptors, a chartered body of teachers. Born in Bury St Edmunds in humble circumstances, Payne was an outsider. In terms of British society, including that of education, he was a marginal person. He did not belong to any charmed circle. His way in the world was made by the exercise of his own talents. Though possessed of a strong sense of history, Payne did not have an unalloyed commitment to traditional institutions and ways of thought. Even in respect of the College of Preceptors, a body in which he obtained high office and in which he assumed a pioneering role, he was, on occasion, a stern critic. This chapter examines four areas of Payne's criticisms and reform proposals with regard to the educational thinking and practice of his day. These were: the education of girls and women; boys' public schools; elementary schooling; the training of teachers.

The education of girls and women

In Payne's day by far the largest group of outsiders in British society were girls and women. Apart from the monarch herself, women were excluded from central government; indeed they were not even entitled to vote in parliamentary elections. Nor were they admitted to such learned professions as the Church, Law and Medicine. One means of calling attention to the injustice of such exclusions was through education, and particularly through examinations. Examinations provided a means whereby the intellectual abilities and attainments of males and females could be measured against each other.

Although the three principal school establishments with which he was personally connected – the Rodney House Academy, the Denmark Hill Grammar School and the Mansion Grammar School – were private schools for boys only, Payne had innumerable contacts with the world of female education, and his criticisms and reform proposals were made from a sound knowledge of the subject. In his years at Camberwell he gained an immediate, indeed intimate, understanding of the inside of a female educational community from his residence at Grove Hill House where Eliza kept her school. It should be noted that, for the first 30 years of their lives, Eliza Payne's experience as a teacher was quite as substantial as his own, and that this experience continued after their marriage. Though the middle years were spent in heavily male environments, as an examiner for the Theory and Practice of Education for the College of Preceptors, Payne received regular confirmation of the attainments of some female teachers. After his retirement from Leatherhead Payne was, in the context of the Council of the College of Preceptors, to work closely with two leading female educational reformers – Frances Buss and Beata Doreck. In 1873 both were awarded Fellowships by the College, and Buss proudly reported to the governors of her school that 'Miss Doreck and I are, as yet, the only women on whom such an honour has been conferred.'[1] Thereafter the letters FCP stood proudly after Buss's name both in life and in death. In June 1871, it was Payne who nominated Beata Doreck for membership of the Council of the College of Preceptors,[2] and it was Payne who contributed a substantial appreciation of Doreck to the *Educational Times* on the occasion of her death in 1875. In so doing, he paid tribute to Doreck's initiative in the establishment of the professorship: 'the honour of bringing it to birth belongs mainly to Miss Doreck; who was, however, warmly supported and aided throughout by her fellow Councillor, Miss Buss'.[3] The College of Preceptors established a scholarship in Doreck's memory, to be awarded on the results of the College's Diploma examinations for teachers. At the Christmas examination of 1876 the scholarship was awarded to a teacher at the North London Collegiate School, Sophie Bryant, who in 1894 succeeded Frances Buss as headmistress.[4]

Buss and Payne shared many educational experiences. Both were largely self-taught, both had a keen interest in history. Both were required to enter teaching from an early age, and to devote their not-inconsiderable energies to building up highly successful private schools. Through Payne, Buss came to admire Jacotot and to apply some of his principles at the North London.[5] Payne had strong connections both with the North London and with its sister establishment, the Camden School for Girls. He was frequently present on formal occasions: for example in 1871, together with Emily Davies, Edwin Abbott, Headmaster of the City of London School, and Joshua Fitch, Payne was on the platform at the Camden School prize-giving.[6] He also attended the prize-giving for the two schools held on 21 October 1872 at Willis's Rooms.

The North London not only had a library for the use of pupils but also a special collection of volumes for teachers, and Payne donated books to both.[7] He also gave courses of lessons and lectures at the school. For example, in 1872 Payne delivered a series of nine lessons on the history of the English language to the children of the first and second classes,[8] and in 1875 a parallel series on the 'Development of early French'.[9] The short course of four lectures given in 1874 – on 'Learning and knowing', 'Attention', 'Memory' and 'How to read with understanding' – would doubtless have been equally applicable to teachers and pupils.[10] In July 1874, at the invitation of Frances Buss, Joseph Payne carried out a three-day inspection of the teaching at the North London Collegiate School.[11] This inspection, by no means uncritical, was an instance of the issue which formed the closest bond between Buss and Payne, and which led to the establishment of the professorship – the need to improve the quality of education by means of the training of teachers.

Frances Buss's concern for the training of teachers for girls' secondary schools might well have been inherited from her mother who was sufficiently anxious, when establishing her private school in Clarence Road, Kentish Town from which the North London sprang, to undertake a course of elementary teacher training at the Home and Colonial College. Certainly it was developed by contact with Payne and Maria Grey. Indeed, in December 1871 it was Grey who recommended

Joseph Payne as the most suitable person to give a 'higher course of professional instruction'.[12]

On 13 January 1872, at a Preceptors' Council meeting chaired by Payne, approval was given for such a series of lectures 'On the Theory and Practice of Education'. The first of these was to be delivered on 25 January at the College, but the course was 'to be given in connection with the North London Collegiate and Camden School for Girls', and subsequent lectures were indeed given at the schools themselves.[13] A substantial programme of 30 lectures was constructed, to be delivered by Charles Lake, Payne's collaborator in the reform of the Preceptors' examinations. These lectures would be aimed at 'preparing the student directly for the examination of the College of Preceptors in the "Theory and Practice of Education" and indirectly for the examination in Logic and Moral Philosophy (Higher Proficiency) of the University of London'.[14]

The sessions were held in Camden Street on Thursday evenings at 5 p.m. They began with a lecture of some three-quarters of an hour, and were followed by questions and discussion.[15] Lake's lectures were not repeated in 1873, the year in which Payne launched his first professorial course, but M.A. Garvey, a barrister and one of the schools' trustees, gave a short series of six lectures commencing on 23 January 1873 on 'The Science and Practical Art of Teaching' to the teachers of both schools.[16]

At this time, following the reorganization into the North London and Camden Schools, Buss was contemplating turning one house, 202 Camden Road, into a day training college capable of training 100 students at a time. She had already adopted Maria Grey's suggestion of recruiting 'student teachers',[17] and in 1872 secured the support of her governors to appoint the first two, Edith Fletcher and Charlotte Offord, from January 1873.[18] Her vision of what such a training might include was entirely consistent with Payne's views, and with the professorial course which he taught from 1873.

> Our students should learn the history of great teachers, their methods, etc., should learn how to teach and what to teach; how to develop the mental, moral, and physical capacities of their pupils (by moral I mean also spiritual). We would affiliate to our College the National Schools, the School Boards of the neighbourhood, and *our own* girls' schools, so that every student in training should have the opportunity of seeing actual schools in work.
>
> I have not mentioned this last to any one but Mr Payne, for several reasons, one being that I am ambitious for the cause of education and especially for the *mixture* of sexes; if the College of Preceptors would take up the idea, it might be better left to them.[19]

Although, in Payne's lifetime, the College of Preceptors was unable to establish a training college for secondary teachers, the professorial lecture course had Buss's firm support. The North London Collegiate School was one of seven London schools and colleges to which students from Payne's class at the College of Preceptors were to be sent to experience 'the opportunity of good teaching'.[20]

Buss urged, indeed as in the case of Fanny Franks, sometimes required, her teachers to attend Payne's course.[21] Doreck also commended the classes and it would appear that they were generally appreciated. Many of those who attended subsequently became headmistresses themselves, and attributed their success to Payne's influence.

In 1873, Frances Lord wrote approvingly to Buss about Payne:

> I am attending Mr. Payne's lectures, as you told me to do. My sister Emily goes too, and, as a teacher, makes remarks that Mr. Payne thinks well of. If she ever takes up Kindergarten work (as I want her to do), she will, I am sure, be greatly helped by these lectures. My friends, the Wards, find, as we do, that the questions Mr. Payne asks draw largely on common observation such as we have been practising and have been wanting to know the value of.[22]

Indeed, it appears that Fanny Franks and Emily Lord, teachers of younger girls at the North London and Notting Hill High School respectively, were so inspired by Payne's lecture on Froebel that in their holidays they set off to seek further training from Madame de Portugall in Geneva. Madame de Portugall, who had been trained in Berlin and taught in Manchester, and was the examiner for the first London Froebel Society's Certificate, was inspector of schools in the canton of Geneva where Froebel's methods were widely used.[23] Another appreciative student, apparently spurred on by Payne to greater heights, was Sophie Bryant who began teaching at the North London in 1875, and who subsequently recorded that:

> When Miss Buss accepted my services to teach mathematics, she sent me also to Professor Payne; and whatever educational science I now possess, the clue to it was put into my hands by him. His lectures had that characteristic of combined originality, lucidity, and suggestiveness which is the fruit of intuitive gift in a strong, sincere nature. His sympathetic discussion of his students' essays after the lecture was a model illustration of the principles he expounded. At the basis of his methodology, as I remember it, lay the foundation principle that, in its ultimate analysis, 'all teaching is self-teaching', whence it follows that the primary function of the teacher is to induce in the learner, by sympathetic insight and suggestion, the self-teaching attitude appropriate to the subject in hand. With this master clue to method in their minds, his students were led on to study the learner as normally self-teacher in an interesting world, and to develop ways of teaching particular subjects accordingly.[24]

After completing Payne's course Bryant proceeded to a BA in 1881 and to a DSc in 1884. In addition to succeeding Buss as headmistress of the North London she served on the Bryce Commission on Secondary Education, the Consultative Committee of the Board of Education and the Senate of the University of London. Bryant played a significant part in the founding of the London Day Training College and chaired its Local Committee. An enthusiastic mountaineer, she died in 1922 while climbing Mont Blanc.

Payne appreciated, with respect to education both in Britain and in the United States, the importance of female educational institutions in which female principals, professors and teachers could provide important role models for girls, but he also saw the advantages of co-education. The professorial classes which Payne taught in the 1870s, although containing a preponderance of females, were open equally to men and women, and Payne reported that 'He had not detected the least inconvenience or difficulty in the fact of their meeting together for the purpose of instruction.'[25] Indeed it would appear that the mixing of sexes had the potential for some lively exchanges. One of Payne's students, P.E. Japernoux, a private teacher of French, acknowledged that 'As regards your lectures I greatly enjoy them and I learn many new ideas by them.' He also confessed to being 'excessively shy and consequently foolish', and was experiencing some difficulty in getting a nine-year-old girl to translate Charles Dickens's *A Christmas Carol* into French. Japernoux asked that the extra discussion class should be held on Tuesday as he had engagements on every other evening of the week, and wished to state that, in spite of what Jacotot or other educators or philologists might say or write, 'as regards teaching a foreign language, say French, to English pupils, even to beginners, without grammar rules, I do not see how it can possibly be done'.[26] Payne would have welcomed such a discussion, particularly in a co-educational group. He wished to draw upon a range of teaching and learning experiences, both of males and females. His lectures on the history of education were distinguished by a specific attention to the role of girls and women, an attention which was probably not to be equalled in general courses on the history of education until recent times.

At the heart of Payne's approach to the education of girls and women was a belief that men and women, boys and girls, were essentially human beings with equal mental capacities, and that this basic identity was far more important than physiological differences based upon sex. Payne's classic statement of this belief, which was coupled with a reference to the superior moral capacities of females, was made at Sheffield in 1865 at the annual congress of the National Association for the Promotion of Social Science. The Social Science Association (as it was generally known) founded in 1857 with Henry, Lord Brougham as its first president, provided an important platform for critics and reformers. Payne attended several of its annual congresses and in 1870 became a member of the Association's Council. Education was the theme of one of its five sections, and female education featured prominently in its proceedings. Payne's statement came during a discussion on the topic of better provision for the education of girls of the middle and upper classes, introduced by papers from Dorothea Beale, F.D. Maurice and Elizabeth Wolstenholme. Payne sought to move the discussion:

> from facts to principles. Where we have to deal with a common mind, both the subjects taught and the mode of teaching must be in a great degree common. We are not teaching a different, but the same kind of human being. The mind has properly no sex. It is the mind of the human being, and consequently there must be a similarity of instruction of both sexes. It has been said that the female mind is not by nature so susceptible of attention to what is called truth; I rather think, as regards the point of conscience, the balance must be thrown the other way, and that there is really a more conscientious regard to truth among women than among men.[27]

Payne recognized the differences between the girls' and boys' schools of his day, and believed in the need for greater similarity in curricula and teaching methods. He also, however, acknowledged that all schools (girls' and boys') shared many common problems. Although the Taunton Commissioners had drawn attention to the 'Want of thoroughness and foundation; want of system; slovenliness; inattention; unnecessary time given to accomplishments; want of organization'[28] in girls' schools, Payne sought to distinguish between those criticisms which were pertinent to girls' schools alone and those which were generally applicable. Payne acknowledged the excessive time given to accomplishments in many girls' schools for the middle and upper classes, and supported Dorothea Beale in her suggestion that there should be a reduction in such spheres as art and music, particularly for those girls who had little aptitude for those subjects. On the other hand, Payne was well aware that in some boys' schools games had become an easy alternative to serious study, and urged that there was much to be gained by all pupils, girls and boys, in studying difficult but worthwhile subjects, including those which would promote both 'accuracy and reasoning'.[29] He believed that other of Taunton's criticisms, for example, those relating to deficiencies in thoroughness and system, and the prevalence of inattention in classrooms, were attributable in large part to a failing common to schools for boys as well as for girls – the shortage of properly educated and trained teachers.

Payne's promotion of the education of girls and women took place in various contexts – in lectures, in examinations, in the advocacy of teacher training, in the Society for Home Study.[30] But the most obvious manifestation of his commitment to the cause of improved female education, and of the esteem in which he was held by its supporters, came in November 1872 when Payne was chosen as chairman of the Women's Education Union.

The National Union for improving the Education of Women of All Classes (to give the Women's Education Union its full title) originated from the work of Maria Grey, who had married into one of the leading Whig families, and stood, unsuccessfully, as a candidate in the first London School Board elections. In November 1871, the Women's Education Union was formally inaugurated at a meeting at the Royal Society of Arts. Its several objects, as listed at the front of the first volume of its *Journal*, included:

1   To bring into communication and co-operation all individuals and associations engaged in promoting the education of Women, and to collect and register, for the use of Members, all information bearing on that education.

2   To promote the establishment of good Schools, at a moderate cost, for girls of all classes above those provided for by the Elementary Education Act.

3   To aid all measures for extending to Women the means of Higher Education after the School period, such as Colleges and Lectures for Women above eighteen, and Evening Classes for Women already earning their own maintenance.

4   To provide means for Training Female Teachers, and for testing their efficiency by Examinations of recognized authority, followed by Registration, according to fixed standard.

5   To improve the tone of public opinion on the subject of Education itself, and on the national importance of the Education of Women.[31]

The Union's first president was one of the daughters of Queen Victoria, Her Royal Highness the Princess Louise, Marchioness of Lorne. She was no mere figurehead, indeed the preliminary meeting of those interested in the formation of the Union 'was held, by her invitation, in her dining room at 1, Grosvenor Crescent'.[32] Its first list of Vice-Presidents (6 females and 17 males) included such noted names as Henry Austin Bruce, a former Vice-President of the Committee of Council on Education, and the Committee's first secretary, Sir James Kay-Shuttleworth. But the real direction of the Union was in the hands of its central Committee, which was composed of 14 men and 14 women. Payne was a member of this Committee from its inception, as the official representative of the College of Preceptors.[33] Other male Committee members included Kay-Shuttleworth, Canon Alfred Barry, the Principal of King's College, London, James Bryce, the historian and politician who in 1895 gave his name to the report of a Royal Commission on secondary education, and Edward Carleton Tufnell, the inspector of poor law schools, who represented the Society of Arts. Female members included Maria Grey, who chaired the early meetings, her sister Emily Shirreff, joint editor of the *Journal*, and

Frances Buss, who represented the London Schoolmistresses' Association. At the first annual meeting, in November 1872, Maria Grey declined to continue in the role of chairman, accepting instead the post of 'honorary organizing secretary'.[34] Accordingly Joseph Payne, 'whose zeal for education and thorough knowledge of the subject point him out as most fit for this position',[35] a noted tribute indeed in such a talented company, was called to the chair, and occupied the position with distinction until ill-health forced his retirement early in 1876.

Payne's duties were not confined to the chairing of meetings. One way in which the Union sought to improve educational opportunities for girls and women was through the endowment of scholarships and prizes. Payne played a prominent part in this work. In February 1874 he placed a letter in several newspapers, including *The Times*, calling attention to the Union's plan to establish a scholarship of £25 for three years to enable girls to proceed from elementary schools to those of the Girls' Public Day School Company or North London Collegiate Trust. In March he was in correspondence with George Croad, Clerk to the London School Board, over the administration of the scheme.[36] The Union had already established five scholarships in connection with the University Locals and other examinations and, in April 1874, a Miss Meson won the prize of £25 offered by the Women's Education Union for the best performance by a woman in the examination of the students in Payne's professorial class.[37]

Payne not only played a leading part in the Women's Education Union, he was also to the fore in the foundation and early work of its sister society, the Girls' Public Day School Company. In June 1872, he was on the platform in the Albert Hall when the Company was inaugurated at a large public meeting presided over by Lord Lyttelton. Payne spoke in support of the Company's first scheme 'to open a public Collegiate day school for girls in South Kensington, in which provision will be made for the training of teachers'.[38] He was one of the original Company shareholders,[39] a member of its Council, and indeed chairman of the Council in 1872.[40] In January 1873 Payne was present at the opening of the Company's first school in Norland Square, Chelsea, and also attended on 28 March when Princess Louise paid a visit to the school. A further eight schools – those at Notting Hill, Croydon, Norwich, Clapham, Nottingham, Bath, Oxford and South Hampstead – were founded during Payne's lifetime.[41]

Payne was aware of the importance attached by pioneers of girls' public secondary schooling to the recruitment of good staff, and particularly approved of the 'provisions made in the school scheme of the Company for the training of teachers'.[42] One example of this conjunction of interests came in 1873 when Payne's 26-page pamphlet on *The Importance of the Training of the Teacher* was published as the fourth in a series produced under the auspices of the Women's Education Union.[43] The Union's *Journal* also gave some prominence to Payne's lecturing activities. For example, in 1873 Emily Shirreff used a report on the meeting of the Social Science Association at Norwich to draw attention to Payne's successful professorial lectures in London, and also to a short course which he had delivered in Edinburgh.[44] In February 1875, it published a three-column account of the sixth in a series of lectures which Payne had delivered in the lecture theatre of the Royal Dublin Society in connection with the General Association of Ireland, a lecture which had attracted 'a large attendance of ladies'.[45] In May 1876, the *Journal* included a short notice of his death in which Payne was characterized as a 'valued friend and member of the Union . . . one of its earliest adherents'.[46] The Committee would particularly miss his expertise and leadership in the recently commenced work of training teachers for girls' secondary schools. In the following issue a substantial tribute appeared, based upon Hodgson's letter published in the *Educational News* of 20 May.[47]

It was not until 29 May 1876, a month after Payne's death, that the Committee of the Women's Education Union approved Maria Grey's draft proposal for a training college to prepare women to teach in secondary schools. The Union's training committee became the provisional committee for the Teachers' Training and Registration Society, which in 1878 opened the College in Bishopsgate which from 1886 was to bear Maria Grey's name.[48] Yet there were firm links between Payne's work and the new college. As Irene Lilley, the historian of Maria Grey College, has written in respect of the relationship between Payne and Grey: 'It was his concept of professional education and his analysis of theory which underlay her schemes. His published lectures gave shape to her own opinions.'[49] When, in 1876, Maria Grey prepared the draft scheme she envisaged three elements: instruction in the subject to be taught, instruction in the science and art of teaching, practice in teaching. The first, she thought, was being supplied by the women's colleges at Cambridge, through University College, London and the University Extension Movement. For the third, she looked to the schools of the Girls' Public Day School Company and others. But for the second, for the core of the new college course, she proposed to draw on 'a nucleus which requires only to be more fully developed, the lectures of the Professor of Education at the College of Preceptors on the science and art of education'.[50]

Another, and more visible link, one which has continued to the present day, was the Joseph Payne Memorial Prize. When Payne died in 1876, Frances Buss sought to establish a memorial to him:

> Because I have not enough to do, I am working up an attempt to raise a little memorial to Mr. Payne, the ablest teacher I have ever known – except Dr. Hodgson – and the man who has raised the noblest ideal before the profession. It cuts me to the heart to see his name lost to posterity ... I want the memorial to be a prize or scholarship in the new Teachers' Training Society.[51]

Naturally Maria Grey was amongst those who collected money for the fund, and herself contributed £5.[52] In 1881 Joseph Frank appears to have made at least two contributions,[53] and the prize was duly established in the following year. In 1883 the winner was Miss Dunlop, who later became principal of the Saffron Walden Training College, and in the following year Miss Walker, who subsequently was principal of the St. George's Training College in Edinburgh. Each received the not-inconsiderable sum of £7. 6s. 2d.[54] The value of the prize varied according to the performance of the capital, which was invested in Consols. For example, in 1899 when Winifred Mercier who went on to a post as History lecturer at Girton, was the recipient, the dividend had fallen to £6. 12s. 4d.[55] Buss's concern for the future reputation of Payne was justified. Not until 1933 did the College of Preceptors, in conjunction with the newly established Institute of Education of the University of London, launch the Joseph Payne Memorial Lectures.[56]

Two points may be made in concluding this section: the first that Payne's contribution to the advancement of the education of girls and women was recognized in his own day; the second to summarize the nature of that contribution.

Contemporary recognition of Payne's commitment was shown in obituary notices, some of which focused upon two themes: his role as the first professor, and his work for the education of girls and women. Thus Payne's local newspaper, the *Paddington, Kensington and Bayswater Chronicle*, declared that 'much of the success achieved by the Women's Education Union and Girls' Public Day School Company must be traced to his unflagging zeal',[57] while the monthly *Educational Guide to English and Continental Schools* began its tribute with a reference to Payne's work for the education of women.[58]

Payne argued for the equality of mental capacity between the sexes, and rejected claims of female inferiority. He welcomed the attainment by women of positions of authority in professional spheres such as education and medicine. While recognizing that single-sex schools and colleges might more speedily promote access by women to such positions, he also approved of the development of co-educational institutions. In the 1870s, his work to promote the training of teachers and the development of a science and art of education took place largely in a female context, and with the full support of the leading female educationists of his day. Finally, he acted as a link between such bodies as the College of Preceptors, the Girls' Public Day School Company and the Women's Education Union, and had the unique distinction of chairing Council meetings of all three associations.

Public schools for boys

In the first half of the nineteenth century Eton, Westminster, Winchester, Charterhouse, Harrow, Rugby and Shrewsbury, together with two day schools, St Paul's and Merchant Taylors', emerged as the great public schools of England. In 1861, their status was confirmed by the terms of reference of the Clarendon Commission which investigated these nine schools. Pre-eminent amongst them, however, both in terms of size and influence and as a matter for public concern, was Eton, founded in 1440 by Henry VI. One third of the report was devoted to Eton, which had already been subjected to severe criticism at the beginning of the decade, and which was attended by one third of the 2,696 boys in the nine schools.

Payne was not a great admirer of the public schools. He acknowledged the contributions of reformers such as Thomas Arnold of Rugby but, on balance, regretted what he saw as the schools' fundamental deficiencies – privilege, custom, corruption and immorality on the one hand, and inefficient teaching, limited curricula and an over-concern with games on the other. His views, which were probably shared by many other proprietors and teachers in private schools, were strongly confirmed by the unhappy experiences of his eldest son, John Burnell, as a master at one of the new nineteenth-century foundations, Wellington College, under its first headmaster, Edward White Benson. Indeed in a lecture on the training of teachers, delivered on 14 April 1869 to an evening meeting at the College of Preceptors, Payne launched into a virulent attack on Benson for his opposition to the training of teachers for secondary schools and for his criticism (on the basis of one example) of the effectiveness of teacher training in Germany.[59]

Payne's strongest condemnation of the public schools, which appeared in a substantial article, entitled 'Eton', in the *British Quarterly Review* of January 1868,[60] took as its starting point the report of the Clarendon Commissioners, issued in four volumes in 1864.[61] The *British Quarterly Review*, first published in 1845, continued until 1886. Its founder and first editor was Robert Vaughan, himself a Congregational minister, who believed that the press might be as important as the pulpit. Its basic religious viewpoint was that of Evangelical Nonconformity, but its essential watchword was freedom, 'of freedom in the largest sense – freedom in Education, freedom in Trade, freedom in Religion – of freedom and fairness in everything!'.[62] As such it provided a perfect medium for the expression of Payne's most radical educational views. Interestingly, neither this article on Eton, nor two other *British Quarterly Review* articles of 1868 and 1870 upon education in the United States which contained strong denunciations of traditional British attitudes and institutions, were included by Joseph Frank in the collected works. Whether the basis for such exclusion was a problem over copyright, a belief that these pieces were already well-known and easily available, or some concern over their highly critical nature, is not clear.

One of Payne's major problems as a critic and reformer in educational matters lay in the nature and role of the state and of government. He did not have great faith in the quality of government in his own day, either at central or local levels. In 1856 he complained to his Member of Parliament, William Evelyn, a Conservative, about his support for Church rates, and accused him of being 'in opposition to the principle of religious equality'.[63] The Leatherhead Poll Book for 1857 shows that in the election of that year Payne voted for two candidates with interests in education: John Briscoe, a Liberal, who would 'promote the education of all classes of the people', and Henry Drummond, a Conservative, the President of the Western Literary Institution, who founded the Professorship of Political Economy at Oxford. Payne strongly resented the aristocratic and patriarchal dimensions of government, and its continuation by means of patronage. His alternative concept was of an enlightened 'commonwealth' (a concept which owed much to his appreciation of the United States) a commonwealth which would both promote, and be promoted by, the education of all its 'citizens' (another of Payne's favourite terms).

For Payne, all children, girls and boys, rich and poor, were entitled to a basic schooling as citizens of the commonwealth, and at public expense where parents were unable to pay fees. Good-quality schooling for children of the upper classes was also a legitimate matter for public concern. One of the great problems for outsiders such as Payne was to provide a justification for governmental interference, by means of commission and legislation, into institutions such as public schools and universities, which were not dependent upon public finance. Payne, unlike the legislators of 1988 who refused to require independent schools to follow the National Curriculum established in that year, argued that even in public schools 'the commonwealth is to have a voice in the matter of the education of those who are to be the *heads* as well as those who are to be the *hands* of society'.[64] He thus supported the establishment of the Clarendon Commission, and not only welcomed its criticisms of the many weaknesses of the nine great schools, but also drew attention to the dilatory way in which the schools responded to the reforms required of them.

Payne urged the reform of the public schools, but his more radical aim was the destruction of the old-boy network and of the assumption that old Etonians, and other public school products, had a natural right to high positions in state and society.[65] In a powerful and prophetic passage Payne declared that:

> These positions are by right ours – the people's – to give, not theirs by right to receive … We want in every department of public business, really efficient men. We want in every public servant the most perfect combination we can obtain of extensive knowledge, mental ability, and moral character. Does Eton, as we know it now, appear peculiarly qualified for the supply of such men? We think not. Yet, at Eton, perhaps for centuries to come, will the upper classes of English society receive their school training.[66]

Payne's specific criticisms of Eton may be considered under four broad heads: management and finances; curriculum and methods of teaching; moral education; quality of products.

One of the main criticisms of private schools was that the interests of the pupils were frequently sacrificed to the proprietors' needs to make a living. Payne, no doubt, relished the opportunity to criticize the efforts of the Provost of Eton, Dr Goodford, and of the Bursar and Registrar, Messrs Dupuis and Batcheldor, in this respect. He drew attention to 'the £6,385 a year which goes into the private purse of the provost and fellows, instead of into the public chest of the college',[67] and noted that as a result 'the begging box is sent briskly round'[68] to parents and former pupils whenever new buildings or other items of extraordinary expenditure were required. Even when money was raised by this method to build a sanatorium, a large proportion of it mysteriously disappeared. Payne observed that the result of this plundering of the funds by the provost and fellows, a plundering justified by custom, religious duty and the need to exercise hospitality, was that Eton had no laboratory, gymnasium, museum, choir, masters' common room or library for the general use of the school. Worst of all, whereas in the original foundation the provision for board (food and drink) was three shillings per week for the provost, for the fellows eighteen pence and for the collegers tenpence, by the nineteenth century the provost was taking £434 per year, the fellows £92, whilst the sum allotted for the boys had not been increased. Payne acknowledged that some of the worst privations and abuses in respect of the boys' board and lodgings, for example, the notorious Long Chamber, had been corrected, but he still concluded that in regard to management and finances the instances he had cited were sufficient 'to show how disgracefully the trust reposed in the college authorities of Eton has been abused'.[69]

Withering as were Payne's criticisms of the mismanagement of Eton in general, and of its finances in particular, he was equally savage upon the curriculum and teaching methods employed in the school. The curriculum was centred upon the Classical languages of Greek and Latin to the virtual exclusion of everything else, except 'the inexorable demands of the boats, cricket, the racket and fives courts, football and the lounging about the streets'.[70] Though the actual report of the Clarendon Commission, even when critical, was couched in judicious and diplomatic language Payne, by hunting through the examination of witnesses, managed to light upon Lord Clarendon's own incredulous and indignant response to the description of the Eton curriculum by the Headmaster, Dr Balston, a response which Payne quoted in full.

> Nothing can be worse than this state of things, when we find modern languages, geography, history, chronology, and everything else which a well-educated English gentleman ought to know given up, in order that full time should be devoted to the classics, and at the same time we are told [by Dean Liddell and others] that the boys go up to Oxford, not only not proficient, but in a lamentable state of deficiency with respect to the classics.[71]

As to the quality of teaching, Payne praised the abilities and diligence of the masters themselves but judged that their best efforts were largely frustrated by Eton's traditional usages and methods: the large classes, use of cribs, correction of verses by the tutors, and 'repetitions' by boys from Classical authors. All such practices, Payne believed, contributed to the negation rather than the promotion of true learning and scholarship. Indeed he pronounced the system of teaching to be 'a positive absurdity'.

Moral education was another cause for complaint. The general tenor of the school, Payne believed, was set by the excessive number of holidays, taken not only on saints' days and their vigils, but also on a variety of pretexts, such as the appointment of an old Etonian to a colonial bishopric, or a birth in the family of a fellow. It was also influenced by the considerable liberties enjoyed by the pupils, their initiation ceremonies, drunkenness and bullying, institutionalized in the fagging and monitorial systems.

As to the products of this education, Payne attributed the much-praised 'gentlemanliness' of Eton boys to their families and origins, rather than to their schooling. Though there were some exceptions, even those boys who sought to proceed to the universities frequently were found seriously wanting in academic attainments, while the great majority of the pupils, Payne believed, benefited but little from a school ethos which was characterized by 'enormous idleness, indifference to every kind of intellectual excellence, gross ignorance, habits of drinking, wasteful expenditure of money, and general self-indulgence'.[72]

Payne did not advocate the complete abolition of the public schools. Like many a critic, before and after, he was intrigued by their unique nature, and wary of excessive governmental intervention in educational matters. He was, nevertheless, an advocate of root and branch reform, both within the schools themselves and in respect of their position and influence within society and the state.

Elementary schooling

Many of Payne's criticisms of elementary (he himself used the term 'primary') schooling were similar to those which he levelled against the public schools. He castigated the attainments of pupils who had been through the system, and attributed the low standards to faults in organization, ethos and teaching methods. Though annual statistics of attainment under the Revised Code of 1862, whereby children were examined in the three Rs of reading, writing and arithmetic, were published under government auspices and freely available, Payne's use of these statistics excited both concern and controversy. This stemmed from two causes: Payne subjected the statistics to further analysis (e.g. by including pupils who might have been entered in the examination but were not) and by concentrating upon failures rather than successes.

For example, the annual report for 1866 showed that 90 per cent of those examined passed in reading, 84 per cent in writing and 73 per cent in arithmetic, giving an average of 82 per cent overall. This appeared to be a highly creditable level of performance. As Payne pointed out, however, the requirements of the tests were minimal in the extreme. Furthermore, of the one million children aged six and over whose names were on the books of government-inspected schools, 196,000 could not be presented because they had made fewer than 200 attendances during the year, while a further 139,000 were simply not presented for examination – probably because they would not pass. Some 231,000 failed to satisfy the examiners in whole or part. Another significant weakness was that while children were supposed to progress through the six Standards of the Revised Code and take a new and higher Standard each year, this was far from being the case. Indeed, about half of the children aged ten or over, who should have been presented in Standards 4, 5 and 6, were actually examined in Standards 1, 2 and 3. Poor as these results were, Payne's analysis of the statistics in the annual report for 1871 showed a decline, rather than an improvement in levels of performance, a decline possibly associated with changes which stemmed from the Education Act of 1870. Such calculations indicated that the great majority of children never reached the sixth Standard. This, for Payne, was a travesty, for it was one of his maxims, and applicable to all educational situations, whether for boys or girls, rich or poor, public or private, that 'efficient teaching implies the success of the great majority of the pupils, not the success of the small minority'.[73]

Payne's indictment of the state-supported elementary school system of his day began as part of a general paper which he read on 3 June 1872 at a sessional meeting at the Social Science Association's Rooms in London. That paper was entitled 'On the Importance and Necessity of improving our ordinary methods of School Instruction' and covered middle-class as well as elementary schools.[74] In September of the same year, however, he presented a more forceful case which concentrated upon elementary schooling alone, under the provocative title 'Why are the Results of our Primary Instruction so Unsatisfactory?' The tone of this presentation was calculated to shock.

> This, then, is the final result of the working of 15,000 schools, conducted by 26,000 teachers, at a cost of about one million a year. All this stupendous machinery is contrived and kept in motion to send out into the world annually about 16,000 children with the ability to read, write and cipher moderately well; and at least 80,000 furnished with little or nothing 'which may better them in life'.[75]

How then could such failure be explained? Payne attributed it to two basic causes: the first 'the idea of education entertained by the Committee of Council';[76] the second the poor quality of teaching. Payne believed that these two causes were strongly interrelated: the second proceeded in large part from the first. He was a vehement and consistent critic of the Revised Code of 1862: it was the negation of his vision of education.

Payne's following castigation of the Code constituted a classic statement of his concept of the nature of education, and contained a warning not only for his contemporaries but for succeeding generations.

> We need have no hesitation in pronouncing it to be mechanical in conception, mechanical in means, mechanical in results . . . The results which we have seen could not in the nature of things be other than they are. They are the legitimate products of a system which assumes the name without possessing the spirit of true education. Nowhere have I ever met, in the course of long practice and study of teaching, with a more striking illustration of the great truth, that just in proportion as you substitute mechanical routine, drill and cram, for intelligent and sympathetic development of the child's powers, you shall fail in the very object you are aiming at. Making quantity not quality the test of your results, you shall fail in securing either quantity or quality. The experiment which has now been tried for ten years in England ought henceforth to take a place in the annals of education as an example to deter.[77]

Payne believed that the Revised Code cast a blight upon all who came under its aegis: inspectors, teachers and pupils.

The poor quality of teaching, Payne argued, depended not only upon the Revised Code and its ethos, but also upon the nature of those who administered it. He was a severe critic of the inspectorate. For Payne the three qualities required in an inspector were: 'a thoughtful study of education', 'a thorough acquaintance with school work, gained by long and successful experience' and 'a knowledge of the best methods of teaching generally, as practised in other countries as well as in our own'.[78] He believed that these posts, 'belong of right'[79] to those who taught in schools and that inspectors should be recruited from among the most intelligent, hardworking, experienced and successful elementary schoolteachers. In fact, however, Her Majesty's Inspectors (HMI) were drawn from men whose reputations rested upon their ability to write Greek iambics, and upon the proud boast that they had never previously set foot in an elementary school.

Many inspectors, some of whom had a disdain for their work, saw their task principally in terms of examining as many children as possible in a day. The teachers attempted to play their part in achieving this goal by drilling the children into mechanical answers. In consequence children were not taught to read as such, but simply to learn by heart certain passages which they could parrot forth on the day of the inspector's visit. This meant that the children fulfilled the requirements of the Code and the schools received their governmental grants, but in reality little education had taken place. Payne quoted from the reports of concerned inspectors, for example, that of HMI Jolly of 1870, which acknowledged that reading grants were given to children who could not really read. Jolly reported that children were not taught how to overcome difficulties themselves, for example, to decipher an unknown word. Instead they relied upon the teacher, whose basic aim was to get all the children to learn by heart the standard reading text.

There were many critics of Eton in the 1860s, and Payne's strictures might be located both within that context, and as part of a longstanding rivalry between those who taught in boys' public and private schools. Payne, however, had few connections himself with the elementary school world, and his criticisms of the national system, as under the aegis of the Revised Code of 1862, provoked considerable controversy and some powerful responses. Such responses came from two sources. The first was from that broad body of opinion which believed that the prime aim of elementary schooling, even under the Revised Code, was still religious and moral. Children should be taught their duty towards God and their betters, and to recognize the latter and defer to them. This was in distinct contrast to Payne's belief that the purpose of education was to enable people to better themselves. The second group of opponents were those whose ability and reputation had been directly impugned by Payne: the inspectors and teachers.

The storm provoked by Payne's Plymouth paper of 1872 led to a special conference on primary education in London in April 1873, convened by the Education Department of the Social Science Association. There was but a small attendance, mainly of teachers, but at least two of Payne's Preceptors' colleagues, Barrow Rule and J.M.D. Meiklejohn, were present. The former stated that he was not prepared to lay the blame for the present unsatisfactory state of primary education upon the teachers; the latter argued that the current division into six Standards was impracticable. Payne, who spoke first, reiterated the points he had made at Plymouth: standards of attainment were lamentable; the main problem was the poor quality of teaching; this quality was the result of the system operated by the Education Department of the Privy Council. As in Plymouth he was followed by Revd Brooke Lambert who, once again, took exception to Payne's calculations, and read from a letter from Joshua Fitch to the effect that Payne's claims as to inefficiency were 'very seriously exaggerated and calculated to mislead those of the public who were not familiar with the condition of elementary schools'.[80] Later in the meeting, however, it appears that Lambert and other doubters acknowledged the accuracy of Payne's figures.

Though the names of Payne and Fitch had been linked together in several educational causes – for example, in College of Preceptors' lectures and in promoting the Girls' Public Day School Company – there were residual differences, and a serious and public dispute broke out between them. Though Fitch had been an early critic of the Revised Code, as a former HMI he no doubt personally felt the force of Payne's denigration of the elementary school system in general, and of the role of the inspectors in particular. Accordingly, in a *Fortnightly Review* article entitled 'Statistical fallacies respecting public instruction', Fitch stated that 'as I happen to have been an inspector during the year to which Mr. Payne's figures refer, and so to have had made some small contribution to the results which he sets forth, I shall venture to offer some reasons for questioning the general accuracy and value of those reports'.[81] Payne, in his turn, was hurt by some of Fitch's allegations, but maintained that, whatever differences there might be over precise calculations of achievement under the Revised Code, there were many eminent educationists who, to use the words of Edwin Abbott, believed that the principal effect of the Code was to 'degrade teaching and perpetuate stupidity'.

Another line of attack on Payne was that he had raised the whole issue as a means of castigating the achievements in Church schools. This, too, he was strenuously to deny, arguing that standards were no better in undenominational schools, nor indeed in middle-class schools, whether private or endowed. On this latter point he was able to refer back to his quotation in the paper of June 1872 from Fitch's own report for Taunton on endowed schools in Yorkshire:

> Three-fourths of the scholars whom I have examined in endowed schools, if tested by the usual standard appropriate to boys of similar age under the Revised Code, would fail to pass the examination either in arithmetic or any other elementary subject.[82]

Payne was, by no means, wholly opposed to examinations. He recognized their worth, for example, in enabling girls and women to challenge male monopolies, and as a means of recruiting to the civil and armed services on the basis of talent rather than of patronage. But he also believed that in schools and colleges excessive examination could be the enemy of true education. In October 1873, at the annual meeting of the Social Science Association held at Norwich, during a discussion of the effects of competitive examinations upon education, chaired by Hodgson and to which Lake and Meiklejohn had presented papers, Payne deplored the practice 'of continually pulling up the plants to see the conditions of the roots, the consequence of which was that all good natural growth was stopped'.[83]

The training of teachers

Payne's central purpose in life was to improve the quality of education in schools. Central to the achievement of that purpose – and equally applicable to secondary schools for girls, public (and private) schools for boys and to elementary schools for the children of the working classes – was an improvement in the quality of teachers. This theme ran throughout Payne's professional life, as it runs throughout this book. His involvement began in 1830 with the pamphlet on Jacotot; from the 1840s it found a new expression in his role as examiner for the College of Preceptors. Once himself retired from teaching, Payne furthered the cause through his several lectures and publications. From 1873 his advocacy was enhanced by his new status as Professor of the Science and Art of Education. Several dimensions of this concern for the quality of teachers have already been covered in previous chapters. The following chapter provides a detailed examination of Payne's concept of a science and art of education, knowledge of which he believed to be essential for every teacher. The purpose of this section is to consider Payne's critique of the lack of quality in teachers and the effect this had upon the status of teaching as a profession.

In Payne's day there was a complete free trade in education. Any man or woman, indeed any boy or girl, however ignorant, however lacking in moral principles or business acumen, could set up a school. Such a situation was justified by the application of market principles. Parents would naturally choose good schools for their children. These would flourish, while bad schools would wither and die. In consequence there was no need to require any prior test of the competence of teachers before they set up schools; 'liberty of teaching' could prevail.

The basic purpose of the College of Preceptors, and one with which Payne was in full agreement (though he frequently queried the effectiveness of its methods) was to raise the status of the teaching profession by providing the public with a guarantee of fitness and responsibility. He pursued this end by various means, both through the work of the College, and through associated bodies, for example, the Scholastic Registration Association, of which he became a Vice-President. Payne's critique of the situation involved two main dimensions. The first was to question the widely held view that in respect of teaching in secondary schools no training was either desirable or possible. The second was to examine the type of training provided in those colleges which prepared teachers for elementary schools.

The traditional means whereby masters in boys' public and grammar schools offered evidence as to their scholastic ability and moral rectitude was through their possession of a university degree and their clerical status. For example Benson, who like other public school headmasters was to progress to a bishopric, and even to the see of Canterbury itself, required his assistant masters at Wellington to take holy orders. It was widely believed, and in many quarters the belief lasted until well into the twentieth century, that these masters neither needed to be, nor could be, trained in the art of teaching. Benson, himself, declared that 'only experience can prove whether a man can teach or not', and added that 'probably a period of not less than two years would be required to ascertain this point'.[84] This belief, which might place pupils in the hands of a succession of incompetents throughout their school careers, was especially galling to those like Payne who had no university degree or clerical status upon which to rely. It provided a particular problem for females who had no access to such qualifications.

In 1876 when Maria Grey was canvassing support for a women's training college for secondary teachers, she received a stern rebuff from the Bishop of Exeter who declared that:

> I am not an advocate, have never been an advocate, for Institutions for the Training of Teachers *above* the Elementary. In providing for Elementary schools, such institutions were a necessity. But they are *not* a necessity for teachers of schools *above* the Elementary. And unless a necessity, I think them a great evil.[85]

In contrast, Payne believed that all teachers, male and female, secondary and primary, should undergo training and should acquire a preliminary certificate of competence before being allowed to proceed to posts in schools. Payne sought to base membership of the teaching profession upon such proofs of competence. As a model he described the situation in Germany where intending teachers were required to demonstrate their knowledge of subject matter, attend lectures on the principles and practice of teaching, give classes in front of experts and finally undertake a year's probationary teaching, before becoming full members of their profession.[86]

Herbert Quick, a graduate of Trinity College, Cambridge and a clergyman, who spent two years in Germany before beginning a teaching career which spanned a variety of grammar, preparatory and public schools, including Harrow, admitted the validity of Payne's arguments. On 13 June 1872, prompted by Payne's recent paper to the Social Science Association, he recorded that:

> Mr. Joseph Payne has made a vigorous onslaught on the state of education in England...What he would have is a more systematic training of teachers and a stop put to *didactic* teaching. The teacher is to be the guide merely. This theory is undoubtedly the right one, but there are great difficulties in working it in a school, and most school teachers give it up altogether. If intelligent teaching is to be found anywhere in England it ought to be in schools like Harrow, where we have for masters the very pick of the Universities. But, whatever may be the cause, our men here do not take much interest in the theory of their profession, and the results of their teaching, as tested by the average boy when he goes to Oxford or Cambridge, do not seem satisfactory.[87]

Nevertheless, it must be acknowledged that in spite of the efforts of Payne, and of others, very few teachers were trained for secondary schools until well into the twentieth century. Amongst male teachers in public and grammar schools, class and gender prejudices suggested that training was appropriate only for those who taught in elementary schools, or for women teachers at secondary level. Even the day training colleges, though attached to universities, were concerned with elementary training. In consequence in 1909–10, the first year of the Board of Education's regulations for secondary training, only 35 men and 139 women were recorded as having completed a course of training for work in secondary schools. The corresponding figures for 1913–14 were 38 and 167.[88]

While Payne's criticisms in respect of secondary schools, therefore, centred upon contemporary British presumption that no training was necessary, his criticisms of elementary schools, many of which were run by teachers who had undergone training and certification before taking up their posts, and whose pupils were subjected to an annual examination, concentrated not upon the lack of training, but upon its lack of quality. Payne acknowledged that students in training colleges in Britain were subject to a strenuous regime: tested for admission and annually thereafter; visiting model schools to see examples of good practice; giving criticism lessons themselves in the practising schools; instructed in school management – the keeping of registers and timetables. Indeed he advocated the setting up of further colleges so that these benefits might be more widely spread, and supported the College of Preceptors' scheme for the establishment of a training college in London for intending secondary teachers. Nevertheless, Payne found two major faults with the colleges of his day.

The first of these was the nature and extent of denominational control. The great majority of the training colleges which existed in Britain in the 1870s came under the auspices of the Anglican Church. Payne regretted the denominational ethos of the elementary teacher training of his day and strongly opposed the use of public money to establish further denominationally controlled colleges or to enlarge those which already existed. In Payne's view the Elementary Education Act of 1870, with its promise of non-denominational religious teaching in the new board schools, reinforced the need for non-denominational training colleges. Since the school boards were not empowered to create training colleges, national colleges were required, colleges in which 'there must be no recognition whatever of the denominations to which the students belonged, nor of the denominational character of the schools which any of them were to enter'.[89]

The second feature of existing training institutions to attract Payne's criticism was that the ethos of the Revised Code affected the colleges as well as the schools. Teachers in training were brought up in an atmosphere of mechanical drill and routine, their horizons circumscribed by the limited range of subjects and attainments prescribed under the Code. Payne also believed that there was too much lecturing and not enough lessoning in the colleges. The consequence of this limited approach was that the colleges neither taught, nor professed to teach, the science and art of education. In the colleges, as in the schools, the theory prevailed 'that education consists in telling, preaching, expounding, lecturing, cramming the memory, mechanical drilling of the lower faculties, or driving to learn'.[90] In opposition to this limited regime Payne presented his own theory of education as one which was characterized by:

> awakening the mind to the consciousness of its power by bringing it into vital contact with facts of daily experience, cultivating by suitable exercises its faculties of observation, perception, reflection, judgment, and reasoning, aiding it to gain clear and accurate ideas of its own; training it, in short, to form habits of thinking.[91]

Payne believed that no person should become a teacher who was not versed in three types of knowledge: a knowledge of the subject of instruction; a knowledge of the nature of the being to be instructed; a knowledge of the best methods of instruction.[92] Products of existing training colleges, he thought, were restricted, essentially by government policy, to too-narrow a knowledge of the subject or subjects of instruction. Their knowledge of children was limited by their complete ignorance of psychology. Their knowledge of the best methods of instruction was hampered by a national fixation with cramming which left prospective teachers without any appreciation of the great practitioners and theorists of the art of teaching who had lived in previous ages, or who resided in other countries.

Thus Payne's critique of the colleges of his day foreshadowed the creation of a new concept and context for the training of teachers. Payne was not against instruction in the practicalities of school management – the organization of classes and the keeping of registers – nor any of the other useful dimensions of the training regimes of his time. But he wanted students additionally to acquire that which was currently being denied to them – a sound knowledge of the science and art of education. In the 1870s, Payne's professorial course provided a blueprint for this new concept. From the 1890s a new context arose, institutions of university rank, unconnected with any denomination, where students might study pedagogy and the psychological, historical and comparative dimensions of education under the guidance of persons of professorial status.

Notes

1 North London Collegiate School Archives (NLCSA). Report presented on 10 October 1873, Head Mistresses' Reports to Governors, 1871–85, p. 48.
2 College of Preceptors' Archives (CPA). Minutes of the Council meeting of 17 June 1871, Council Minute Book, 1870–89, p. 56.

3 *Educational Times*, 1875, XXVIII(174): 157.
4 CPA. Minutes of the Finance Committee meeting of 14 April 1877, Finance Committee Minute Book, 1874–1914, p. 20.
5 S.A. Burstall, *Frances Mary Buss: An Educational Pioneer*, London: SPCK, 1938, p. 70. In 1830, at the age of 22, Payne had published an influential pamphlet on the French educational reformer, Jean Joseph Jacotot.
6 A.E. Ridley, *Frances Mary Buss and Her Work for Education*, London: Longmans, Green & Company, 1895, p. 108.
7 NLCSA. Minutes of the Governors' meeting of 9 December 1872, Governors' Minute Book, 1870–5, p. 64; Report presented on 7 April 1873, Head Mistresses' Reports to Governors, 1871–85, p. 36; Report for 1873, Prize Day Reports and Lists, 1870–80, p. 98.
8 NLCSA. Report presented on 21 October 1872, Head Mistresses' Reports to Governors, 1871–85, p. 27.
9 NLCSA. Report for 1875, Prize Day Reports and Lists, 1870–80, p. 124.
10 NLCSA. Report for 1874, Prize Day Reports and Lists, 1870–80, p. 114; Report presented on 13 April 1874, Head Mistresses' Reports to Governors, 1871–85, p. 53.
11 NLCSA. Archive box, 'History of School 1850–75', copy of a 13-page handwritten report, addressed to Buss, of Payne's inspection of the school on 24, 27 and 28 July 1874.
12 NLCSA. Archive box, 'FMB and family', Grey to Buss, 23 December 1871.
13 *Educational Times*, 1872, XXIV(130): 259; and 1872, XXIV(131): 277.
14 NLCSA. A copy of the lecture programme bound in with the report for 12 February 1872, Head Mistresses' Reports to Governors, 1871–85.
15 Ibid.
16 A copy of the lecture programme bound in with the report for 7 April 1873, Head Mistresses' Reports to Governors, 1871–85. See also a report of a lecture by M.A. Garvey to the teachers of the North London Collegiate Schools on the subject of the 'Science and Art of Teaching', *Educational Times*, 1873, XXVI(146): 56–8.
17 NLCSA. Report for 1871, Head Mistresses' Reports to Governors, 1871–85, p. 9.
18 NLCSA. Minutes of the Governors' meeting of 9 December 1872, Governors' Minute Book, 1870–5, p. 64.
19 Quoted in Ridley, op. cit., p. 206.
20 Quoted in J. Kamm, *How Different from Us: A Biography of Miss Buss and Miss Beale*, London: Bodley Head, 1958, p. 149.
21 Ridley, op. cit., pp. 70–1.
22 Quoted in Ridley, op. cit., pp. 274–5.
23 E. Lawrence (ed.), *Friedrich Froebel and English Education*, London: Routledge & Kegan Paul, 1969, pp. 32, 45.
24 F. Watson (ed.), *The Encyclopaedia and Dictionary of Education*, London: Pitman, 4 vols 1921–2, III, p. 1264. See also Ridley, op. cit., p. 178.
25 *Transactions of the National Association for the Promotion of Social Science (TNAPSS)*, 1873, p. 368.
26 Author's Collection, Japernoux to Payne, 13 June 1873.
27 *TNAPSS*, 1865, p. 362.
28 *TNAPSS*, 1871, p. 370.
29 *TNAPSS*, 1865, p. 362.
30 *TNAPSS*, 1873, p. 368.
31 *Journal of the Women's Education Union*, 1873, I(1).
32 L. Magnus, *The Jubilee Book of the Girls' Public Day School Trust, 1873–1923*, Cambridge: Cambridge University Press, 1923, p. 17.
33 CPA. Minutes of the Council meeting of 25 November 1871, Preceptors' Council Minute Book, 1870–89, p. 68.
34 *Journal of the Women's Education Union*, 1873, I(1): 8.
35 Ibid.
36 *Journal of the Women's Education Union*, 1874, II(14): 19, 50.
37 *Educational Times*, 1874, XXVII(156): 12.
38 Magnus, op. cit., p. 53; E.W. Ellsworth, *Liberators of the Female Mind*, Westport, CT: Greenwood Press, 1979, p. 184.
39 J. Kamm, *Indicative Past: A Hundred Years of the Girls' Public Day School Trust*, London: Allen and Unwin, 1971, p. 49.

40 Ibid., p. 204.
41 Magnus, op. cit., pp. 52–93.
42 *Journal of the Women's Education Union*, 1873, I(1): 40.
43 Frances Buss had presented copies of the first two pamphlets in the series to the library of the College of Preceptors. CPA. Minutes of the Council meeting of 20 April 1872, Preceptors' Council Minute Book, 1870–89, p. 87.
44 *Journal of the Women's Education Union*, 1873, I(11): 195.
45 *Journal of the Women's Education Union*, 1875, III(26): 30.
46 *Journal of the Women's Education Union*, 1876, IV(41): 70.
47 Ibid., IV(42): 86–7.
48 Maria Grey College Archives (MGCA). Archive box, 1870–1919: A 3, Folder 1870–9; B 36, Folder 1880–9.
49 I.M. Lilley, *Maria Grey College, 1878–1976*, Twickenham: West London Institute of Higher Education, 1981, p. 6.
50 MGCA. Archive box, 1870–1919, A 2, Folder, 1870–9.
51 Quoted in Ridley, op. cit., p. 274.
52 NLCSA. Archive box, 'FMB and family', Grey to Buss, 8 July 1876.
53 MGCA. Teachers' Training and Registration Society Subscription Book, 1878–84. Joseph Frank Payne, Payne's second son, whose edited collections of his father's lectures and essays were published in 1880 and 1892.
54 MGCA. Scholarships Awards Book, 1878–1936.
55 In 1912, a particular problem arose when legal costs for transferring the Payne Memorial Prize Fund to new trustees amounted to £15. 1s. 3d, a sum reduced by the Board of Education to £8. 18s. 9d. Since, in that year, the interest was only £6. 2s. 7d, it was resolved to pay the legal fees from other College funds. MGCA. Minutes of the Finance Committee meeting held on 29 January 1912, Teachers' Training and Registration Society Finance Committee Minute Book, 1900–15, p. 195.
56 J.V. Chapman, *Professional Roots: The College of Preceptors in British Society*, Epping: Theydon Bois, p. 118.
57 *Paddington, Kensington and Bayswater Chronicle*, 6 May 1876.
58 *Educational Guide to English and Continental Schools*, June 1876. See also the *School Guardian*, 6 May 1876.
59 *Educational Times*, 1869, XXII(97): 27–32.
60 *British Quarterly Review*, 1868, 47: 34–69.
61 PP 1864, XX, *Report of Her Majesty's Commissioners appointed to inquire into the Revenues and Management of certain Colleges and Schools, and the Studies pursued and Instruction given therein.*
62 *British Quarterly Review*, 1845, 2: 291.
63 Author's Collection, Evelyn to Payne, 4 March 1856.
64 *British Quarterly Review*, 1868, 47: 38.
65 In 1989 over a quarter of the 200 wealthiest people in Britain had attended Eton. If females and those educated abroad were to be excluded from the total the fraction of old Etonians would rise to a third.
66 *British Quarterly Review*, 1868, 47: 68–9.
67 Ibid., p. 39.
68 Ibid., p. 41.
69 Ibid., p. 43.
70 Ibid., p. 51.
71 Ibid., pp. 60–1.
72 Ibid., p. 68.
73 J.F. Payne (ed.), *Lectures on the Science and Art of Education, with Other Lectures and Essays, by the late Joseph Payne*, London: Longmans, Green & Company, 1880, p. 296.
74 Ibid., pp. 283–305.
75 'Why are the results of our primary instruction so unsatisfactory?' Paper presented to the annual congress of the Social Science Association in Plymouth, *TNAPSS*, 1872, p. 245.
76 Ibid., p. 247.
77 Ibid., pp. 247–8.
78 J.F. Payne, op. cit., p. 289.
79 Ibid., p. 290.

80 For a substantial report of the conference see the *Daily News*, 18 April 1873, although Payne subsequently complained to the editor that he had been misquoted.
81 *Fortnightly Review*, November 1873, p. 617.
82 J.F. Payne, op. cit., p. 298.
83 *TNAPSS*, 1873, p. 355.
84 Quoted in J.F. Payne, op. cit., p. 114.
85 Quoted in Lilley, op. cit., p. 5.
86 J.F. Payne, op. cit., p. 116.
87 F. Storr (ed.), *Life and Remains of the Rev. R.H. Quick*, Cambridge: Cambridge University Press, 1899, p. 175.
88 Figures from P.H.J.H. Gosden, *The Evolution of a Profession: A Study of the Contribution of Teachers' Associations to the Development of School Teaching as a Professional Occupation*, Oxford: Basil Blackwell, 1971, p. 214.
89 *TNAPSS*, 1872, p. 267.
90 Ibid., p. 251.
91 Ibid.
92 J.F. Payne, op. cit., p. 139.

CHAPTER 7

CONTEMPORARY EDUCATIONAL REFORMERS

Speeches made in the author's role as Public Orator when presenting these educational reformers for honorary degrees and fellowships of the Institute of Education, University of London

Marie Clay (presented in 2002)

Marie Clay's own education began in Wellington, New Zealand, at the East Girls' College and at the Wellington Teachers' College. Her first degrees were gained from the University of New Zealand and she also studied in the United States and completed a doctorate at the University of Auckland in 1966. After teaching in primary schools and working as a psychologist her main career was at the University of Auckland. Appointed to a lectureship in 1960, she progressed rapidly through the academic ranks, being awarded a chair in 1975 and twice serving as head of the Education department.

Her interests in child development and in clinical problems led Marie Clay to focus upon early intervention to combat problems with literacy. Reading recovery, as it became known, is now practised in several countries. She has been the recipient of numerous national and international awards, including honorary degrees from universities in the United States. In 1987 her services to education, to children and to the teaching of reading in three continents were recognized in a very substantial and public way when she was created Dame.

Marie Clay's academic path was not easy. As the first woman academic in the Education department at Auckland and the first woman professor at Auckland she frequently found it necessary to confront a traditional and at times sexist male culture. Initially introduced as 'the woman who used to be an infant mistress', or expected to prepare tea for special events, Marie Clay gently but firmly secured the necessary changes. Her organization, self-discipline and neatness became legendary. For example, other colleagues would take home briefcases full of work to be completed each evening and bring them back undone the next morning. Marie Clay would take home one task each night, carrying the necessary papers in an old-fashioned wicker basket, and always return with that task completed. Even her holiday home, which she generously lent to other staff and to their families, had tidy cupboards with every spice jar clearly labelled.

Marie Clay's interest in children's reading began when on teaching practice she was required to undertake a case study of one child who was having difficulty with reading. In the 1950s, while at home with her own pre-school age children, she became a play-centre mum, participating in all the activities that such a responsibility required but also teaching remedial reading at her kitchen table. She was particularly struck by the rapid progress of two 11-year-old boys which she described as alarming, alarming in the sense that it was inexplicable in terms of the theories existing at that time. In 1972, Marie Clay published her first critique of the concept of learning disability and began what she was later to describe as 'my long and lonely swim against the accepted tide of theory and practice'. Subsequent publications included *An Observation Survey of Early Literacy Achievement*, *Writing Begins at Home* and *Becoming Literate: The Construction of Inner Control*.

Reading recovery began in 1976 at the University of Auckland in a lean-to building behind an old house in Wynyard Street, with one teacher teaching hard-to-teach children behind a one-way screen and Marie Clay herself observing and recording. In 1977 the team was enlarged to seven, and a teachers' manual produced. Field trials were carried out in schools. The success of this project was considerable. In 1979–80 100 teachers were trained in Auckland, and national implementation in New Zealand took place 1983–8. From a birth cohort of 50,000 6-year-old children in 1994, a prevention programme was provided for 14,500, of whom 9,000 became independent readers and writers in that year, 3,400 were identified as completing in the following year and 1,043 were referred for specialist reports.

In the 1980s reading recovery began in Victoria, Australia and in Columbus, Ohio. By the 1990s it had reached Canada and the United Kingdom. The Institute of Education, University of London became a major centre for the work. Marie Clay was a visiting professor, 1991–3, tutors were trained and training programmes established for tutors and teachers across a wide spectrum of counties and boroughs. Marie Clay's challenge to teachers of young children became two-fold. The first element was to teach as many children as possible to read well. The second was for those whose reading was not progressing, to give them a second chance at literacy learning (i.e. reading recovery) before categorizing or labelling them as special kinds of learners.

There are numerous tributes to Marie Clay's inspirational role, commonsense, modesty, kindness, openness to new ideas and ability to focus on the task in hand. Two stories must suffice. Once on an internal flight in New Zealand to present a keynote conference address, she was so moved by a recently completed thesis (which later became a successful book) on the transformational power of story and reading in the life of a multiply handicapped girl, that she decided to abandon her prepared text and to share the account with the audience.

On another occasion, during a farewell speech at the University of Auckland, she referred to the times when she would take her own children to a family property in the country and how they marvelled at the extent to which pathways they had cleared in the bush on the previous visit had become overgrown. She likened this to some of her own academic work, expecting that many of the paths she had taken would be abandoned. Her audience on that occasion, in common with audiences around the world, knew that this was untrue. Marie Clay's work in the teaching of reading has stood, and will continue to stand, the test of time.

Elliot Eisner (presented in 2004)

Elliot Eisner was born in Chicago in 1933. Chicago was then the United States' second largest city, distinguished by its railroads and stockyards, by its engineering feat of reversing the flow of the Chicago River and by skyscrapers such as the buildings of the Civic Opera House and the *Chicago Daily News*. The young Elliot grew up in a Jewish community on the west side of Chicago, a community that he described at that time as being populated with delicatessens and synagogues – virtually one on every corner.

Between the ages of 5 and 13 he attended two elementary schools, but was not an A grade student. Indeed, as he later recalled, 'arithmetic was problematic and frustrating, my handwriting was and is at present not particularly good, spelling was a relentless bore, and English grammar was largely meaningless'. But he was good at art and his third grade teacher, Eva Smith, persuaded his mother to enrol the young Elliot at Saturday morning art classes at the School of the Chicago Art Institute. Art became, and would always remain, a great source of pleasure and inspiration.

High school was even more frustrating than elementary school and he graduated in the 32nd percentile. His chief interests in high school, as he recalls, were three in number – art, sports and girls. He left school at 17 and spent the next four years studying painting at the School of the Art Institute of Chicago and at Roosevelt College, emerging with a BA in Art and Education at the age of 21. Through this formal study, Elliot Eisner learned valuable lessons about the importance of both emotional and intellectual commitment to study and work.

The young Elliot Eisner's interest in education also grew in a milieu that lay outside the formal school system. This was a neighbourhood boys' club, called the American Boys Commonwealth (popularly known as the ABC) where as a child Elliot spent many happy hours working with clay, plaster and paint, and learning to draw and to weave. During his college years Elliot Eisner returned to the club to teach arts and crafts to children and adolescents in the very art room in which he had been taught as a child.

The neighbourhood was changing. Some of the adolescents came from poor families and were described in the terminology of the time as juvenile delinquents or pre-delinquents. Establishing rapport was often difficult, but Elliot Eisner came to see how much art could contribute to young people whose self-esteem and aspirations had been shattered by difficult home circumstances and failures at school. This interest led him to complete a master's thesis at the Illinois Institute of Technology with the title, 'The therapeutic contributions of art in group work settings'. In his book, *The Kind of Schools WE NEED*, Elliot Eisner recorded that at this time 'I became as much interested in the children with whom I worked as in their art: no, even more so.'

Three elements can be identified in Elliot Eisner's own education and subsequent career. The first was the influence of his home, family, neighbourhood and city. His sense of social consciousness and responsibility towards others and his sense of intelligence and education were nurtured in discussions at the dinner table with his parents, and in his teaching experiences in difficult informal circumstances at the ABC. It was developed and broadened by four years of school teaching, from 1956 to 1958 at the Carl Schurz High School in Chicago, and from 1958 to 1960 in the famous Laboratory School at the University of Chicago. In spite of his academic reputation and status Elliot Eisner continues to explore the mysteries that are involved in teaching and learning. For example, he spent three months in third grade classrooms in two schools at Stanford and returned to the University with an enhanced sense of, 'seeing the ways in which a group of eight year olds can differ in size, temperament, maturity, interests, energy level and personal style'.

Elliot Eisner does not proclaim any single method of instruction. He remains fascinated by the complexities and uncertainties of education and is highly suspicious of the attempts by governments, whether central or local, to find administratively efficient solutions to complex educational questions. Instead he champions the particular over the general, and affirms that teaching, at its best, is an artistically pervaded constructive activity which is characterized by flexibility and nuance. And at the heart of his thinking is always how it was, how it is, to be a young teacher in an inner city school.

The second element is his commitment to art and to the arts more broadly both in themselves and in education. As he wrote in his book, *Educating Artistic Vision*:

> Work in the arts develops the ability to care, to care not about the monumental but about the little things, the inner aspects of experience – the shimmer of a droplet on a golden leaf, the cool grayness of an early winter morning, a rusted crumpled pile of wire laying near an old brick wall. When experienced, the arts contribute to the fund of *our* experiences, develop our perceptivity, and hence the ability to savor the previously insignificant. In this sense the arts develop the sensibility necessary for human concern . . . the arts thereby enable us *to make sense* of the world.

This commitment to a very broad definition of education as initiation into a whole range of worthwhile activities is reflected not only in the content of Elliot Eisner's published work but also in its very style. His books and journal articles are eminently readable. His writing is not full of jargon or abstruse terms. He uses images to make complex ideas comprehensible.

His commitment to this broad definition of education, intelligence and achievement has also been reflected in his support for non-written forms of assessment, for example practice-led doctorates which give due recognition to studio-based work and design.

The third element is his academic standing and international influence. Elliot Eisner acquired two higher degrees from the University of Chicago. He revelled in the University's ambience and in the quality of its Education faculty – which at that time included such luminaries as Bruno Bettelheim, Jack Getzels, John Goodlad, Robert Havighurst, Philip Jackson and Joseph Schwab.

His first University post was at the Ohio State University, but in 1961 he was appointed to the staff of the University of Chicago. In 1965 he became Associate Professor of Education and Art at Stanford University in California. Five years later he was appointed to a full professorship. His current title is Lee Jacks Professor of Education and Professor of Art.

Elliot Eisner is a national figure in the United States, but he is also European in outlook and his published work has had a global impact. For example, Roy Prentice has described how Elliot's book *Educating Artistic Vision*, published in 1972, had a huge impact upon virtually every art teacher in the United Kingdom. His achievements have been widely recognized by the award of honorary degrees not only in the United States but also in Europe. The most recent of these awards was the 2004 Brock International Prize for Education – an award bestowed for a lifetime of work in the field of education.

Beryl Gilroy (presented in 2000)

Beryl Gilroy was born in British Guyana – as it then was. An avid reader as a child, she obtained a first class teacher's diploma and there made her name as a teacher of infants. She also worked for five years as a lecturer in a training college for UNICEF and became only too aware of the ways in which inadequate diet affected the capacity of children to learn.

School in Guyana was a serious place – a place of hard work and endeavour. Teachers assumed that all children had the capacity to learn; there was no concentration upon individual differences. Teaching was routine, chanting of alphabet and tables, regurgitation of facts and the application of corporal punishment by strap or cane. Syllabuses were approved by the inspectorate and days were governed by strict timetables, bells and work records. But education was important, for education was a means of escape from the mire of poverty and ignorance in which countries like Guyana had been left to founder.

In 1951, attracted by the work in child development pioneered at the University of London's Institute of Education, Beryl came to Britain. Here she studied with Dorothy Gardner and Charlotte Fleming, completing an advanced diploma in child psychology in 1954, followed by an academic diploma in education and a degree in psychology. Beryl had hoped to support herself in London by teaching, but in spite of her qualifications and experience, she found it impossible to secure a teaching post in this country. At every turn she was confronted by racial prejudice. As she wrote in her autobiography, *Black Teacher*, 'The fact was that, as a Guyanese, I simply could not get a teaching post.'

So, after a visit to the Employment exchange, in July 1953 she set out one day armed with a list of addresses and cards to look for other employment. The first encounter was hardly propitious, for Beryl Gilroy and the personnel officer were wearing identical green and black floral dresses – priced at four guineas; purchased from Richard shops. Beryl sought to break the ice by asking 'Do you say snap or shall I?' and was promptly informed that the job had been filled earlier that morning. But eventually she secured employment at the Multi-Choice Mail Order Stores in London's East End, where for the sum of one guinea (one pound and one shilling) a day, she filed in numerical order the thousands of payment cards that came in each week.

Here she learned about that strange phenomenon – the English working classes. Her next job was as a lady's maid, a post which involved much preparation of meals and darning of stockings. In this capacity she learnt about that even stranger phenomenon – the English upper classes. Other jobs followed, but finally in the spring of 1954 she secured a teaching post in a north London Catholic school, where she started with a class of 42 seven-year-olds.

There were many good aspects to this school but it was not a temple of progressivism. For example, one of her fellow teachers not only advocated the streaming of the five-year-olds, but also declared that 'Research, especially educational research, threatened the future of Britain ... All the famous psychologists of the day were raving lunatics who practised academic cannibalism, by devouring all that was good and sane in English education.'

Teaching in this, and subsequent schools, was tough. There was much poverty – financial, physical and spiritual. There was racism. And yet for Beryl Gilroy there was an even deeper sense of unease, that she who had been so successful and confident a teacher in Guyana should daily be beset by so many and varied concerns. Nevertheless, she was able to analyse this.

> Suddenly I realised that my role as a teacher had changed. From being the dominant character in the learning situation I was now a partner, concerned not only with outcomes and aims but with attitudes, pace of learning, and individual differences in children. No longer were they a class, but individuals with patterns of thinking, perceptions and imagination different not only from those of their peers but different indeed from my own.

She became interested in children with special learning difficulties and thus renewed her studies in psychology. Marriage and motherhood led to a break from teaching. But Beryl Gilroy started a playgroup and then returned to teaching – first part time and then full time. In 1968, she was appointed to a post as deputy head-teacher at Monlein Infants School and in the following year as headteacher of Beckford Infants School – the first black headmistress in Camden. Both of these posts were in multi-racial schools.

Beryl Gilroy's talents flowed out into even broader channels. She obtained further qualifications, at the University of Sussex and at the Tavistock Clinic. She became a counselling psychologist and an education consultant. In later years she obtained two doctorates, one earned and one honorary. She contributed to radio and appeared on television. But above all she wrote. Between 1970 and 1975 she produced a series of children's books, and then in 1976 a book which is first and foremost amongst her writings and particularly in its relevance for teachers and teaching. The autobiographical *Black Teacher* is a marvellous work – sad, witty, humorous, perceptive – but above all a deeply moving and disturbing reflection upon the lives of London children. Her novels include the prize-winning *Frangipani House*, a haunting story of Mama King, who is placed in the Frangipani House, a dreary, claustrophobic old peoples' home, from which she escapes to live in the dangerous, dirty, vital world of the beggar community.

Her major historical work is *Stedman and Joanna: A Love in Bondage*. This eighteenth-century story is located in the Netherlands, England and Surinam, and is based upon the journal of John Gabriel Stedman, a soldier in the Scots Brigade of the Dutch army. Her poetical writings include *Echoes and Voices*, charmingly subtitled *Open-heart Poetry*. This volume gives us the voice of many speakers – a carefully crafted collection of gentle, poignant verse.

Some 50 years ago Beryl Gilroy came to London to study at the Institute of Education. She has been a lifelong learner and a lifelong teacher. Indeed, until 1998 she was still working as a consultant both in Europe and in the United States. In 1982, she returned to the Institute as a research fellow to work with Dr Jagdish Gundara in the Centre for Multicultural Education.

Charles Handy (presented in 1999)

Charles Handy was born at Clane in County Kildare in Ireland, and it thus entirely appropriate that he should be presented for this fellowship on 17 March, St Patrick's Day. He was educated at Oriel College, Oxford where he achieved a first class honours in Greats – classics, history and philosophy. Although critical of much of the education he received at school, the young Charles did benefit from the commitment of one particularly inspirational teacher and from the Oxford tutorial system which, as he says, 'taught him to think for himself'.

He then worked for Shell International as a marketing executive, economist and management educator in South-East Asia and London. One of his early jobs had the grand sounding title of Regional Co-ordinator Marketing (Oil) Mediterranean Region. For a young classical scholar such as Charles this must have been very sat-isfying, redolent perhaps of the glory that was Greece or the grandeur that was Rome. But, as Charles Handy himself has acknowledged, the title and the three pages of job description were somewhat tempered by a sentence in the final para-graph which said 'With authority to initiate expenditure up to a maximum of £10'.

He then went to study at the Sloan School of Management at the Massachusetts Institute of Technology where in 1967 he was awarded a Master of Business Administration (MBA). He returned to this country to establish the only Sloan programme outside of the United States, at the United Kingdom's first Graduate

Business School in London. In 1972 he was appointed a full professor at the London Business School, specializing in managerial psychology, and in 1974 was appointed a governor of the School.

By the mid-1970s Charles Handy was very successful: 'I was a professor, gallivanting around to conferences, consulting, lunching, dining'. But then, following the death of his father – a quiet man, the rector of the same protestant country parish in Kildare for some 40 years, retiring at the age of 72, for the last 14 of them serving as Archdeacon of the Diocese – Charles Handy took a change of direction. His account of his father's funeral, contained in the preface of his book, *Waiting for the Mountain to Move and Other Reflections on Life*, is one of the most moving of tributes to a parent that one could ever read. For Charles Handy had been somewhat disappointed in his father who, it seemed to him, 'had settled for a humdrum life in the same little backwater'. And yet:

> As I stood by his grave, surrounded by people he had helped to marry and whose children he had later baptized and then seen marry in his church in their turn, as I saw the tears in the eyes of the hundreds of people who had come from everywhere to say farewell to this 'quiet' man, I turned away and began to think.
>
> Who, I wondered, would come to my funeral with tears in their eyes? What is success and who was successful, me or my father? What is life for and what is the point of our existence in this world?...I went back to England. It was a long hot summer that year. I resolved to change my life and my priorities.

And so it was that between 1977 and 1981 Charles Handy gave up his professorial post and became Warden of St George's House in Windsor Castle. This was a private conference and study centre set in a courtyard behind St George's Chapel, and established by Prince Philip and the Dean of Windsor, Robin Woods, to be a place of retreat and reflection upon ethics and values in society for busy people in a busy world. While there, Charles Handy was invited by the Dean and canons to preach the sermon at the Sunday morning service in St George's Chapel, the first time that a layman had preached there since it was built in the sixteenth century. Indeed, the proximity of the chapel meant that Charles Handy daily attended early morning service in the little upstairs chapel and on high days even more frequently. On one occasion this led his surprised mother-in-law to remark, 'Charles, you've been to church three times today already and it's only Thursday!'

Charles Handy is best known as Britain's foremost business guru. His books have sold over a million copies. Titles such as *Understanding Organizations*, *The Age of Unreason*, *Gods of Management*, *The Empty Raincoat*, *Beyond Certainty* and *The Hungry Spirit* are required reading around the world. *The Empty Raincoat*, published in 1994 and reprinted seven times in that year, won the JSK Accord prize for the best business book of the year. This prolific output continues and his next book is to be a joint production with Elizabeth Handy, his wife and business partner and a portrait photographer, whose marvellously evocative recent book, *Behind the View*, provides a visual record of change and continuity in the Norfolk village of Bressingham. The new book, entitled *The New Alchemists*, will provide picture and pen portraits of Londoners who have created, as it were, something out of nothing.

Today, Charles Handy describes himself as a social philosopher, emphasizing the fundamental values of life on the one hand, while also charting and explaining the changing economic world in which we live, on the other.

Charles Handy's contribution to education has not simply been in terms of business education. His publication of 1984, *Understanding Schools as Organizations*, provides a series of insights which are as pertinent and refreshing as they were 15 years ago. So, too, are his comments on the 1988 Education Reform Act, of which he said 'I would like to suggest that they insert somewhere in that Act three old-fashioned words – curiosity, forgiveness and love – words which, to my mind, still lie at the heart of all learning.'

And in an education world that is so dominated by league tables which measure a very limited range of achievements, and in which it is proposed to link the pay of teachers to the performance of pupils in such league tables, his words about the several types of intelligence – intellectual, musical, creative, practical, physical, social and psychic – have a particular resonance.

> To me, now, it is an article of faith that everyone is intelligent in some way. The challenge is to find the way. Some never do. They are our sadness. But for the future let us at least make sure that all of our children discover that they are intelligent in their own particular way, in or out of school, before they get trapped into jobs or lives where they cannot shine. Then no one need feel stupid anymore.

Michael Marland (presented in 2002)

Michael Marland was educated at Christ's Hospital School and Sidney Sussex College, Cambridge where he read English and History, was president of the University Amateur Dramatic Club and a founder member of the Musical Comedy Association. He has been a teacher all his life, and virtually all of that professional life has been spent in London schools. In 1961, after teaching for a year in Germany and for three years in Kent, he was appointed head of English at Abbey Wood School. Three years later, he became head of English and then director of studies at another south-east London school, Crown Woods. In 1971, at the tender age of 37, Michael Marland was appointed headteacher of Woodberry Down School. In 1980, he was the founder headteacher of North Westminster Community School (London's first multi-campus school). This post he held for some 20 years until his retirement in 1999.

At North Westminster, he introduced a series of initiatives designed to provide a much broader approach to education that would justify the use of the term Community School. For example, a home–school liaison officer was appointed and heritage language schemes adopted. A performing arts department was established. The ILEA was persuaded into developing a community Studio Theatre. This not only provided a venue for school and community performances, but also attracted professional and international artists, including Jessye Norman and Willard White.

Michael Marland was a 24-hours-a-day headteacher. He immersed himself completely in the life of the school. Even when walking (his preferred mode of transport between the school's three sites) he would talk endlessly into his trusty dictaphone, producing masses of material for his secretaries to type up. They, in turn, tried everything they knew to keep his perambulations to a minimum.

As a headteacher he was a man of vision – a great believer in treating all pupils as full and accepted members of society. Eminent writers such as Fay Weldon, Margaret Drabble and Keith Waterhouse were persuaded to come into the school to judge short story competitions and to talk to pupils about their (the pupils') writing and to offer public praise where it was merited. At North Westminster

Michael Marland always led by example in curriculum and pedagogy, for example, by initiating and personally teaching a core course to years 10 and 11 in the area of 'Science, Technology and Society'.

Similarly, even though at times national teacher disputes, both official and unofficial, impinged on staff relationships at North Westminster, as elsewhere, Michael Marland maintained his passionate belief in, and commitment to, all kinds of staff development. For example, he established a periodicals club, at which staff met regularly to discuss articles of educational interest. He also promoted staff awareness of such issues as bilingual and multilingual education and of the need to support arts in the curriculum. This concern for staff development extended to inviting staff of all grades and levels out to meals with the stream of VIPs who constantly visited the school. His reputation as a generous host, always prepared to share his own cogent views on any educational topic that arose, became legendary.

This penchant for being a bon viveur was apparent even in his schooldays, where he was once observed by a science master ascending from the staff kitchen in a dumb waiter clutching two bottles of red wine – doubtless to see whether the wine travelled well in a vertical direction. Michael's sartorial elegance is also well known, and in particular his adherence to the bow tie. This, too, may be traced to his schooldays, and the distinctive uniform of the scholars of Christ's Hospital, and was later confirmed by a youthful rivalry with Kenneth Tynan.

But in spite of being a 24-hours-a-day headteacher, Michael Marland was not constrained by the community of North Westminster. He was the founder chair of the National Association for Pastoral Care in Education and in 1974 wrote a pioneering work entitled *Pastoral Care*. He was also the founder chair of the Royal Opera House Education Committee, while his sponsorship of an intercultural curriculum in arts, humanities and literature led to the foundation in 1968 of the Longman Imprint Books, a literature series for secondary pupils. This series brought the works of such postwar writers as Stan Barstow, Doris Lessing and Alan Sillitoe into classrooms throughout the country. Michael Marland edited a number of collections and anthologies for Longman, for example *The Experience of Love* in 1980 and *Short Stories for Today* in 1984. The intercultural dimensions of this wider approach to literature and to literacy are shown by the titles of such anthologies as Doris Lessing's *Nine African Stories* and Richard Wright's *Black Boy*. Recent titles have included *Global Tales* and *Stories from Asia*.

Michael Marland has served on a host of bodies and committees concerned with curriculum, literature, libraries and information dissemination. One of his most distinguished contributions was as a member of the Bullock Committee, whose report, *A Language for Life*, had a considerable influence and led to Michael Marland being awarded the CBE in 1975. His historical perspectives on language and languages were well demonstrated in a volume of 1987, entitled *Multilingual Britain: The Educational Challenge*. For not only did he show that some 70 per cent of the world's population today is bilingual, but he also drew on the multilingual heritages of this island, for example, the use of Latin, French and English in medieval England, and of other historic cultures. He was a pioneer of the academic study of school management. This was exemplified by his book, *Head of Department*, written in 1971, the year in which he founded the Heinemann School Management series, which he continues to edit.

Michael Marland has written many books and articles on education and teaching, indeed he is a veritable champion of books themselves. Service as chair of such bodies as the Books in the Curriculum Research Project, Educational Publishers Council, National Book League Executive, National Book League

Review Panel and National Textbook Reference Library are evidence of his commitment.

And the best known book that he has written and that most used by prospective and practising teachers (and also employed by many trainers of teachers) is surely the slim volume of 100 pages entitled *The Craft of the Classroom: A Survival Guide to Classroom Management in the Secondary School*. This was first published in 1975 and has been regularly reprinted ever since. Indeed a generation of Postgraduate Certificate in Education (PGCE) students was advised that there were two essential commodities to take in their pockets or bags on teaching practice – the first a stick of chalk; the second a copy of *The Craft of the Classroom*. The sticks of chalk may have been replaced by overhead projectors and Powerpoint, but the basic message of *The Craft of the Classroom* remains as valid and pertinent as ever. For the book's final paragraph sums up the essence of good teachers and of good teaching:

> You will sometimes feel that you have succeeded, but disappointments will be frequent. I know only too well that some people could conscientiously apply all the detail I've listed and yet not get across at all. The craft won't work without a spirit compounded of the salesman, the music-hall performer, the parent, the clown, the intellectual, the lover and the organizer, but the spirit won't win through on its own either. Method matters. The more 'organized' you are, the more sympathetic you can be. The better your classroom management, the more help you can be to your pupils.

Koïchiro Matsuura (presented in 2003)

Koïchiro Matsuura was born in 1937. As a little boy living in the district of Yamaguchi, he saw death, grief and fear raining down from the skies in the shape of incendiary bombs which turned streets of houses into great fireballs. Yamaguchi is but two hours by road from Hiroshima. At 8.15 on the morning of 6 August 1945 there was a blinding flash of nuclear explosion when a uranium bomb with the destructive force of 20,000 tons of TNT was detonated some 2,000 feet above Hiroshima. Some 66,000 people died instantly with 145,000 dead by the end of the year. Three years after the end of the Second World War the 11-year-old Koïchiro was taken on a first visit to Tokyo. Although the Imperial Palace still stood largely intact in the centre of the city, he could see far out into the distant suburbs, because everything else had been reduced to rubble.

Growing up in a postwar Japan characterized by great hardship and material deprivation, Koïchiro Matsuura was one among many young Japanese who deplored and rejected the militaristic and misguided policies of the past and determined to dedicate himself to peace. To further this aim, he decided to enter the diplomatic service where he became committed to an unremitting search for tolerance and disarmament and to channelling human potential not into war or aggrandisement, but into the service of education, science, communication and culture.

Mr Matsuura's early studies were in law at the University of Tokyo. These were complemented by further work in economics at Haverford College in the United States. He entered the Ministry of Foreign Affairs in 1959 and subsequently served in a variety of roles: as third secretary at the Japanese embassy in Accra in Ghana; as first secretary of the Japanese delegation to the OECD; as Counsellor at the Japanese embassy in the United States and as Consul General in Hong Kong.

He experienced a similar variety of posts within Japan itself, and from 1992 to 1994 served as Deputy Minister for Foreign Affairs. This was followed by ambassadorial posts, culminating in the appointment as Japanese ambassador to France, 1994–9. Along the way Mr Matsuura learned English, French and Spanish, and was awarded honours and decorations in Djibouti, France, Indonesia and the United States. He also produced six major publications: three in Japanese, two in French and one in English, in the fields of diplomacy, economics and history.

In 1999 he succeeded Dr Federico Mayor as Director General of the United Nations Educational, Scientific and Cultural Organization (UNESCO). The Constitution of UNESCO, framed in November 1946, proposed 'to contribute to peace and security by promoting collaboration among the nations through education, science and culture in order to further universal respect for justice, for the rule of law and for human rights and fundamental freedoms'.

Mr Matsuura's childhood experiences in Japan were critical in determining his choice of purpose and career. His speeches and writings provide further insights into his continuing vision. For example, he has described how in March 1998 he stood in the research centre of the National Museum of Ethiopia in Addis Ababa and saw the bones of what may be the oldest known hominid, our common ancestor, nicknamed 'Lucy', who had lived some three million years ago. He reflected that we may all be distant descendants of Lucy, and as such in whatever continent we live, from Africa to Europe, from Asia to the Americas, we are members of a single family. And he remembered the words of the great Muslim poet, Sa'dî Shiraz:

> All humans form a single being
> he who touches one of its limbs, touches me –
> and if he wounds it, he wounds me.

In his address delivered in November 1999 on the occasion of his installation as Director General of UNESCO, Koïchiro Matsuura declared that one of his absolute priorities would be:

> to assist and reinforce basic education wherever needed – with due regard for the local culture. Basic education for young children, both boys and girls, is the single key to their future, to any hope for employment, livelihood, and social emancipation. It is also the first and necessary step towards democratizing access to higher education or vocational training. Indeed, basic education is the true driving force for sustainable development in the world. I shall pursue this effort on behalf of basic education in every practical way throughout my term in office.

He also invoked the 'ancient tradition, dear to all civilizations, that there exists a subtle link between the inner harmony of human beings, and the balance of the natural world around us – as if we projected thereon our own inner turmoil, or inner peace'.

Donald Woods (presented in 2000)

Donald Woods was born in the Transkei territory and his early years were spent on the south-eastern side of South Africa. He grew up speaking Xhosa better than he spoke English, for this was the language of his playmates and of his nursemaid,

Maggie Mzondo. Donald's Xhosa name was 'Zweliyanyikima', 'the world shakes', a prophetic appellation.

In 1948 the Afrikaner Nationalist party came to power in South Africa, and began to pass a series of laws to subject every area of the country and every facet of life to apartheid. Shortly afterwards, at the age of 18, Donald Woods went to the University of Cape Town to study law. There his ideas about law and justice were much influenced by the teaching and example of one of the lecturers, the barrister Harold Levy. His own racial prejudices were challenged, and one sentence by Abraham Lincoln became a cornerstone of his beliefs, 'What is morally wrong can never be politically right.' He also met black people from other countries and began to consider to what extent the inferior position of black people in South Africa was a consequence of environmental circumstances. As he later wrote:

> I thought that if a black baby born in the Transkei were brought up in Buckingham Palace, it would grow up to attend Oxford or Cambridge and would speak, think and react like a member of the British royalty. For me this was a startling concept, because it challenged all my racial prejudice.

At this time, Donald Woods also became interested in politics and journalism. He joined the new Federal Party, which totally rejected apartheid, and took a job with an anti-government newspaper, the *Daily Dispatch*, in East London. A year later, in 1958, Donald Woods came to London. Some of the sights were fascinating – including Speakers' Corner in Hyde Park. He had a series of jobs: with a local paper, *Weekly Post Newspapers*, based in West London, with the *Western Mail* in Cardiff and then with the *Daily Herald*. He also visited the United States and Canada. In 1960, he returned to South Africa and to the *Dispatch*. In 1965 he was appointed editor.

Under Donald's editorship the paper conducted a number of campaigns against bigotry and racism. One result of this was to increase the number of telephone threats made against the newspaper and against staff members and their families. Donald Woods's life was changed forever when he met Bantu Stephen Biko. As he wrote:

> Steve Biko was the greatest man I ever met... He had from an early age the unmistakable bearing and quality of a unique leader... the style of leadership was his own – it was unpushy, un-self promotional, yet immediately acknowledged by his peers... I was 13 years older than Steve, yet I always had the feeling that I was talking to someone older and wiser, and like many others I often sought his advice on all manner of problems... He had a rocklike integrity and a degree of courage that sent one's regard for the potentialities of the human spirit soaring skyhigh.

Yet the South African government placed Steve Biko under a banning order. On 18 August 1977, he was arrested and interrogated. On 6 September, he was taken to Room 619 of the Sanlam Building in Strand Street, Port Elizabeth, tortured, beaten, including several blows to the head which caused him to lapse into a coma. He died on 12 September.

Donald Woods, himself, was placed under a banning order, which meant that he was forbidden to travel, to write anything – even a postcard – or to associate with more than one person at a time. The Security police monitored his phone calls and opened his mail. They made threatening phone calls and even fired shots at his house. The Woods's youngest child, Mary, was sent a tee shirt saturated with ninhydrin, an acid-based substance, which severely burned her face and shoulders.

In 1978, Donald Woods and his family made their daring escape from South Africa, via Lesotho and Botswana, and came to London. The original edition of his book, simply entitled *Biko*, was published in 1978 and 1979 in 12 languages. From that date onwards Donald Woods lectured, wrote and broadcast against the policy of apartheid in South Africa.

When Donald, his wife and five children arrived in this country in 1978, they had no money and no possessions. The South African government seized everything. He made a new career as a lecturer. For example, over a period of 12 years he lectured at 462 American universities, in each and every one of the 50 states. In many universities, as at Amherst in 1978, the students said 'What can we do to help?' To which Donald Woods would reply, 'Fund and support a black South African student through your university course.' Through this and other fundraising activities, such as the Lincoln Trust, Donald Woods played a significant role in helping black students from South Africa to study at universities in the United States and in the United Kingdom. In 1978, he was the first private citizen to address the United Nations Security Council.

In 1987 the *Biko* book, together with Donald Woods's autobiography, *Asking for Trouble*, provided the basis of the film, *Cry Freedom*, produced and directed by Sir Richard Attenborough. In the film, Donald Woods was played by Kevin Kline, Wendy Woods by Penelope Wilton and Steve Biko by Denziel Washington. Donald Woods had previously turned down a substantial financial offer from a major American film maker because it involved relinquishing rights over the story – and thus over the truth. In sharp contrast, Donald and Wendy were fully involved with the making of Attenborough's film. There is no sensationalism, and in many cases the facts were underplayed rather than over dramatized so that the South African government could have no justification for challenging the accuracy of the film. Donald and Wendy advised on all aspects of production, even on the accents of Timothy West and John Thaw. Kevin Kline brought a tape recorder to Donald Woods's home in order to capture his particular inflections.

Donald Woods is an expert in written style and also has a fluency in some 20 different languages. He continues to take the greatest interest in education in South Africa, and his latest book, currently in press, is entitled *Rainbow Nation Revisited*. Taken together, the *Biko* book, Donald Woods's autobiography, *Asking for Trouble* and *Cry Freedom* played a fundamental role in undermining the racist regime.

Ten years ago, in February 1990, Nelson Mandela was released from imprisonment. Four years later, a new chapter in the history of South Africa began. Problems remain, but a basis for a truly rainbow nation has been laid. Donald Woods now lives in Surbiton. He has close connections with his local university at Kingston and has received two honorary degrees from universities in the United States and two from those in this country. In the New Years Honours List, he was created a CBE.

Ted Wragg (presented in 2002)

Ted Wragg was educated at King Edward VII Grammar School, Sheffield, and at the University of Durham, where he obtained first class honours in German and a first class PGCE. Postgraduate study was for an MEd at Leicester and a PhD at Exeter. He taught for eight years in secondary schools, before being appointed lecturer in education at Exeter. He was Professor of Education at the University of Nottingham for five years, returning to Exeter as Professor and Director of the School of Education in 1978.

Four themes have been apparent during his long tenure of office at Exeter. The first has been his immense knowledge of the many issues connected with teacher education and his ability to represent those within the University of Exeter as a whole. The second has been his commitment to teacher education as a proper university responsibility, coupled with a profound respect for teaching as a profession. The integration of professional relevance and academic respectability became the distinguishing feature of the Exeter School of Education, against a national and political background which tried to keep them apart. Under his direction Exeter became one of the largest university departments of education in England, second in size, indeed, only to the Institute of Education, University of London. The third theme is the impressive concern and humanity with which he treats all staff and students, always making himself available to those with problems, however busy his schedule might be. And finally there is his boundless energy, directing a department of 1,000 students, making a major contribution to national bodies and debates, providing incisive comments in the University Senate, teaching on a range of courses, both undergraduate and postgraduate, sustaining his own impressive corpus of research and writing with no fewer than 50 books at the last count, even coaching the University football team, and even, on occasion, and I quote, 'scorching up the M1 to catch another Sheffield Wednesday defeat'.

His national commitments have included service as President of the British Educational Research Association, Chair of the School Broadcasting Council for the United Kingdom and of the Educational Broadcasting Council for the United Kingdom, and membership of the SSRC Educational Research Board, of the UGC Education Committee and of the Qualifications and Curriculum Authority (QCA). Since 1986, he has been the editor of *Research Papers in Education*. His own research interests are represented in the titles of his several publications, for example, *Teaching Teaching* (1974); *Teaching Mixed Ability Groups* (1976); *A Handbook for School Governors* (1980); *Classroom Teaching Skills* (1984); *An Introduction to Classroom Observation* (1994).

In all of these activities Ted Wragg has shown himself to be a truly outstanding educator and an influential figure on the national and international scenes. But this work and these publications have been complemented by other books, collections of articles from the *Times Educational* and *Times Higher Education Supplements* and the *Guardian*. Examples include: *Swineshead Revisited* (1982); *Pearls from Swineshire* (1984); *The Wragged Edge* (1991); *Riches from Wragg* (1990); *Mad Curriculum Disease* (1991) and *The Last Quango* (1996). These articles and volumes have brought Ted Wragg fame and a cult following, and not only among members of the teaching profession.

For example, commenting on *The Ted Wragg Guide to Education*, published in 1995, the comedian, Rory Bremner, wrote:

> Thank God for Ted Wragg. His humour is a tonic and an inspiration: the sort that has you gnashing your teeth with rage one minute and clutching your sides with laughter the next. This book should be part of the National Curriculum for anyone who wants to know about education, and required reading for rational beings and ministers alike.

Similarly, Neil Kinnock declared of the same volume that:

> Ted Wragg writes about education (and a lot of other things) with a combination of wit, passion and knowledge that is not equalled by anyone else. The 'Guide' should be compulsory reading for Secretaries of State – even those with learning difficulties would benefit.

Presentation ceremonies such as this have not escaped Ted Wragg's humorous attention. For example in 1979, in an article entitled 'Standing on ceremony' in the *Times Higher Education Supplement*, Ted Wragg while acknowledging that he 'enjoyed ceremonies as much as the next man', wondered 'what a visiting Martian might make of degree ceremonies when the cream of the nation's youth and its leaders dress up for mutual congratulation in garb that would in other circumstances lead to speedy arrest'.

He also recalled a former Exeter colleague who in his retirement speech regretted that he had been forced to give up processing in academic dress through the town for the annual university service, 'since local yobs had taken to calling out "Get some work done" and "Hello Mavis" at the parading dignitaries'.

Ted Wragg has been and still is an immense presence – as a person, as an educator and as a humorist. As Professor Tim Brighouse explained:

> As fast as the unintended blunders of bureaucrats and ministers sap the energy, idealism and commitment of the teaching profession, so Ted Wragg's Friday back page refuels their determination to stick to their life's work ... With his column, and his example at Exeter in research and teaching, Ted Wragg has achieved more for real improvement in the classroom than all the efforts of twenty pieces of legislation, eight Secretaries of State and thousands of circulars ... The real corridors of power are on the back page of [Friday's *TES*] and in the classroom next Monday morning ... He has the uncanny knack of creating energy, humour and generosity as fast as others unwittingly consume it.

PART 4

CURRICULUM AND STANDARDS

CHAPTER 8

A CURRICULUM FOR THE NATION

R. Aldrich and J. White (eds), *The National Curriculum beyond 2000: The QCA and the Aims of Education,* London: Institute of Education, 1998, pp. 41–63

Introduction

The National Curriculum is to be revised for the twenty-first century.[1] As part of that revision process the Qualifications and Curriculum Authority (QCA) has declared 'that there is a need to develop a much clearer statement about the aims and priorities of the school curriculum as a necessary preliminary to any review'.[2] This is most welcome. It is a shame upon us all that, at the end of the twentieth century, children in schools in England are following much the same curriculum as at the end of the nineteenth. It is also a shame upon us all that maintained schools in this country do not have the resources and facilities to provide the quality and breadth of curriculum which our children need and deserve.

Innumerable books and articles have been written about the school curriculum, its purposes and aims. Many contrasting opinions and emphases have been expressed. Nevertheless, at the end of the twentieth century there is a widespread view in official, as well as in professional circles, that the 'present statutory arrangements, including the National Curriculum, lack a clear vision of what the parts, individually and collectively, are designed to achieve'.[3] Such agreement is hardly surprising. The original aims of the National Curriculum were set out in the most general terms. The Education Reform Act of 1988 stated that a maintained school should have a 'balanced and broadly based curriculum' which

> promotes the spiritual, moral, cultural, mental and physical development of pupils at the school and of society; and prepares such pupils for the opportunities, responsibilities and experiences of adult life.

The precise relationship between these broad aims and the ten subjects of the National Curriculum was never made clear. In 1995, this lack of clarity was further compounded with the formation of the Department for Education and Employment (DfEE). The aims of education were then redefined without reference to a redefinition of the curriculum itself. The new department declared that:

> The Government's principal aim for the education service at all levels and in all forms of learning is:
>
> To support economic growth and improve the nation's competitiveness and quality of life by raising standards of educational achievement and skill and by promoting an efficient and flexible labour market.[4]

Since then a new government has come to power, and new educational aims and goals have been set out in the White Paper, *Excellence in Schools*, published in July 1997.

This situation, whereby the aims and objectives of formal education and of the curriculum are regularly and dramatically redrawn by politicians and administrators of central government, without any reference to the school curriculum which they have established, is odd to say the least. It is particularly odd that this should be happening during a five-year moratorium on curriculum change. It suggests that the politicians and administrators of central government believe that radical changes can be made in the aims of education while the curriculum remains the same. It also suggests that the aims of education and of the compulsory school curriculum have become matters of politicking rather than of substance. It is rather like a traveller deciding to go from London to Manchester, while still taking the train to Leeds for which she has a ticket.

In the other contribution to this volume[5] my colleague, John White, has, with his customary incisiveness, tackled the central question: *how should the aims of the revised curriculum be determined?* Two further questions are considered in this section. The first is: *what are the main strengths and weaknesses of common curricula in general and of the National Curriculum in particular?* The second, given that the aims and content of school curricula have been debated for centuries: *what lessons may be drawn from an historical perspective upon these issues?*

Three preliminary points need to be made here to indicate the position from which these questions are to be approached. The first is to re-affirm my frequently stated contention that the application of historical perspectives to human events makes it possible 'to distinguish what is important and long lasting from that which is unimportant and transitory, to identify continuities and changes, and to make judgements as to worth'.[6] The second point is to concur with the analysis of two further Institute of Education colleagues, Peter Gordon and Denis Lawton, who have maintained that 'curriculum change is the result of complex patterns of interaction between influential individuals and general processes of social, political and economic change'.[7] Finally, I endorse the conclusions drawn by John White in his paper as to: the very limited value of making lists of general curriculum aims which have neither internal coherence nor any specific connection with curricular content and delivery; the superiority of liberal democracy over other forms of government (a point I have argued elsewhere)[8] the nature of a democratic political role in the determination of curricular aims and of curricula; the need to avoid sectionalism and to provide for a careful drawing of lines between political and professional spheres of power; the roles of teachers and other educational professionals within democratically determined general aims and broad curricular frameworks; the importance of co-operation between families and schools; the place of knowledge, understanding and dispositions.

The remainder of this paper is arranged in three parts. It begins with a review of the National Curriculum as it exists at present. Strengths and weaknesses, arguments for and against, are identified and discussed. The second part provides one historical perspective by examining the *Thoughts* of John Locke, the most important educational and political thinker in British history. Finally, conclusions are drawn and answers provided in respect of fundamental curricular aims and curricular provision.

Strengths and weaknesses

Two broad types of argument in favour of the value and strengths of the National Curriculum may be noted here. The first are those that are adduced in favour of common curricula in general. For example, it is maintained that a common curriculum provides all children with access to that knowledge which is considered to be most worthwhile. It thus avoids the weaknesses apparent in educational systems in which some types of knowledge – including those that are considered to be the most important and prestigious – are reserved to certain groups of children – on social class, gender or other grounds. Differentiated curricula, indeed, may both reflect and reinforce differentiated societies. For example, until well into the second half of the twentieth century, undergraduate student access to the universities of Oxford and Cambridge was restricted to those who could demonstrate their proficiency in the Latin language. No instruction in Latin, however, was provided in many secondary schools. In consequence pupils in such schools were excluded, on curricular grounds, from the two most prestigious seats of higher education in England.

Another argument of this general nature is that a common curriculum furnishes a valuable framework for progression. This has two major benefits. First, it ensures that children do not omit certain topics and repeat others as they move from one year or school to another. Second, a common curriculum may serve as a basis for measuring educational standards and progress – of individual pupils, of schools and teachers, of local educational authorities and of the nation as a whole.

The second, and more specific, type of argument in favour of the National Curriculum of 1988 was the belief that this was an idea whose time had come. Although its introduction and implementation aroused much controversy and opposition, opponents were principally motivated by their loss of control over the curriculum, a control which they had enjoyed for some 40 years. By the 1960s, there was considerable support for the idea of a common curriculum based upon a common culture and delivered in common schools. Indeed, by 1975 Denis Lawton was arguing that 'pupils should have access to the same kind of curriculum unless good reasons can be shown for providing different curricula; the onus is on those who wish to provide different curricula, to demonstrate that this will be "fair"'.[9] In 1982, Malcolm Skilbeck entitled his inaugural professorial lecture at the Institute of Education, University of London, *A Core Curriculum for the Common School*.[10] Both Lawton and Skilbeck, however, acknowledged the deficiencies of the Schools Council for Curriculum and Examinations, the body established in 1964 to provide for research and development in these two areas. Many curriculum development projects were promoted – some 172 between 1964 and 1978 – but the Schools Council was less effective in providing the type of core curriculum which they both envisaged. Lawton criticized the Schools Council for its 'cafeteria approach';[11] Skilbeck concluded that while the Schools Council under its revised constitution of 1978 might have been regarded as the best means of establishing a core curriculum, failure to do so led to its justified demise.[12] The National Curriculum of 1988, therefore, may be interpreted as the logical outcome of a movement which commanded widespread professional and political support. Indeed, several initiatives by Labour governments, for example, the reorganization of secondary schools under the terms of Circular 10/65, and James Callaghan's Ruskin College speech of 1976 with its emphases upon basic curricula, improved standards and accountability, may be counted as steps on the way towards a common curriculum for a common school. Nevertheless, as Lawton and Skilbeck (among others) acknowledged, little progress was made. It took the very considerable political will and skill of a Conservative Prime Minister, Margaret Thatcher, and a Conservative Secretary of State for Education, Kenneth Baker, to achieve a common curriculum.

Arguments against the National Curriculum may similarly be divided into two broad groups. The first group are those based not only upon opposition to the National Curriculum of 1988, but also upon opposition to the very principle of a common curriculum. All children, it is argued, are different, and therefore all children need different curricula. Such differences, particularly during the primary school years when all children must acquire the basic skills of reading, writing and arithmetic, may be ones of degree rather than of kind. Nevertheless, it is maintained that curricula should not be based upon the priorities of the producers, but as far as possible upon the needs and choices of the consumers – pupils and their parents. Paradoxically, for many on the political Right the National Curriculum appeared to be an aberration, given that the majority of the clauses of the Education Reform Act of 1988, and the general tenor of Conservative educational and other legislation since 1979, had given such prominence to market forces.

The second type of perceived weakness and attack focused upon the National Curriculum of 1988 itself, and encompassed both content and control. Some critics questioned the idea that the National Curriculum was a natural development. It was argued that the professional insights of teachers, academics and inspectors in the 1970s and 1980s had been jettisoned. The ideal of a common curriculum based upon areas of knowledge and experience, and which drew upon professional expertise and research findings, had been replaced by a backward-looking, subject-based curriculum under political and bureaucratic control.[13]

As the following comparison indicates, in re-assuming control of the school curriculum, central government appeared to ignore the curriculum development work of some 30 years, reverting instead to a simple list of subjects which almost directly replicated a list produced in the first decade of the twentieth century.

1904 Secondary School Regulations	*1988 National Curriculum*
English	English
Mathematics	Mathematics
Science	Science
History	History
Geography	Geography
Foreign language	Foreign language
Drawing	Art
Physical Exercise	Physical Education
Manual work/housewifery	Technology
	Music

The National Curriculum of 1988 was presented by its proponents and supporters as forward-looking, a curriculum for the twenty-first century. In fact it is largely a traditional curriculum – traditional in its division into subjects and in the very nature of those subjects themselves. It is a National Curriculum which, it has been argued, has been designed to facilitate national testing and to incur minimal expenditure in terms of new types of teachers or facilities.

One further criticism may be noted. While the National Curriculum is compulsory in maintained schools in England (though not in the same form in other parts of the United Kingdom) it does not have to be followed in independent schools. From the beginning it was clear that 'the government believe it would not be right to impose the National Curriculum on independent foundations'.[14] This differentiation between what is required of maintained and of independent schools means that in this sense the National Curriculum of 1988 may be seen not as a common curriculum, but as a divisive one. In the nineteenth century the term, 'National Education', was not used to describe the education of all the children in the nation, but rather of the children of parents who could not, or would not, pay the full costs themselves. The term 'National', in the National Curriculum of 1988, therefore, shows some continuity with this previously divisive, and to some extent demeaning, concept of 'National Education'.

Two points may be made in concluding this section. The first is that common curricula in general and the National Curriculum in particular, have both supporters and opponents, strengths and weaknesses. The second, that it is possible to argue that while the principle of a common curriculum is to be welcomed, the current National Curriculum provides an unsatisfactory example, and is flawed in several respects: its inflexibility even in the face of radical changes in respect of the government's stated aims for education and the linking of education and employment in one ministry; its over-dependence upon subjects; its failure to provide a national base which includes the whole of the United Kingdom and independent as well as maintained schools.

An historical perspective

John Locke (1632–1704) is the most important political thinker in English history. He was the principal founder of philosophical liberalism, and a champion and codifier of liberal principles in an intolerant age. He is also the most important educational thinker in English history. Locke summed up the educational wisdom and intellectual achievements of previous ages and, through his writings, transformed and transmitted them to future generations. Times, of course, have changed since the seventeenth century, but much of what Locke had to say is timeless. In any discussion about the relationship between a democratic society and the construction of curricular aims and of a school curriculum, John Locke should occupy a central place.

Locke's contemporaries and successors were well aware of his importance and influence. As Samuel Pickering has written:

> By 1704, John Yolton argued, 'Locke's epistemological, moral, and religious doctrines' had been so 'thoroughly disseminated both in England and abroad' and had been 'so much discussed, criticized, and praised' that 'no responsible thinker in the eighteenth century could afford to omit reference to Locke'. Of *Some Thoughts*, Richard Aaron wrote simply, 'few other English books have influenced educational thought so deeply'.[15]

Locke's importance and influence were widely appreciated and, during the eighteenth century, at least 25 English and 16 French editions of his principal educational work, *Some Thoughts Concerning Education*, were produced, together with others in Dutch, German, Italian and Swedish.[16]

That is not to say that Locke's ideas can simply be translated into the twenty-first century. The social, political and economic conditions of seventeenth-century England were very different from those of today. So too, were some of the educational conditions; for example, compulsory school attendance was not required for a further 200 years, while access to grammar schools and to universities was restricted to males. Nevertheless, certain continuities may also be noted. The universities of Oxford and Cambridge and several grammar schools are still in existence. Some of these schools are now in the independent sector; others in the maintained. Grammar schools were the most distinctive type of school in the medieval and early modern periods. Originally founded in large numbers to teach Latin, the international language of scholarship, law and of the Church, to boys, by the seventeenth century there was less demand for Latin, and many of the new grammar school foundations were making provision for the teaching of English subjects as well.[17] Other establishments, for example, charity or parish schools, concentrated upon the basics – which in the seventeenth and eighteenth centuries would have been religion and reading. Most education, of course, still took place outside of school, and was social, religious and vocational, both in content and in context.

Some of the religious dimensions of formal education have lasted until today, but over the last two centuries the growing predominance of secular over religious educational aims has been apparent. In Locke's day, as throughout the 300 years following the Reformation of the 1530s, although formal educational institutions were largely local in character, ultimate control of education was in the hands of the state and of the state Church. Religious and social aims predominated in curricular matters. In August 1840, instructions issued by James Phillips Kay (later Kay-Shuttleworth) on behalf of the Committee of the Privy Council, the new central authority for education, to the first two members of Her Majesty's Inspectorate of Schools, John Allen and Hugh Seymour Tremenheere, advised that:

> Their Lordships are strongly of opinion that no plan of education ought to be encouraged in which the intellectual instruction is not subordinate to the regulation of the thoughts and habits of the children by the doctrines and precepts of revealed religion.[18]

Some 20 years later, however, the Revised Code of 1862 marked an important change in emphasis. Although inspectors were still required to examine children in religious knowledge, the system of payment by results introduced in that year was based upon the performance of pupils in the three secular subjects of reading, writing and arithmetic. The growth of secular, as opposed to religious, aims in curriculum matters is but one of the fundamental changes that can be observed across the centuries. Others include the incorporation of science into the curriculum, a process furthered by the National Curriculum of 1988 which extended the grammar school curriculum of 1904 to all secondary and primary schools. Even more fundamental changes have seen a reduction in the differentiation in curricular aims and provision which existed in the seventeenth century – a differentiation based on social hierarchies and gender. Until the beginning of the twentieth century much of the education of the children of the poor was aimed at teaching them to recognize their betters (which in the case of girls included their future husbands) and to defer to them.

But though there have been changes in curricular aims and in curricula, there have also been continuities. The personal, social and moral education of children, construed and constructed across the centuries within a religious framework, remains a central concern. The promotion of civil peace and social cohesion through education is as important in the twenty-first century as it was in Tudor and Stuart times. The issue of securing an appropriate balance between moral, academic and vocational education has been a constant, as has the place of formal schooling within education in general. There is no space here to consider all of the curriculum continuities and changes which connect and divide the seventeenth and twenty-first centuries. They have been treated in a recent work[19] which also provides historical perspectives upon the accompanying themes of access, standards and assessment, teaching quality, control, economic performance and consumers. But it is important to note that key tensions about curricular aims, content, context and delivery – child-centred or subject-based, academic or vocational, religious or secular, moral or knowledge-centred, common or diverse – are nothing new. They have long histories.

John Locke's claim to be the most important educationist in English history depends upon three factors. The first is that he was himself an educator, both of children and of adults. The second, that Locke's range of interests and qualities traversed a number of fields. Indeed, he made important contributions to knowledge, not only in education but also in political philosophy, science, medicine, psychology, economics and theology. The third is that in each of these fields Locke acts as a hinge between the medieval and modern worlds. As Peter Gay has concluded, 'John Locke was the father of the Enlightenment in educational thought as in much else...His treatise on education stands at the beginning of the long cycle of modernity, but it stands, too, at the end, and as the climax, of a long evolution – the discovery of the child'.[20]

There is no space in this paper to provide a substantial account of Locke's political philosophy. His place in British history is bound up with the concept of the 'Glorious Revolution' of 1688, but he is equally admired in the United States. As Tarcov has claimed:

> there is a very real sense in which Americans can say that Locke is *our* political philosopher. The document by virtue of which we Americans are an independent people...derives its principles and even some of its language from the political philosophy of John Locke.[21]

Similarly, only a brief summary of his life is possible here. Born in 1632 at Wrington in Somerset, Locke's father was an attorney and small landowner who served as a captain in the Parliamentary army during the Civil War against King Charles I. In 1647, at the age of 15, Locke was sent to Westminster School in London, then under the direction of the famous headmaster, Dr Richard Busby, a scholar, a firm believer in flogging and a supporter of the Royalist cause. In 1652 Locke gained a scholarship to Christ Church, Oxford. There he was attracted by elements of the new learning, and followed a wide curriculum – the traditional studies of classics, rhetoric, logic, morals and geometry, together with mathematics, astronomy, history, Hebrew, Arabic, natural philosophy, botany, chemistry and medicine. In 1660 he was appointed to a lectureship in Greek, and held a number of College offices before taking up a post in 1667 as tutor and physician in the household of Anthony Ashley Cooper, Baron Ashley. At Exeter House in the Strand, Ashley's London home, Locke fulfilled a variety of roles. He acted as tutor and medical adviser to Ashley's sickly young heir, and subsequently arranged his marriage to Lady Dorothy Manners. He attended Lady Dorothy during her several deliveries and miscarriages and oversaw the education of her seven children. In 1672, his employer was created first Earl of Shaftesbury and Lord Chancellor. Locke thus gained some entry to the political world, and indeed held minor public office as Secretary of Presentations of Benefices and Secretary of the Council of Trade and Plantations. Between 1675 and 1679 Locke was in France, where he travelled and read widely, and spent some months acting as tutor to Caleb, the son of Sir John Banks. Following Shaftesbury's disgrace, and death in Holland in January 1683, Locke also took up residence in Holland, where he lived until 1689.

The last years of his life were spent as a paying guest in the house of Sir Francis and Lady Masham at Oates in Essex.

Locke lived in the most turbulent age in modern English history. He was a boy during the Civil War, and a pupil at Westminster when, on 30 January 1649, King Charles I was executed at Whitehall, just a short distance from the school. His employer, Shaftesbury, was twice imprisoned in the Tower of London, and forced to flee for his life. Locke was stripped of his government posts, and came under considerable suspicion as a traitor, not least in Royalist Oxford. Even in Holland, Locke thought it prudent to adopt an assumed name and to keep on the move. A cautious, careful man, not until February 1689, following the proclamation by Parliament of William and Mary as king and queen, did Locke deem it safe to return to England. His new-found political favour was demonstrated by William's offers of the post of ambassador to the Elector of Brandenburg (which Locke declined) and the post of Commissioner of Appeals. For Locke, however, the most important outcome of life under the new regime was that he now deemed it possible to publish his major works: the *Letters Concerning Toleration* (1689, 1690, 1692 and posthumous fragment), *An Essay Concerning Human Understanding* (1690), *Two Treatises of Government* (1690), the *Reasonableness of Christianity* (1695), and the work upon which his reputation as an educator mainly rests, *Some Thoughts Concerning Education* (1693).

This very brief account of Locke and his times indicates his range of experiences – educational, political, commercial, medical, scientific, religious and philosophical. His educational ideas were the products of these experiences, and his approach to the aims and content of the curriculum was broad and balanced. This breadth of experience must have been complemented on the many occasions on which he feared for his freedom, and indeed for his life, by a depth of understanding of those values and knowledge which should be counted as being of greatest worth.

Some Thoughts Concerning Education, though first published in 1693, was based upon a series of letters which Locke wrote between 1684 and 1687 from Holland to a friend and distant relative, Edward Clarke, who had asked about the education of his son. The *Thoughts*, therefore, are not a systematic treatise on education, but are based upon a considered response to a specific situation and request. They were not intended as a blueprint for the schooling of all children. Locke's advice was aimed principally at parents and tutors. He certainly did not believe that in his own day the education suitable for the son of a gentleman could be universally applied. Nevertheless, fundamental elements of universality do occur in Locke's writings. The *Essay Concerning Human Understanding* was a general inquiry into the origins, certainties and extent of human knowledge, and the first French translation of the *Thoughts* appeared in 1695 under the title *De l'éducation des Enfans*. Indeed, in his preface to this edition Pierre Coste stated that although Locke's work was particularly designed for the education of gentlemen,

> This does not prevent its serving also for the education of all sorts of children, of whatever class they are: for if you except that which the author says about exercises that a young gentleman ought to learn, nearly all the rules that he gives, are universal.[22]

Although the historical circumstances in which Locke lived and wrote must be borne in mind, there is no doubt that his thoughts about the importance, purpose, methods and content of education have considerable relevance for the twenty-first century. Education was his priority, and Locke's belief in the importance of education is demonstrated by his statement in the first paragraph of the *Thoughts* that 'of all the men we meet with, nine parts of ten are what they are, good or evil, useful or not, by their education'. For Locke, the purpose of education was to produce virtuous and healthy human beings. As far as possible, teaching was to be by example rather than by rules, by the formation of good habits, and by a humane approach characterized by rationality rather than by corporal punishment. The curriculum, though broad, should be adapted to the child's interests and abilities. Such principles are universal and may be universally applied.

The *Thoughts* began with a quotation from Juvenal (*c*.55–*c*.140), the Roman lawyer and satirist, that 'A sound mind in a sound body is a short, but full description of a happy state in this world'. *Mens sana in corpore sano*, indeed, is a valuable statement of the aims of education and of life in general, both for children and for adults, and as applicable in the year 2000 and beyond as in the first, second or seventeenth centuries. As a doctor, Locke placed considerable emphasis upon the physical well-being of children. Indeed, the first section of the *Thoughts* deals with child health and contains much good advice on 'plenty of open air, exercise and sleep, plain diet, no wine or strong drink, and very little or no physick'.[23] The relevance of this advice is immediately apparent. The current National Curriculum does not give sufficient attention to physical well-being. Many state schools and colleges are forced to provide education in outmoded, inadequate and dilapidated buildings. Few have adequate exercise facilities and playing fields. Some, indeed, have been forced by financial constraints to dispose of land rather than to acquire it. One of the most obvious discrepancies between the facilities and curricula of independent and maintained schools is to be found in their respective provisions for physical exercise. For some children, it is only through holiday camps conducted at independent schools that they are able to enjoy the exercise and sports facilities which should be theirs by right under a proper national curriculum. For the majority of children, however, such access is permanently denied. Locke's concern about diet is also pertinent for our times. While this might not be thought to be a curriculum matter, it is a shame that public concern for the diet of children, once demonstrated in the provision of school meals and milk, has been allowed to lapse. Such provision was introduced at the beginning of the twentieth century because it was recognized that the capacities of some children to learn were being seriously inhibited by poor nutrition. At the end of the century, poverty and ignorance ensure that many children in this country still suffer from an inadequate diet.

Locke's views on a sound mind embraced many dimensions. He did not advocate cramming the mind full of indigestible and unintelligible information, but emphasized rather the importance of the formation of good habits from an early age, of paying attention to the child's real needs, of using esteem and disgrace rather than corporal punishment in the disciplining of children, and of the need for good parental example. These precepts are of a methodological or pedagogical nature, but Locke's hierarchy of values – virtue, wisdom, breeding and learning – designed originally for the son of a gentleman, provides important perspectives upon the knowledge-based society and its subject-based National Curriculum.

For Locke, one of the most knowledgeable men of his day, virtue was the true end of education. Almost half of the sections in the *Thoughts* are concerned with this aim. Virtue was to be promoted by simple acts of religious observance and faith, by the denying of selfish desires and by a concern for credit and good reputation. For a gentleman, virtue was 'absolutely requisite to make him valued and beloved by others, acceptable or tolerable to himself'.[24] This did not mean any holier-than-thou attitude. Locke's concern for virtue as the chief end of education was of a practical kind, and expressed in his support for certain virtues. These have been well summarized by Tarcov who has written that 'The Lockean virtues are self-denial, civility, liberality, justice, courage, humanity, curiosity (or, more properly, industry), and truthfulness.'[25]

Wisdom, for Locke, was similarly of a practical kind – managing one's time, money and resources to the best advantage, with openness and sincerity. He made a sharp distinction between cunning and wisdom. Wisdom was an essential quality for securing a good reputation, whereas 'a cunning trick helps but once, but hinders ever after'.[26] Wisdom, which can only be fully developed in adulthood, is hard to come by, involving as it does the acquisition of a true knowledge of the world and of the individuals in it.

Good breeding meant treading a middle way between 'sheepish bashfulness' on the one hand, and a bullying, hectoring, disrespectful manner on the other. Locke's aim was the cultivation of civility, which he identified as 'this first, and most taking of all the social virtues'.[27] His golden rule for achieving this virtue was 'not to think meanly of ourselves, and not to think meanly of others'.[28] Children, however, could not be taught civility by rules alone. Shamefacedness and confusion in thoughts, words and looks could only be overcome by encouraging children to behave in all company, whether in the home or outside, 'with that freedom and gracefulness, which pleases, and makes them acceptable'.[29] Locke's emphasis upon the importance of reasoned discussion and respect for the views of opponents is particularly apposite today when so many areas of life – including politics and the media – are characterized by confrontation. He abhorred 'frequent interruptions in arguing, and loud wrangling' and noted that:

> The Indians, whom we call barbarous, observe much more decency and civility in their discourses and conversation, giving one another a fair silent hearing, till they have quite done; and then answering them calmly and without noise or passion. And if it be not so in this civilized part of the world, we must impute it to a neglect in education, which has not yet reformed this ancient piece of barbarity amongst us.[30]

Finally, Locke came to learning. He acknowledged that his readers might

> wonder, perhaps that I put learning last, especially if I tell you that I think it the least part. This may be seem strange in the mouth of a bookish man...this being almost that alone, which is thought on, when people talk of education, makes it the greater paradox.[31]

How is that paradox to be explained? In relegating learning to the last place in curricular aims, Locke sought to reverse the widespread assumption that education consisted mainly of teaching children large amounts of factual academic knowledge. He particularly wanted to draw attention to the excessive concentration upon Latin and Greek in the grammar schools of his day and to the excessive punishments employed to instil such learning into children. Locke wanted all children to learn the basics – to read, to be able to express themselves clearly both orally and on paper, and to count – but he was opposed to the unexamined domination of the curriculum by traditional subjects.

As Locke well knew, in his own day (as in ours) the very scope and nature of knowledge was being transformed. Yet in Locke's day, as in ours, the acquisition of certain types of academic knowledge predominated in many schools, to the detriment both of other types of academic knowledge, and to moral, personal, social, aesthetic, physical, practical and vocational education. Schools were dominated by a narrow, subject-based curriculum which reflected custom and tradition. This situation had arisen as a result of a failure to consider the true aims of education and to apply them to the curriculum. 'How else is it possible' Locke asked, 'that a child should be chained to the oar, seven, eight or ten of the best years of his life, to get a language or two?'[32]

Locke's advice on curriculum was sound and balanced: reading should be taught at the earliest possible age, with picture books rather than sacred scriptures as texts; drawing and writing, including shorthand for the purpose of making quick notes; French and Latin by the conversational method; arithmetic, geometry, accounts, geography and history; science; accomplishments; and at least one (and preferably two or three) manual trades, even for the sons of gentlemen. Locke, who was himself a keen gardener, saw several purposes in manual training: the promotion of physical well-being, relief from too much bookish learning, the ability to earn a living.

Conclusion

Five conclusions may be drawn.

The first is that since the introduction of the National Curriculum in 1988 the relationship between the aims of education as expressed by central government and the school curriculum has been unclear. Indeed, there would appear to have been virtually no connection at all. The decision of QCA to begin the process of review by focusing upon aims, rather than upon a list of subjects is most welcome. The current list of subjects is no starting point for the creation of a national curriculum for the twenty-first century. Not only should the list of aims precede the list of subjects, the very concept of a curriculum which is essentially presented as a list of subjects should be called into question. Connections between curricular aims, location, content and delivery must be made clear. They must also be respected. There should be no future restatements of aims and purposes without acknowledgement of the effects of such restatements upon the location, content and delivery of the curriculum.

One effect of beginning the process of curricular revision with aims rather than with subjects is to emphasize the need for such aims to be broadly understood (and to the greatest possible extent shared) by all those concerned with education – pupils, parents, teachers, administrators, politicians, employers. A truly national curriculum will involve all of these groups not only at the level of planning, but also of delivery. A national curriculum should not simply be confined to the education provided in schools, but should be framed with reference to education throughout the community, in the family and home, in the club and church and in the workplace. It is clear that a genuine reform of the existing National Curriculum will not simply require changes to the current list of subjects. It will also necessitate a re-consideration of the relationship between school subjects and areas of knowledge and experience, a change in the relationship between schools and education, a strengthening of the family and workplace as educational environments, and a modification or supplementation of the role of classroom teacher by means of the family or group tutor. A new partnership is required, one which will include the media, and be based upon mutual recognition of roles and responsibilities. The practical problems associated with such fundamental reform may be considerable. There are bound to be costs, not least in respect of teachers, facilities and equipment. There will also be wider costs, consequent upon an appreciation of the educational importance of the environments in which children are brought up. But the first and the most substantial task is to replace the confrontational and proprietary culture that has built up around education and which so soured the introduction of the National Curriculum of 1988.

The third conclusion is to note that in recent years, principally as a result of central government interventions, the historical (and philosophical) dimensions of educational study have been virtually eliminated from the education and training of prospective and practising teachers, and from discussions of educational planning and policy making. At this historic moment in time, when a revised national curriculum is to be put in place for the twenty-first century, it is essential to recognize that such questions as 'What are the aims of education?' or 'What knowledge is of most worth?' have long histories. John Locke is but one of those who have considered such questions and whose answers provide important perspectives upon our current discussions. It is to be hoped that the current revision of curricular aims will make full use of historical perspectives. Such perspectives make it possible to explore both the nature and processes of continuities and changes and to identify those elements which are of permanent and greatest worth. In a piece of this length it has only been possible to provide an introduction to such perspectives and to furnish the briefest of summaries of the life and educational thought of one individual who died some 300 years ago. A much fuller picture, and more substantial analysis could be provided by considering perspectives drawn from the work of other prominent thinkers about the curriculum. These might include such diverse and more modern figures as J.H. Badley, the founder of Bedales School, and Lawrence Stenhouse, director of the Humanities Curriculum Project funded by the Nuffield Foundation and the Schools Council and founder of the Centre for Applied Research in Education at the University of East Anglia.[33] Nevertheless, as Peter Gay has rightly concluded, although the society, and therefore the educational structures of Locke's day were very different from our own, and though many of Locke's specific recommendations may seem to be irrelevant or out of date, the roots of what is valuable in modern educational philosophy are to be found in *Some Thoughts Concerning Education*.

> And more: if we want to remind ourselves why we really wish to educate children, if we seek a philosophy that insists on the relevance of subject matter to experience without neglecting the pleasure of cultivation for its own sake, that emphasizes recognition of the child's needs without ignoring the uses of discipline, that urges the relation of morale to learning without denying the virtue of hard study, that seeks to form men and women fit for modern life without forgetting that this fitness requires cultivation of the higher sensibilities and a profound knowledge of the great literature of the past – if we seek such an educational theory we would do well to read, and reread, Locke with care.[34]

Since the seventeenth century, the amount of learning in the world has greatly increased – particularly in such areas as science and technology. Today, these subjects occupy a pride of place similar to that once enjoyed by religion and the classical languages. In the twenty-first century this process of change is bound to continue, and most children and adults will need a greater and/or different range of knowledge and of skills in order to participate successfully in society. This will require the creation of a national curriculum that is both more responsive to change, and better tailored to the aptitudes and abilities of individual pupils.

A significant modification of the prescription of subjects and of specific programmes of study is needed. Not that everything will change; many of the traditional elements in knowledge and learning – for example, reading, writing and mathematics – will retain their importance.

Though much of the knowledge and many of the skills required in the twenty-first century may change, the nature and primacy of values will remain constant. Locke's emphasis upon the importance of virtue, wisdom and civility is enduring; his advice that 'Learning must be had, but in the second place, as subservient only to greater qualities',[35] provides a timely corrective to narrow, subject-based curricula in any age. The values that Locke espoused – self-denial, civility, liberality, justice, courage, humanity, industry and truthfulness – are universal. Such qualities are essential not only for the well-being of the individual, but also for the well-being of society and of the state. In the long run it profits none of us if individuals, groups or nations gain considerable knowledge and power and yet lack the qualities necessary to exercise such knowledge and power for the general good.

Notes

1   I am most grateful to William J. Reese, Deborah Spring and John White for comments on earlier versions of this paper. The quotations from the *Thoughts* are taken from J.L. Axtell's 1968 edition of Locke's educational writings and have been rendered into modern form.

2   Qualifications and Curriculum Authority, *Aims for the School Curriculum 5–16*, London: QCA, 1997, p. 1.

3   Ibid.

4   Department for Education and Employment, *The English Education System: An Overview of Structure and Policy*, London: DfEE, 1995, p. 1.

5   J. White, 'New aims for a new National Curriculum', in R. Aldrich and J. White (eds), *The National Curriculum beyond 2000: The QCA and the Aims of Education*, London: Institute of Education, 1998, pp. 1–40.

6   R. Aldrich, *Education for the Nation*, London: Cassell, 1996, p. 3.

7   P. Gordon and D. Lawton, *Curriculum Change in the Nineteenth and Twentieth Centuries*, London: Hodder and Stoughton, 1978, p. 2.

8   R. Aldrich, *The End of History and the Beginning of Education*, London: Institute of Education, 1997, pp. 13–20.

9   D. Lawton, *Class, Culture and the Curriculum*, London: Routledge and Kegan Paul, 1975, pp. 116–17.

10 M. Skilbeck, *A Core Curriculum for the Common School*, London: Institute of Education, 1982.

11 D. Lawton, *The End of the Secret Garden? A Study in the Politics of the Curriculum*, London: Institute of Education, 1978, p. 13.

12 Skilbeck, op. cit., pp. 38–9.

13 D. Lawton and C. Chitty (eds), *The National Curriculum*, London: Institute of Education, 1988.

14 Quoted in R. Aldrich, 'The National Curriculum: an historical perspective', in Lawton and Chitty, op. cit., p. 29.

15 S.F. Pickering, *John Locke and Children's Books in Eighteenth-Century England*, Knoxville, TN: University of Tennessee Press, 1981, p. 9.

16 Ibid., p. 10.

17 R.S. Tompson, *Classics or Charity? The Dilemma of the Eighteenth-Century Grammar School*, Manchester: Manchester University Press, 1971, p. 58.

18 *Minutes of the Committee of Council on Education, 1840–1*, p. 3.

19 R. Aldrich, *Education for the Nation*, London: Cassell, 1996, pp. 23–39.

20 P. Gay (ed.), *John Locke on Education*, New York: Teachers College, 1964, p. 1.

21 N. Tarcov, *Locke's Education for Liberty*, Chicago, IL: University of Chicago Press, 1984, p. 1.

22 Quoted in J.L. Axtell (ed.), *The Educational Writings of John Locke*, Cambridge: Cambridge University Press, 1968, p. 52.
23 *Thoughts*, section 30.
24 Ibid., section 135.
25 Tarcov, op. cit., p. 189.
26 *Thoughts*, section 140.
27 Ibid., section 143.
28 Ibid., section 141.
29 Ibid., section 142.
30 Ibid., section 145.
31 Ibid., section 157.
32 Ibid., section 147.
33 R. Aldrich and P. Gordon, *Dictionary of British Educationists*, London: Woburn Press, 1989, pp. 14–15, 237–8.
34 Gay, op. cit., p. 15.
35 *Thoughts*, section 147.

CHAPTER 9

EDUCATIONAL STANDARDS IN HISTORICAL PERSPECTIVE

H. Goldstein and A. Heath (eds), *Educational Standards*, Oxford: Oxford University Press, 2000 (*Proceedings of the British Academy*, 102), pp. 39–56

Introduction

The *Oxford English Dictionary* lists some 30 usages of the word, 'standard'. Two broad categories amongst such usages are those of a military or naval ensign and an exemplar of measure or weight. The term, 'standard', first appears in English with reference to the Battle of the Standard, fought at Northallerton between the English and Scots on 22 August 1138. A contemporary chronicler, Richard of Hexham, described the standard as a mast of a ship surmounted by flags around which the English grouped, which was called a standard because 'it was there that valour took its stand to conquer or die'. In this sense the 'raising of one's standard' meant (and still may imply) setting forth to engage in battle or other stirring deeds.

The second sense, of an authorized exemplar of measure or weight, for example, the standard lengths built into the wall of the observatory at Greenwich, is connected to the first inasmuch as early usages state or imply 'the king's standard'. Just as the royal standard in battle was the place around which all should rally and from which commands were issued, so the royal or official standards or measures were those which subjects should employ in business and commercial dealings. This sense of a measure to which all objects or persons should conform was extended into many spheres of life, becoming a definite degree of quality, viewed as a measure of an adequate level for a particular purpose or as a prescribed object of endeavour. In 1862, with the introduction of the Revised Code into elementary schools, the word 'standard' took on a further meaning, defined by the *Oxford English Dictionary* as, 'Each of the recognised degrees of proficiency, as tested by examination, according to which school children are classified'. From the end of the nineteenth century, the demise of centrally controlled annual examinations led to the gradual disappearance of this particular connotation of the word 'standard'. Today, however, standards in education are as prominent an issue as they were a century and more ago. In 1998, a School Standards and Framework Act stands on the Statute Book, a Standards and Effectiveness Unit with more than 100 members of staff has been created within the Department for Education and Employment (DfEE), while the Standards Task Force is chaired by the Secretary of State, David Blunkett, himself, with Chris Woodhead, the Chief Inspector of Schools, and Tim Brighouse, Director of Education for Birmingham, as vice-chairs.

Dictionary definitions demonstrate that the terms 'standard' and 'standards' have many different meanings. These meanings have changed over time, and will continue to do so. Confusion can, and does, occur, even in official documents.

For example, the third section of the White Paper, *Excellence in Schools*, published in 1997, is entitled 'Standards and accountability'. Its first sub-heading declares, 'Raising standards: our top priority', and it reports that 'in the 1996 national tests only 6 in 10 of 11 year-olds reached the standard in maths and English expected for their age'.[1] Here, the term, standard, is being used in the sense of an accepted level against which all should be judged. But the raising of standards referred to in the sub-heading presumably does not apply (at least not initially) to raising the expected standards which 4 out of 10 children were already failing to reach. Rather it refers to raising the unacceptable standards or levels of achievement of those who were failing to reach the expected standard. Indeed, the White Paper states categorically that by the year 2002, '80% of 11 year-olds will be reaching the standards expected for their age in English; and 75% of 11 year-olds will be reaching the standards expected for their age in maths'.[2] It remains to be seen whether any modification of the expected standards will be needed to ensure that these percentages are achieved.

Further questions may be identified here, questions which are historical in that they relate to continuities and changes in human purposes and judgements over time. For example, if an educational standard is defined as an authorized exemplar or measure, who defines that standard? Is it intended to be the same for all pupils of the same age? Are all pupils expected to achieve it, or is its purpose to select some and to reject others – as in the case of the 11-plus examination which governed transition from the primary stage before the introduction of comprehensive secondary schools, or in the use of General Certificate of Education Advanced level grades in selection of entrants to higher education? Standards, in common with examinations, curricula and education itself, have a history which has been contested by contemporaries and historians alike. Since 1988, government policies to improve the quality of education have been based upon the concept of an expected standard of achievement for all children of a particular age. This situation may be strongly contrasted with the advice given in the Plowden Report of 1967 which

> concluded that it is not possible to describe a standard of attainment that should be reached by all or most children. Any set standard would seriously limit the bright child and be impossibly high for the dull. What could be achieved in one school might be impossible in another.[3]

In further contrast, in 1971 Cox and Dyson included the following ironic 'progressive' definition of standards: 'Irrelevant academic concept designed to exclude, or penalize, students distinguished for *either* concern *or* creativity *or* both.'[4]

Today, it is argued by central government and its agencies not only that it is necessary to define national standards, but also that the levels of educational attainment of many children are lower than they should be because the expectations of many teachers, parents and pupils are too low. Teacher, pupil and parental perceptions of importance and standards, however, may conflict. For example, Schools Council Enquiry I, *Young School Leavers*, published in 1968, showed that parents of 15-year-old leavers, unlike their teachers, placed the greatest emphasis upon doing well in studies that would enable their children to get jobs. This was understandable, given that until very recent times most children in Britain left school at the earliest opportunity and proceeded directly into employment. Similarly, in October 1998, the *Times Educational Supplement* reported that 'Parents do not share ministers' high level of concern about academic achievement in schools.'[5] Expectations of standards, in common with definitions, therefore, exhibit changes, as well as continuities, over time. Levels of expectations in terms of educational achievement are the product of a long and contested history in which governmental priorities, economic and religious doctrines, employment requirements and social factors, including those of class and gender, as well as the expectations of teachers, parents and pupils, have loomed large.

The use of the term 'historical perspective' in the title of this paper, and the application of historical perspectives to contemporary educational issues,[6] also merit a brief explanation. History may be defined as the disciplined study of human events with particular reference to the dimension of time – principally in the past, but also with some acknowledgement of present and future. Such acknowledgement is essential, if only because that which is now past was once both a future and a present. Contemporary contests around the issue of educational standards frequently draw upon historical perspectives. For example, George Walden, a Conservative education minister, 1985–7 and columnist for the *Daily Telegraph*, has recently traced the perceived low standards of the English education system of today to the long-standing social class divide between private and state schools. Walden argues that while the seven per cent of children in private schools flourish, as indicated by levels of achievement in public examinations at ages 16 and 18, and by the 90 per cent of pupils from private schools who proceed to higher education, the remaining '93 per cent are still locked into a second-class system of education'.[7] One major reason for this inferiority, according to Walden, is that teachers in private schools 'have remained largely immune to the social dogmas and experimental methods inflicted on generations of state school pupils'.[8] Other commentators, however, including many teachers in state schools, would lay greater emphasis upon the link between educational standards and financial resources. Figures produced by Walden himself show the annual cost per secondary day pupil in state schools as being £2,250, with a pupil–teacher ratio of 18.4:1, as opposed to secondary day pupils in private schools with a cost of between £3,600 and £8,700 and a pupil–teacher ratio of 9.8:1.[9]

The journalist, Melanie Phillips, is another contemporary high-profile commentator on educational standards. Her book, *All Must Have Prizes*, also published in 1996, begins with a catalogue of evidence to demonstrate 'Standards sliding'.[10] Phillips, a columnist for the *Guardian, Observer* and *Sunday Times*, declares that today, 'The rot sets in at primary school level and runs throughout the system.'[11] Her key chapter seven, entitled 'The Unravelling of the Culture', is historical. It traces 'the collapse of external authority that lies at the heart of the breakdown in education',[12] from the Enlightenment and Rousseau, through a list of malign progressives which includes Holmes, Dewey, Nunn, Isaacs, Piaget, Simon and Stenhouse.

Changes

Substantial changes in educational standards across time may be simply demonstrated. For example, in Britain, as in the Western world in general, there was an overall, though uneven, rise in literacy levels across several centuries. Significant studies of such phenomena include those by Cipolla (1969),[13] Clanchy (1979),[14] Cressy (1980),[15] Stephens (1987)[16] and Vincent (1989).[17] One important feature of these historical studies is their emphasis upon such factors as occupation and general culture in the increase (and occasional stagnation and decrease) in literacy levels. Thus Cressy notes that stagnation in the development of literacy during the second half of the eighteenth century has been associated by some historians with the 'social disruptions of the industrial revolution'.[18] Vincent explores the changing patterns of nineteenth-century male and female literacy, and highlights the contribution to literacy development of the penny post, and such associated features as Christmas and Valentine cards and the picture postcard. In 1858 'the Postmaster General had drawn attention to the fact that as many letters were being delivered in Manchester alone as in the whole of Russia'.[19]

Broad comparisons of literacy across centuries and cultures help to confirm the complex definitional problems associated with educational standards. In medieval Britain, education was construed primarily in vocational and religious contexts. Boys learned the skills of their fathers, and girls of their mothers; all were taught the basic elements of the Christian faith. Teaching and learning were essentially oral. The majority of people had neither the opportunity nor the immediate need to acquire literacy. Literacy, itself, is a term which is as difficult to define as to measure. The two skills of reading and writing have often been quite separate. In the early modern period, following the development of printing in the fifteenth century and the religious Reformation of the sixteenth, increasing numbers of people in Protestant countries learned to read the Bible and other religious works. This did not, however, necessarily mean that they also read secular literature, or that they learned to write. The nature and extent of literacy (and numeracy) needed for an individual to function effectively in a particular society has clearly changed over time. Current debates about literacy levels should be set in a series of contexts which include the impact of such recent developments as the popular newspaper and typewriter in the nineteenth century, and television and the computer in the twentieth.

There is evidence to indicate that the steady improvement in literacy standards which took place across five centuries in Britain has not been maintained in the second half of the twentieth century. In a recent paper, presented at conferences in 1997, Greg Brooks of the National Foundation for Educational Research argues that during the period from 1948 until 1996 literacy standards in the United Kingdom changed very little. Indeed, there was a slight fall among 8-year olds (children in year 3) in England and Wales during the late 1980s, followed by a recovery in the early 1990s. This fall might have been associated with the introduction of the National Curriculum, which reduced the amount of time devoted to literacy in primary schools, and with the high number of teachers leaving the profession at that time. International evidence suggests that the levels achieved by high and middling performers in the United Kingdom are comparable to the best in the world, although among children and adults there is a significant proportion of the population who have poor literacy skills. Brooks concludes that the most effective way of raising average levels of achievement would be to 'intervene early in the education of children who are already failing or at risk of doing so, to ensure that they are equipped with the literacy (and numeracy) skills necessary for the rest of their education and for life'.[20]

First reports of a follow-up study to the ORACLE (Observational, Research and Classroom Learning Evaluation) project, carried out in 60 East Midlands primary classrooms between 1976 and 1978, suggest not only stagnation, but also actual decline. In July 1998, Maurice Galton reported in the *Times Educational Supplement* that his comparisons of children in years 4, 5 and 6 at the end of the school years 1976–7 and 1996–7 showed significant decline in the three basic areas of maths, reading and language skills. Galton judged that:

> The fall appears to have occurred in the late 1980s and throughout the 1990s. The one factor which stands out in this period of rapid change is the national curriculum...Teachers said they were under pressure to get through the

curriculum, emphasising instruction and content rather than teaching for understanding... Teachers told us, despite denials from the Office for Standards in Education, that it is easier to pass inspections if you have a secondary-style timetable to demonstrate that the requisite hours are given to the core subjects... It is perhaps ironic that those who have criticised primary teaching most vehemently, such as the Chief Inspector, helped to encourage this form of the national curriculum.[21]

This evidence of stagnation or decline at primary levels in the 1980s and 1990s must be set against other evidence from the secondary, further and higher education sectors. Although commentators such as Phillips cite evidence of decline at all levels, there can be no doubt that over the same period there has been a steady increase in pupils achieving passes in public examinations at ages 16 and 18, while the numbers entering higher education and attaining degrees have more than doubled.

The Revised Code

In 1858, the Newcastle Commission was appointed to examine the condition of popular education in England. It reported in 1861. The Revd James Fraser, an assistant commissioner, investigated elementary schooling in Devon, Dorset, Herefordshire, Somerset and Worcester. This substantial extract from his report indicates the religious, occupational, social class and gender contexts in which the most contentious example of government-directed attempts to raise educational standards took place:

> Even if it were possible, I doubt whether it would be desirable, with a view to the real interests of the peasant boy, to keep him at school till he was 14 or 15 years of age. But it is not possible. We must make up our minds to see the last of him, as far as the day school is concerned at 10 or 11. We must frame our system of education upon this hypothesis; and I venture to maintain that it is quite possible to teach a child soundly and thoroughly, in a way that he shall not forget it, all that is necessary for him to possess in the shape of intellectual attainments by the time that he is 10 years old. If he has been properly looked after in the lower classes, he shall be able to spell correctly the words that he will ordinarily have to use; he shall read a common narrative – the paragraph in the newspaper that he cares to read – with sufficient ease to be a pleasure to himself and to convey information to listeners; if gone to live at a distance from home, he shall write his mother a letter that shall be both legible and intelligible; he knows enough of ciphering to make out, to test the correctness of, a common shop bill; if he hears talk of foreign countries he has some notions as to the part of the habitable globe in which they lie; and underlying all, and not without its influence, I trust, upon his life and conversation, he has acquaintance enough with the Holy Scriptures to follow the allusions and the arguments of a plain Saxon sermon, and a sufficient recollection of the truths taught him in his catechism, to know what are the duties required of him towards his Maker and his fellow man. I have no brighter view of the future or the possibilities of an English elementary education, floating before my eyes than this.[22]

Not that Fraser believed that one half, or even a quarter of children who left school aged 10 did 'carry with them into the business of life even the humble amount of accomplishments which I have named. But they ought to do; and in all the schools which in my list (Table XVIII) I have named as "efficient" I believe they do'.[23]

Under the Revised Code of 1862 a large part of the central government's financial assistance to aided elementary schools was based upon the principle of payment by results. Annual examinations were carried out by Her Majesty's Inspectors (HMIs), who were issued with detailed instructions for the purpose. Reading, and the slate work of younger children in writing and arithmetic, was to be examined in the school. The paper work of older scholars might be marked in the school, but all work done on paper, together with the mark schedule, had to be sent to the Education Department. The six standards established in 1862, which roughly corresponded to children aged between 6 and 12, are shown in Table 9.1.

A major Code revision occurred in 1872. The original Standard I was abolished; the first examination of children would now normally begin at age seven. The existing Standards II to VI were re-numbered I to V. A new Standard VI was added, as shown in Table 9.2. At the same time it was announced that henceforth no pupil could be presented for examination for a second time under a lower standard or for the same standard. Additionally, from 31 March 1873, no day scholar over nine years of age and no evening scholar over 13 could be presented in Standard I, while from 31 March 1874 no day scholar over nine years of age, and no evening scholar above 14 could be presented for Standard II.[24]

The results for England and Wales in the year ending 31 August 1872, the first year of the operation of the New Code, are shown in Table 9.3.[25] Comparison of standards during the period of payment by results is difficult. The addition of 'specific' subjects, which were examined individually, and 'class' subjects in which the overall proficiency of the class was assessed, provided other ways of securing grants. For example, in 1872 of the 118,799 children presented in Standards IV–VI, 71,507 were also examined in one or more of the specific subjects. Of these 49,273 secured passes, of whom 18,958 did so in two subjects, with geography, grammar and English history proving to be the most popular. The most obvious feature, however, was the large increase in the numbers of schools seeking government recognition as public elementary schools for the purposes of obtaining grants. The New Code was introduced in the immediate aftermath of the Elementary Education Act of 1870 which established school boards empowered to levy a rate for education. In consequence, whereas in the period 1862 to 1869 the average number of schools seeking inspection for the purposes of obtaining grants was 492, in 1870 the figure was 1,114 and in 1872, 1,530. The annual report of the Committee of Council on Education for 1872–3 welcomed the increase in applications, and thus in scholars presented for examination. But it also regretted the considerable numbers of scholars who were not entered for any examinations, the great preponderance of scholars in Standards I–III as opposed to IV–VI, and the very high percentage of those aged 10 or over who were presented in Standards I–III.

Joseph Payne, a former schoolmaster who in 1873 became first professor of the College of Preceptors, was one of the major critics of standards under the system of payment by results.[26] Another opponent was John Menet, Vicar of Hockerill, whose 26-page pamphlet, *A Letter to a Friend on the Standards of the New Code of the Education Department*, was published in 1874. In this work Menet posed the question 'Why, then, is the principle of Standards radically bad?'[27] and grouped his answers under eight main themes.

Table 9.1 Standards I–VI as established in 1862

	Reading	Writing	Arithmetic
Standard I	Narrative in monosyllables	Form on blackboard or slate from dictation, letters capital and small manuscript	Form on blackboard or slate, from dictation, figures up to 20: name at sight figures up to 20: add and subtract figures up to 10, orally and from examples on the blackboard
Standard II	One of the narratives next in order after monosyllables in an elementary reading book used in the school	Copy in manuscript character a line of print	A sum in simple addition and subtraction and the multiplication table
Standard III	A short paragraph from an elementary reading book used in the school	A sentence from the same paragraph, slowly read once and then dictated in single words	A sum in any simple rule as far as short division (inclusive)
Standard IV	A short paragraph from a more advanced reading book used in the school	A sentence slowly dictated once, by a few words at a time from the same book, but not from the paragraph read	A sum in compound rules (money)
Standard V	A few lines of poetry from a reading book used in the first class in the school	A sentence slowly dictated once, by a few words at a time, from a reading book used in the first class of the school	A sum in compound rules (common weights and measures)
Standard VI	A short ordinary paragraph in a newspaper, or other modern narrative	Another short ordinary paragraph in a newspaper, or other modern narrative, slowly dictated once by a few words at a time	A sum in practice or bills of parcels

Table 9.2 Standard VI from 1872

	Reading	Writing	Arithmetic
Standard VI	To read with fluency and expression	A short theme or letter, or an easy paraphrase	Proportion and fractions (vulgar and decimal)

Table 9.3 Examination results for England and Wales in the year ending
31 August 1872

Number of day scholars qualified for examination	792,706
Number presented for examination	661,589
Number presented in Standard I	258,946
Number presented in Standard II	172,391
Number presented in Standard III	111,453
Number presented in Standard IV	66,925
Number presented in Standard V	36,843
Number presented in Standard VI	15,031
Number examined under 10 years of age	342,655
Number examined over 10 years of age	318,934
Number examined in Standards I–III	
Under 10 years of age	339,618
Over 10 years of age	203,172
Number examined in Standards IV–VI	
Under 10 years of age	3,037
Over 10 years of age	115,762
Number who passed without failure in any subject	
Standards I–III	
Under 10 years of age	213,395
Over 10 years of age	122,704
Standards IV–VI	
Under 10 years of age	1,814
Over 10 years of age	63,982

The first was that it was impossible to devise standards for the whole country. No two schools were alike. Some were established and settled, others were new and reliant on shifting populations. Some were large with children classified according to standards, others had all pupils in the one class. Some children walked to school along a few yards of pavement, others trudged for hours across muddy field, moorland or fen. Given the variety of school circumstances it was obvious that a single set of standards would be much too difficult for some and much too easy for others.

The second problem was that the minimum requirements laid down by the standards too often became the maximum. If a penalty was imposed for not reaching a particular level, then the chief aim was to avoid the penalty, and not to aspire to anything much beyond it. The grudging spirit in which the Code was operated was indicated by the instructions to inspectors issued from the Council Office in September 1862. These advised that inspectors must be satisfied as before on a range of matters – including the state of the buildings, qualifications of the teachers and keeping of registers – and that the new examination would not supersede judgements in these matters but rather presuppose them. The examination results did not prescribe that '*if thus much is done, a grant shall be paid*', but, *unless thus much is done, no grant shall be paid*'.[28]

Menet's third point was the effect of standards on the quicker and slower children. Quicker children were held back, for there was a serious disadvantage to the school in children passing through the standards too quickly. One standard per year was the most they should progress in order to get the maximum grant. On the other hand, the slowest children could not keep up with the rate of one standard per year. It was for this reason that so many children were presented in the lower standards, and some not at all. From a financial point of view, schools had every inducement to neglect children who had little or no chance of being successful.

His fourth criticism, and that which was most frequently made against the system, was that standards encouraged a dull and mechanical routine of teaching and learning. As HMI Kennedy acknowledged in his report for 1872, under the aegis of standards, most elementary schools merely became glorified infant schools in which nothing but reading, writing and arithmetic were taught at increasing levels of complexity. Such a curriculum stifled true mental progress and development. The teacher's task became to secure as many passes as possible. One of the most telling sections in Menet's pamphlet was his use of quotations from such experienced inspectors as Arnold, Campbell, Fussell, Kennedy, Mitchell, Stewart and Watkins, all of whom contrasted the superior teaching and learning that went on in many schools before the introduction of the Revised Code. For example, Matthew Arnold was quoted from his report for 1872–3: 'I have never concealed from your Lordships that our mode of payment by results, as it is called, puts in the way of the good teaching and the good learning of these subjects almost insuperable obstacles.'[29]

The next criticism concerned the increasingly mercenary approach to education engendered in school managers and teachers. By the end of the 1860s the term 'farming of schools' was widely used in inspectors' and other official reports. Children were seen not as individuals or as learners, but as grant-earners. In some schools the teacher's salary was based directly upon the number of passes and grant earned. Indeed, in some cases, Menet reported, 'the commercial element is still further strengthened by the return of a certain amount in some shape to the children who pass in the Standards'.[30]

Standards also interfered with the organization of a school. In Menet's view, schools should be organized by classes, not by standards. Children should be grouped according to their educational needs, not according to grant-earning requirements. He also asked why standards and payment by results should be applied only to public elementary schools, but not to middle-class, private, grammar or public schools? What would a parent say to a master or mistress in one of these schools who announced that children would be limited to a narrow curriculum, not allowed to progress too quickly through that curriculum, and that only selected scholars who were likely to pass would be entered for the annual examination? Finally, Menet criticized 'the disastrous effects of the Standards...upon Inspection properly so called, as distinguished from mere Examination'.[31]

Menet's solutions were based upon the abolition of the system of standards, and its replacement by a return to an annual examination by properly trained inspectors, 'an examination which would be fairly within the range of each school, according to its circumstances and standing'.[32] He concluded:

> We want, on the one hand, less routine, less mechanism, less complication, fewer pains and penalties. We want in their place, on the other hand, a much fuller and clearer recognition of what Education really is, more freedom for Inspectors, more liberty for Teachers, more cultivation of mind, and more common sense. Let the weights be removed which press on all sides, and everybody concerned will breathe more freely.[33]

The criticisms of Menet and Payne, among others, did not go entirely unheeded. The system which they deplored was further modified, for example, by the addition of a seventh standard in 1882. In the same year, the Education Department's instructions to inspectors allowed them to calculate part of the grant upon 'the estimate you form of the merit of the school as a whole'.[34] Although the quantity and quality of the pupils' passes were still to be the major factors in such an estimate, some allowance could also be made for 'special circumstances', for example, 'a shifting, scattered, very poor or ignorant population'.[35]

Payment by results came to an end in the last decade of the nineteenth century, but the concept and terminology of standards with which it had been associated lasted into the twentieth. The very standards themselves, in tabular form, continued to be included in the elementary school code. In 1912 John Adams, first principal of the London Day Training College, delivered a presidential address entitled 'An objective standard in education' to the Educational Science section at the Dundee meeting of the British Association. In this address, and in his major work, *The Evolution of Educational Theory*, first published in the same year, Adams showed how the old concept of standards had so passed into common usage that people talked about children not as being of a certain age, or of ability, but as 'being in standard so-and-so'.[36] Adams gave a cautious welcome to the work of Binet and Simon in respect of intelligence scales, for, as he observed, standards, which had been 'Primarily meant as means of measuring the money value of the communication of certain bits of information...came in the teacher's hands to be a means of estimating ability'.[37]

Conclusion

Four broad conclusions may be drawn.

The first is that the term, 'standards', has occupied a prominent and contested place in recent British educational history. This is not surprising, given the ever-changing nature and amount of knowledge, coupled with changes in educational and broader societal priorities. It is not difficult to dip into that history to find evidence for, or against, a decline in standards over time. On the one hand, it is clear that literacy standards are higher in the twentieth century than in any previous period. Similarly, a much greater percentage of the population now attends university and is educated to degree level than ever before. In the middle years of the twentieth century, grammar schooling was deemed to be appropriate for 20 per cent of the population. Today 30 per cent enter higher education. Improved educational access and standards have been particularly visible in respect of females. Not until the nineteenth century did female literacy begin to equal that of males, nor women gain access to higher education. On the other hand, there can be little doubt that levels of attainment in some subjects were higher in the later nineteenth century than they are today. For example, it seems likely that: more children knew the Lord's Prayer, Creed and Catechism than today; more boys could work complex sums in multiplication and long division; more girls were skilled in needlework; more children could recite substantial amounts of poetry. Some of these accomplishments were the direct product of the system of standards. Under the Code of 1883, when English was taken as a class subject children in Standard I were required to 'repeat 20 lines of simple verse'. This was followed by '40 lines of poetry' with associated tasks for Standard II, 60 for III, 80 for IV and 100 for V. Standard VI children had 'To recite 150 lines from Shakespeare or Milton, or some other standard author, and to explain the words and allusions.'[38] It is not difficult to gather such evidence about rising or falling standards. What is more difficult, but considerably more worthwhile, is to situate and evaluate it in the context of the time, and in historical perspective.

The standards debate of the second half of the nineteenth century took place in a series of contexts which in some respects were quite different from those of today. But although there are differences, similarities are also apparent. The Revised Code was introduced in 1862, not in implementation of the major recommendation of the Newcastle Report, which called for the introduction of a local system of county boards and local inspectors, but to avoid it. Not until 1870 would local boards be allowed to intrude into the field of public education. In 1862 teachers, who in the eyes of the government had been getting above themselves, would immediately be brought to account by the introduction of 'a little free trade'. Payment by results, it was argued, meant that, in future, government and taxpayers would get better value for money. Elementary education would either be efficient or it would be cheap. But was elementary education made more efficient? Menet's most persuasive argument against the system of standards of his day was that many of the HMIs who operated the assessment regime upon which payment by results was based, were prepared to state publicly that, on balance, it was harmful to good teaching and learning. They, and Menet himself, while fully committed to the need for some form of externally based assessment, concluded that such assessment must be professional and formative as well as managerial and summative.

Evidence from the other side of the world lends support to this conclusion. For in New Zealand from 1877 an almost identical system applied. Its central features – a national syllabus divided into prescribed standards, school inspectors whose role was to apply the assessment system and take no responsibility for its effects – were essentially the same, although without the direct operation of payment by results. In New Zealand, school examination results were published in tabulated form in newspapers, and in 1880 the government declared that 'the school with the lowest average age and the highest percentage of passes in the same standards is the most efficient...a high average age and a low percentage of passes indicates a school of the opposite character'.[39] David McKenzie has recently concluded that the system of external review based upon standards as operated in New Zealand, even without the dimension of payment by results, was essentially mis-educative. The initiatives of better teachers were curbed; weaker teachers taught to the test and some engaged in outright dishonesty. Intended minima soon became maxima; good teaching and educational improvement were stifled. McKenzie supports Matthew Arnold's identification of the underlying problem, namely that the fault lay in the bureaucratic system of evaluation itself, rather than in its specific use for the purpose of payment by results.[40] McKenzie drew upon this historical perspective to argue that criticisms of the Education Review Office in New Zealand 'owe their origin to the failure of the Picot Committee to grasp that a distanced review authority which is required to act judgmentally will be unable to facilitate the co-operative activity that the process of educational review requires'.[41]

The third point concerns the contributions which historians can make in relation to educational research. In 1996, in a lecture entitled 'Teaching as a research-based profession: possibilities and prospects', David Hargreaves argued that much educational research, unlike that in medicine or the natural sciences, was 'non-cumulative, in part because few researchers seek to create a body of knowledge which is then tested, extended or replaced in some systematic way'.[42] The historian can employ a chronological approach to provide a cumulative account, but must also indicate some of the difficulties inherent in creating, testing, extending or replacing bodies of knowledge in educational research. There are continuities in educational history, and it is not difficult to show, for example, that some basic principles of teaching and learning have as much validity in the twentieth century as in the nineteenth. Progress in some matters – for example, better physical health and improved literacy rates – can also be demonstrated over long periods of time. But it is difficult to be prescriptive about all issues of educational practice, and to measure progress (or decline) in all areas, including overall educational standards, essentially because the concept of education (like that of progress) is not value-free. Education, indeed, has been well defined as initiation into worthwhile activities, and it is clear that assessments of what knowledge (and of what standards) are of most worth, have been, and will continue to be, matters of debate. It seems probable that one of the best means of ensuring improvements in educational standards is for that debate to be conducted in a constructive and co-operative way.

Finally, it is important to end on a positive note. The current government's commitment to the raising of educational standards is to be welcomed, as are many of its initiatives to achieve this aim, particularly the establishment of General Teaching Councils for England and Wales. Central government should continue to do what it can to contribute towards the raising of standards. But it should also recognize both the limitations of its own role, and that pupils, parents, teachers, local authorities and others have most significant parts to play.

Education is not susceptible to quick fixes, whether as a result of political intervention or pedagogical fashion. Teaching is not like some other professions, for example, medicine and the law, where high profile and dramatic results may be easily and quickly achieved. The two fundamental factors in raising educational standards are the steady commitment to worthwhile education amongst pupils, parents and society at large, and the recruitment and retention of as many good teachers as possible.

This paper ends, as it began, with definitions. Worthwhile education is about the promotion of knowledge over ignorance, of truth over falsehood, of concern for others over selfishness, over effort over sloth, of mental and physical well-being over despair and debility. If we neglect these truths in order to put a spin or gloss upon education for other purposes – whether we are politicians, journalists, authors, academics, teachers – then we shall be agents in lowering rather than raising educational standards. Good teachers may be defined as those with a sound knowledge of their subjects and of pedagogy, steady application of principles of management and organization, genuine concern for those whom they teach, and the ability to enthuse and inspire.

Notes

1 Department for Education and Employment, *Excellence in Schools*, London: HMSO, 1997, p. 10.
2 Ibid., p. 19.
3 Department of Education and Science, *Children and Their Primary Schools. A Report of the Central Advisory Council for Education (England)*, London: DES, 1967, I, pp. 201–2.
4 C.B. Cox and A.E. Dyson (eds), *The Black Papers on Education*, London: Davis-Poynter, 1971, p. 215.
5 C. Dean, 'Standards are not parents' top priority', *Times Educational Supplement*, 9 October 1998.
6 See R. Aldrich, *Education for the Nation*, London: Cassell, 1996.
7 G. Walden, *We Should Know Better: Solving the Educational Crisis*, London: Fourth Estate, 1996, p. 1.
8 Ibid., p. 44.
9 Ibid., p. 43.
10 M. Phillips, *All Must Have Prizes*, London: Little, Brown and Company, 1996, pp. 1–6.

11 Ibid., p. 5.
12 Ibid., p. 187.
13 C.M. Cipolla, *Literacy and Development in the West*, Harmondsworth: Penguin, 1969.
14 M. Clanchy, *From Memory to Written Record: England 1066–1307*, London: Edward Arnold, 1979.
15 D. Cressy, *Literacy and the Social Order: Reading and Writing in Tudor and Stuart England*, Cambridge: Cambridge University Press, 1980.
16 W.B. Stephens, *Education, Literacy and Society, 1830–70: The Geography of Diversity in Provincial England*, Manchester: Manchester University Press, 1987.
17 D. Vincent, *Literacy and Popular Culture: England 1750–1914*, Cambridge: Cambridge University Press, 1989.
18 Cressy, op. cit., p. 177.
19 Vincent, op. cit., p. 46.
20 G. Brooks, 'Trends in standards of literacy in the United Kingdom, 1948–1996', paper presented at the UK Reading Association conference, University of Manchester, July 1997, and at the British Educational Research Association conference, University of York, September 1997, p. 1.
21 M. Galton, 'Back to consulting the ORACLE', *Times Educational Supplement*, 3 July 1998.
22 PP 1861 XXI, *Report of the Commissioners appointed to inquire into the State of Popular Education in England*, II, pp. 46–7.
23 Ibid., p. 47.
24 Committee of Council on Education, *Report of the Committee of Council on Education 1871–72*, 1872, p. lxxxiii.
25 Committee of Council on Education, *Report of the Committee of Council on Education 1872–73*, 1873, pp. xi–xii.
26 See R. Aldrich, *School and Society in Victorian Britain: Joseph Payne and the New World of Education*, New York: Garland, 1995, pp. 179–85 and Chapter 6 in this volume.
27 J. Menet, *A Letter to a Friend on the Standards of the New Code of the Education Department*, London: Rivingtons, 1874, p. 7.
28 Committee of Council on Education, *Report of the Committee of Council on Education 1862–63*, 1863, p. xviii.
29 Menet, op. cit., p. 13.
30 Ibid., p. 17.
31 Ibid., p. 19.
32 Ibid., p. 23.
33 Ibid., p. 26.
34 Committee of Council on Education, *Report of the Committee of Council on Education 1882–83*, 1883, p. 157.
35 Ibid.
36 J. Adams, *The Evolution of Educational Theory*, London: Macmillan, 1912, p. 304.
37 Ibid.
38 Committee of Council on Education, *Report of the Committee of Council on Education 1882–83*, 1883, pp. 132–3.
39 D. McKenzie, 'The irony of educational review', *New Zealand Annual Review of Education*, 1994, 4: 249.
40 Ibid., p. 251.
41 Ibid., p. 247.
42 D.H. Hargreaves, 'Teaching as a research-based profession: policies and prospects', Teacher Training Agency annual lecture, 1996, p. 2.

PART 5

THE TEACHING OF HISTORY

CHAPTER 10

NEW HISTORY
An historical perspective

A.K. Dickinson, P.J. Lee and P.J. Rogers (eds), *Learning History,* London:
Heinemann Educational Books, 1984, pp. 210–24

Introduction

The 1978 annual conference of the History of Education Society was devoted to
the subject 'Post-War Curriculum Development: an Historical Appraisal',[1] the
third annual conference sponsored by the Society in this field. The first, in 1971,
had considered 'The Changing Curriculum', the second, in 1975, 'The School
Curriculum'.[2] In 1974 a group was formed to explore 'The History of the
Curriculum'. It still flourishes.

Though many historians of education have shown interest in the curriculum – in
conferences, teaching, research and publications – the influence of such work upon
contemporary curriculum development is more difficult to identify. Indeed it
would appear that much of the curriculum debate of the last 20 years, *even in relation to the teaching of history*, has taken place in an ahistorical or unhistorical
context. In the former sense historical perspectives have simply been ignored. In
the latter the past has been misused – raided, distorted and condemned – so that
'Attention is drawn to the past, not for its own sake, but as a means of sharpening
a particular contemporary axe.'[3] The purpose of this chapter is to offer, in a very
modest way, some historical perspectives upon the teaching of history in secondary
schools, and in particular upon the 'new' history of the last decade and more. This
contemporary concept of new history I would take to be as outlined by R. Ben
Jones in 1973.

> The New History lays less emphasis on content and more on the process of
> learning...
> The New History emphasises that the basis of this selection (of content) is
> the educational objectives to be achieved and the historical skills to be
> acquired...
> the approach of the New History is what is popularly called the Enquiry
> Method.[4]

How new?

The new history in schools is new in so far as each movement and event in historical time is new and unique in itself. It is new in so far as the new history is a
response to the challenge and opportunities, and problems, of a particular age, an
age characterized in secondary schools by, among other developments, the rapid

application of the comprehensive principle from 1965, and the first Certificate of Secondary Education (CSE) examinations in history taken in the same year. It is not correct, however, to suppose that inquiry methods, the use of sources, historical skills, educational objectives and learning 'how' rather than learning 'what' are new in themselves. Such procedures have formed an essential part of writings on the aims and methods of history teaching in schools since the beginning of this century at least. Thus from 1911 *A History of England for Schools with Documents, Problems and Exercises* supplied 'the apparatus for work which to some extent is analogous to that provided by the laboratory in the teaching of science'.[5] This book, with its 'Nuffield' or heuristic approach, was a response to the demand from inspectors and history teachers in schools and teacher-training establishments, who were seeking to implement the ideas put forward by M.W. Keatinge in *Studies in the Teaching of History*.

This important work, first published in January 1910 and reprinted in 1913, 1921 and 1927, was concerned with the teaching of pupils in the middle forms of secondary schools. It sought to establish history as an essential part of the curriculum by proving the subject's capacity for rigorous intellectual training. Keatinge wanted to introduce pupils to the methods of the modern scientific historian, to reduce part of the subject in schools to problem form and to confront pupils with evidence. This, however, was not simply to reduce history to a set of mechanical exercises. Though *Studies in the Teaching of History* laid particular emphasis upon scientific methods and the use of contemporary documents, chapters on 'method and moral training' and 'history and poetry' were also included. Above all, Keatinge made no extravagant claims for source work. Pupils would not be constructing their own history, nor writing their own textbooks:

> The boy is no more placed in the position of the historian who weighs and estimates his raw material than the boy in the laboratory who is being put through a course of practical work is...being placed in the position of the scientific discoverer.[6]

In 1929 H. Ann Drummond, Lecturer in Education at the University of Bristol and formerly for two years history mistress at Bedales, described the experiments and conversions of students on teaching practice to the Keatinge method.[7] She confidently declared that 'Most teachers would agree that "sources" should certainly be used in the history course in school, whether elementary or secondary'.[8]

The Learning of History in Elementary Schools appeared in the same year. It came from the pen of Catherine Firth, formerly Director of Studies in History at Newnham College, Cambridge, and subsequently Lecturer at Furzedown Training College. A key chapter on historical method linked the worlds of research, teaching and learning:

> The search for evidence, the framing of hypotheses, their testing, their verification, modification or rejection, and the search again: this is in actual fact the process followed not only by the student in the Public Record Office, but by every teacher who works out a fresh lesson for a class, and by every child who writes his own answer to a 'thinking question'.[9]

Firth believed that though history was essentially chronological and bound up with the dimension of time, the history teacher's basic responsibility was to encourage the double question, 'Is it true?' and 'How do we know?'.[10] Subsequent chapters on 'The activity of children towards historical material', 'The use of original authorities' and 'Independent work', continued the same theme.

F.C. Happold's experiments in history teaching were undertaken at the Perse School, Cambridge, and his methods were set out in an Historical Association pamphlet of 1927. For Happold, historical study in schools meant:

> the ability to collect, examine and correlate facts and to express the result in clear and vivid form, freedom from bias and irrational prejudices, the ability to think and argue logically and to form an independent judgement supported by the evidence which is available, and, at the same time, the realisation that every conclusion must be regarded as a working hypothesis to be modified or rejected in the light of fresh evidence.[11]

The Approach to History, which appeared in the following year, was Happold's 'plea for the substitution of historical training for the mere teaching of history in schools'.[12] Happold emphasized the importance of pupil activity, projects and independent work. Though he declared himself less sanguine than Keatinge about the particular value of using original sources in the classroom, Happold also saw history as a means of acquiring the art of thinking, and as a sound mental discipline. A carefully structured and graded course in historical method was outlined in which 'emphasis is placed not so much on the acquisition of historical knowledge as of correct methods of work and of a capacity for historical thinking'.[13]

The wide-ranging aims and methods of history teaching in schools, as set out by such writers as Allen,[14] Drummond, Findlay,[15] Firth, Happold, Hasluck,[16] Jarvis[17] and Keatinge became the intellectual orthodoxy of their day. In a survey of 50 years of answers to the question 'Why teach history?', Rogers concluded that by the later 1920s 'the value was seen to lie in the methods of study', 'it did not matter so much *what* the pupils learnt so long as they learned *how* to learn it'.[18]

Much of what is claimed as the new history of today, therefore, does not appear to be new at all. Emphases upon sources, historical skills, pupil involvement, inquiry methods and learning 'how', have a firm place in the tradition of history teaching in this country. They need not depend essentially upon Bloom, Bruner or Piaget, nor upon highly contentious notions of structure or doubtful taxonomies for the measurement of historical and other educational objectives and skills.[19]

How historical?

To the historian of education, however, the most significant feature of the new history movement is its unhistorical, rather than its ahistorical basis. It is unhistorical in so far as its proponents imply that all previous history teaching in schools has been content-dominated, superficial and boring. It is unhistorical in so far as the word 'traditional' has been used simply as a term of abuse. For, on the contrary, there is considerable evidence both as to the achievements (as well as the failures) of history teachers of the first half of the twentieth century, and of the nature and quality of their debates about aims and methods.

By the beginning of the twentieth century history was an accepted subject at both university and secondary school levels. In the 1870s separate honours schools were established at Oxford and Cambridge. The *English Historical Review* was founded in 1886, the Historical Association some 20 years later. By 1890 more candidates had taken history in the Oxford Locals than in any other subject. In that year 68,000, some 91 per cent of the total entries for Oxford Locals, Oxford and Cambridge Schools Examination Board, and London Matriculation offered history.[20] Connections between a genuinely 'new' history at university and school levels were forged in this period. Thus essays on the aims and practice of history teaching in schools by W.H. Woodward, Principal of the University Training College, Liverpool, and C.H.K. Marten, history master at Eton and one time President of the Historical Association, were included in a collection of *Essays on the Teaching of History* published in 1901 by the Cambridge University Press.[21] Five of the other contributions were on aspects of history teaching in English universities, and one on university teaching in the United States. Schoolteachers of history, particularly those who had relied on an uncritical use of such textbooks as Mangnall's *Historical Questions*, or Ince's *Outlines of English History*, might well have benefited from the guidance of their university mentors. Thus H.M. Gwatkin, Dixie Professor of Ecclesiastical History at Cambridge, established three chief aims in the practical teaching of history: 'to rouse interest, to give the guiding facts, and to teach the principles of research and criticism',[22] and briefly discussed their implications for school teaching. In his essay on constitutional history, J.R. Tanner gave examples of good practice in the university teaching of the subject. Thus, he reported, one Cambridge lecturer supplied his class with two 32-page pamphlets which included 'a list of books recommended, a statement of the subject-matter of each lecture, and short paragraphs on points of special difficulty, with abundant references to the best sources of information'.[23]

Such connections were extended into the elementary school world. Between May 1909 and June 1911 a conference of some 25 teachers, headteachers, lecturers and inspectors, presided over by A.F. Pollard, Fellow of All Souls, Oxford and Professor of English History in the University of London, was set up by the London County Council (LCC) 'to consider and report as to the methods of teaching history in the public elementary schools of London'. The LCC was committed to a policy of co-operation between elementary schools, secondary schools, training colleges and universities, and since 1909 had produced reports on the teaching of English, geography and arithmetic. The 72-page report on history was published in 1911. It began with a summary of the historical background to history teaching, and then proceeded to an examination of existing teaching methods in London elementary schools. Material for comparative study was provided by accounts of history teaching in the British Dominions, Austria, Belgium, France, Germany, Holland, Hungary, Italy, Japan, Norway and the United States. Two central chapters on the aims of history teaching and suggestions as to the best methods of attaining them were summarized in seven recommendations including:

1   The whole teaching must be governed by the desire to stimulate the use of reasoning power on the part of the pupil rather than of the teacher.
2   Mere knowledge of historical facts is no guarantee of historical understanding.
3   Each school should be allowed at discretion to select for more detailed treatment such aspect or portion of the period as may suit its special circumstances or the character of its pupils.
4   To attain these ends each teacher must omit a considerable portion of what is now considered necessary in a history syllabus.[24]

A concluding chapter on the initial and in-service training of teachers advised that instruction in general principles of pedagogy was insufficient to secure these ends. Historical culture must become an essential element in the curriculum of every training college. The conference outlined five necessary ingredients in this historical culture:

> (a) adequate range of historical knowledge, (b) some acquaintance with the means of ascertaining historical fact, (c) some conception of the nature and meaning of historical evidence, (d) some capacity to comprehend historical value and interpret historical truth, and (e) some facility in methods of expressing and presenting results.[25]

For many years F.R. Worts, Headmaster of the City of Leeds School, had nursed the strongest convictions that the 'academic' approach to history that resulted from the university connections was wrong.[26] The *Memorandum on the Teaching of History* of 1925, produced by the Incorporated Association of Assistant Masters (IAAM), encouraged Worts 'to continue what seemed to be a hopeless task. I no longer felt *contra mundum*'.[27] The *Memorandum* of 1925 drew on the wisdom of a committee of 74 history teachers in grammar and public schools and was edited by a central co-ordinating committee of 12. Within its pages was gathered together 'the accumulated experience of men who do the practical work of teaching'.[28] This included not only the what, why and how of history teaching, but also a protest against the control of school history by university professors, examiners and inspectors. The merits of history as a training of the intellect or training in right living having been raised, the authors wondered whether they should even:

> concentrate on imparting a body of knowledge, leaving time and reflection to do the rest. Formerly this last was regarded as the sole purpose of history teaching; if the pupil knew certain facts and dates, the work was well done, and nothing more was expected. We have moved far since those days, and such knowledge is now regarded in its right perspective – as a means and not as an end in itself. Teachers at any rate think so, though the demands of examination boards and the questions of examiners leave them wondering if such a conception had made much progress beyond the schools.[29]

Worts's own book, *The Teaching of History in Schools: A New Approach*, first published in 1935, was a powerful attack on the 'old' methods foisted on schools by so-called ' "experts" viewing school-life from the fence or the rim of its true experience; they theorise rather than demonstrate'.[30] Worts did not discount the value of much that had been written about the teaching of history but now he argued that any theorizing could and should be based upon practical classroom experience. This would have been less possible in 1900 when the development of history teaching in schools was seen as a logical extension of the development of historical studies at university level, with the graduate history teacher as the agent for securing these advances. By the 1930s such graduates, and the secondary schools in which they taught, had more than come of age. Thus Drummond's book of 1929 was criticized for being based on an 'all-too-short teaching experience'[31] while, in Worts's view, the Perse School, where Happold had been senior history master, could not 'be accepted as a normal standard for the average Secondary school'.[32]

The relative merits of the moral and intellectual aims and dimensions of history teaching in schools had been a matter of concern since the days of Thomas Arnold, a century before. Worts sought to reverse the existing emphasis as he saw it, 'to give precedence to ethical over intellectual values'. He concluded:

(i) That we schoolmasters and mistresses are wrong in attempting to inculcate academic ideas of History into our pupils.
(ii) That we ought not to treat History as a science.
(iii) That the scientific 'historical method' ought to find much less favour in our 'methodology' and school practice.
(iv) That History in schools ought not primarily to be regarded as inducing a certain habit of mind or as an agent of mental discipline...
(vi) ... that History in schools is the witnessing of the 'Pageant of Man' rather than the learning of a 'science', that is not a 'science' and never can be.[33]

On the use of sources, historical materials and research methods below the sixth-form level, Worts commented:

today, certainly the vain hope is held that from a knowledge of original documentary matter, juveniles and adolescents will perceive in 'elementary' fashion the principles underlying the true historian's work of knowing original authorities, of discriminating and adjudging their records, and of using the approved material for the making or the writing of History... It is far better to leave this provision of 'sources', primary or secondary, to its first and simple task, namely, of supplying reading material capable of stimulating interest, adding colour to, and infusing the sense of action and reality into dry and colourless texts.[34]

By 1935 Happold himself had acquired a new perspective, having moved to the headmastership of Bishop Wordsworth's School in Salisbury. *Citizens in the Making* was not concerned to train better historians but rather with the 'fundamental need of the training of better citizens'.[35] In the difficult days of the 1920s and 1930s many teachers were aware of the 'transition in this country from the old order to the new'[36] and saw schools in general, and history lessons in particular, as a key means of ensuring that this transition took place by evolutionary rather than revolutionary means.[37] There was, however, no simple dichotomy between the intellectual and moral approaches to history teaching. Thus in 1929 Firth's book had included a chapter on 'The teaching of local history and the preparation for political citizenship'.[38] A decade later, M.V.C. Jeffreys concluded a classic plea for the line of development approach with a short section on 'social studies' and 'education for citizenship'.[39]

International citizenship was promoted in schools in the United Kingdom by the League of Nations Union, formed in 1918 under the presidency of Lord Grey, the former Foreign Secretary. History lessons, it was argued, should emphasize peace and not war, co-operation rather than antagonism, culture rather than destruction, international rather than national ideals. This theme reached a peak in 1927–8 and Drummond, in her publication of 1929, advocated the establishment of a branch of the Union in every secondary school. Similarly, the much travelled Fred Clarke, whose early writings included a *Social History of Hampshire* (1909), argued in *Foundations of History Teaching*, a book written in 1927 while on a voyage 'Off Finisterre', for the importance of the study of 'humanity' in history, an ideal that had 'come to expression in the form of a League of Nations'.[40]

Doubts, however, about the wisdom of using history lessons for propaganda purposes had been expressed in Historical Association meetings from 1921. In the 1930s, as the inadequacies of the League became more apparent, so the influence of the Union declined, as shown in the poor response to its pamphlet, *History Teaching and World Citizenship* (1938).[41]

In the post-Second World War period the several editions and reprints of *The Teaching of History*, first produced in 1950 by another IAAM committee of history teachers, were worthy successors to the *Memorandum* of a quarter of a century before. Multiple aims included 'the weighing of evidence, the detection of bias, the distinguishing of truth from falsehood, or at least the probable from the impossible'.[42] Variety in method was encouraged and encompassed sections on sources, project work and 'research' methods. On the other hand, excessive lecturing, note-taking and reading aloud from textbooks were deplored. The two editions of the *Handbook for History Teachers*,[43] however, drew on the resources of the university world, both in articles on the teaching of history and in bibliographies for advanced work in schools.

For the first 60 years of the twentieth century, school history teaching in this country relied heavily upon academic historical study and practical classroom experience. Little part was played either by general educational theory or by specific educational research. Thus Ian Steele concluded a recent article by suggesting that:

> the key problem which bedevilled the history teacher in the nineteenth century has still not been resolved: the lack of a coherent theory of history teaching in the context of which aims and objectives, content, learning experiences, evaluation techniques etc., will assume a more identifiable shape. The 'new' history of the 1960s points the way to the future but it seems we are still only at the starting gate![44]

In the past two decades, it has become possible to remedy these omissions. Some advocates of new history, however, by their fundamentally unhistorical approach, have sought to denigrate and destroy earlier foundations and to build anew. This destruction has been justified by such statements as 'Grammar school history teaching aimed principally to equip pupils with a body of factual knowledge',[45] or 'This tradition is now worn out, and must be replaced by one which bases its claims not upon a received corpus of emasculated academic knowledge, but upon the needs of children who will be adults in the twenty-first century'.[46] History teachers and teaching of the past having been summarily condemned and dismissed, school history is to be re-created in accordance with the writings of three educationists, not one of whom was primarily concerned with history as a subject.

Thus *The Teaching of History* of Dennis Gunning rests upon two premises: 'the primacy of concept-learning and the vital importance of skill-learning'.[47]

    (a) From Bruner and Piaget we take the idea of the central importance of concept development.

    (b) From Bloom we take the idea of the possibility of isolating and developing specific, named intellectual skills.[48]

These, however, are not even to be key concepts of the subject nor historical skills as such, for that would be 'too restricting an idea'.[49] Protests from 'traditionalists' are forestalled. 'There is an academic discipline called "History". There is also a school subject called "History". There is no self-evident reason why they have to be the same.'[50] New history in schools is thereby cut off from history as understood by academics, most schoolteachers and children and the general public. Whereas the ahistorical dimension raises the question as to how much of the new history is genuinely new, the unhistorical dimension prompts the query as to how much of it is genuinely history.

The place of history in education

The two previous sections have provided examples of a variety of initiatives, some of them quite inspirational, that have enriched the teaching of history in schools. On the other hand, it is not difficult to furnish evidence that much history teaching in the twentieth century has fallen far short of these high ideals.[51] Emphasis upon such shortcomings, however, has fuelled the belief that inadequate history teachers have consigned the subject to a subordinate place in the secondary school, whence it can now be rescued by the thorough application of new history. For example, John Elliott characterized the years 1918–40 as a time of failure in curriculum reform, so that by the outbreak of the Second World War 'History had failed to become a dominant subject of the curriculum'.[52] This he attributed principally to insufficient and ineffective training in the teaching of the subject, concluding that 'With a less than half-trained and overworked teaching force available, the high hopes pinned on history in 1918 never rose off the ground'.[53] Whether the gap between theory and practice has been wider in history than in other subjects is difficult to determine. Latin, for example, has been advocated for the noblest of reasons – as giving access to a great culture and history, as an agent of mental discipline, as a source of moral example, as an essential basis for grammatical, literary and certain professional studies. Countless generations of schoolboys, and girls, however, have identified Latin in terms of incomprehensible gerund grinding.

The fate of Latin in twentieth-century schools is instructive. Classical study, the staple diet of grammar and public schools since their inception in the medieval period, maintained a pre-eminent position in the education of the upper and aspiring classes until very recent times. In 1914, 92 of 114 boys' public schools had headmasters with classical degrees.[54] All Oxbridge entrants, whether for arts or sciences, were required to have an Ordinary (O) level General Certificate of Education (GCE) pass in Latin until the 1960s. Latin, however, was never a popular subject. Its status in grammar, preparatory and public schools did not depend upon mass appeal, coherent theories of instruction, nor enlightened methods of presentation. It had little enough place in the curricula of elementary or primary schools.

By the nineteenth century Latin had become essentially exclusive, a means of identification and selection, the hallmark of the gentleman or scholar, an elite curriculum device to distinguish the few from the many. Latin was the pivot of a literary, liberal arts, faculty psychology, transfer of training, concept of education. Its status, like that of any subject in the school curriculum, depended to a large extent upon factors quite outside the control of the classroom teacher.

History's position in the primary school curriculum has been much stronger than that of Latin. Indeed there is evidence of a significant history presence in nineteenth-century elementary schools prior to the introduction of the Revised Code in the 1860s with its emphasis upon the three Rs. History's place in the secondary school curriculum was confirmed in the Secondary School Regulations of 1904 which prescribed a broad humanistic, as opposed to a particular vocational or technical curriculum. Thus:

> Not less than $4\frac{1}{2}$ hours per week must be allotted to English, geography and history; not less than $3\frac{1}{2}$ hours to a language (other than English) where only one was taken, or less than 6 hours where two were taken; and not less than $7\frac{1}{2}$ to Science and Mathematics, of which at least three must be devoted to Science. The instruction in Science must be both theoretical and practical.[55]

In the Oxford Local Examinations of 1908 both at junior and senior levels, history was taken by the third highest number of candidates, a total exceeded only by arithmetic and English. In the same year the Cambridge Local Examinations produced a virtually identical pattern, with history again in third place both at junior and senior levels. At this period history was a compulsory subject in the preliminary examinations of such professional bodies as the Institutes of Accountants, Architects, Auctioneers and Surveyors, the Law Society and the General Medical Council.[56] In the inter-war years history became a predominant university subject, particularly at Oxford. A history degree thus became a useful qualification for a secondary school headship. In the mid-1950s open awards in history at Oxford and Cambridge constituted some one-fifth of the total, more than in Classics, and almost as many as in science as a whole. It was indeed an established status subject.[57]

Though the prestige of history as a university and a school subject may be lower today than it was 50 or even 25 years ago, in the second half of the twentieth century the secondary school curriculum, as shown by passes in GCE examinations in England and Wales, is broadly the same as that outlined in the Regulations of 1904. In 1956 history was the fifth most popular subject at O level. Ten years later it had slipped to sixth place, and in 1976 to seventh (see Table 10.1).

At Advanced (A) level history climbed from fifth place in 1956 to fourth in 1966. In 1976 it stood fifth again, having been overtaken by economics with 35,292 passes, a category, however, that included both economic history and British constitution (see Table 10.2).

In 1966 CSE passes at grade 5 or above showed history in fourth place. Ten years later it had been overtaken by both art and craft, and biology with 138,136 passes (see Table 10.3).

In 1966 an inquiry was conducted into the attitudes of young school-leavers. Some 4,618 13–16-year olds, their parents and teachers, and some 3,421 former pupils from the same schools, then aged 19–20, were interviewed. These findings were collected and summarized in Schools Council Enquiry I, *Young School Leavers*. This report has been widely and uncritically adduced by advocates of new history as fundamental proof of the failure of 'traditional' history teaching in secondary schools.[58]

Table 10.1 GCE O level passes: summer examination

	Eng. Lang.	Maths	Eng. Lit.	French	History	Geography	Biology
1956	100,960	77,419	69,313	59,337	51,496	50,215	30,508
1966	193,425	154,168	122,928	96,190	80,605	88,886	74,750
1976	269,252	191,300	146,241	90,892	85,091	102,802	118,193

Source: *Annual Statistics of Education.*

Table 10.2 GCE A level passes: summer examination

	Maths	Physics	Chemistry	Eng. Lit.	History	French	Geography
1956	15,773	14,382	11,964	11,462	10,004	8,328	6,256
1966	40,772	28,556	21,582	31,850	23,103	18,497	17,645
1976	49,996	29,163	24,508	46,446	26,870	17,252	25,528

Source: *Annual Statistics of Education.*

Table 10.3 CSE passes at grade 5 or above, all modes

	English	Maths	Geography	History	Tech. Drawing	Art and Craft	Physics
1966	92,415	89,676	40,944	33,185	28,311	22,389	22,336
1976	447,126	347,106	150,996	131,841	75,677	143,185	91,192

Source: *Annual Statistics of Education.*

In the history of education, *Young School Leavers* occupies a position midway between the Newsom Report of 1963 entitled *Half Our Future*, which considered the education between the ages of 13 and 16 of pupils of average or less than average ability, and the proposed raising of the school-leaving age to 16 in 1972. It concentrated upon:

> what teachers, 15-year-old leavers and parents considered should be the main functions of secondary schools and the ways in which they thought that school curricula and school life in general should develop to meet the needs of the kind of pupils who would be affected by the raising of the school leaving age.[59]

In general terms the report showed that 15-year-old leavers and their parents saw the most significant purpose of secondary schooling as being the provision of basic knowledge and skills that would enable the young school leaver to obtain immediate employment and the best possible career prospects. Thus boys in the 13–16-year-old group placed maths, English, metalwork, engineering, woodwork, science and technical drawing at the head of their list of useful school subjects. Girls in this group similarly chose English, maths, housecraft, commercial subjects, typing and needlework as the most useful subjects in the school curriculum. History, quite understandably, occupied a low place in their lists. Headteachers and teachers of these pupils, however, gave a very low priority both to vocational preparation and to examination achievements. In a list of 24 objectives, headteachers assigned examination achievement and 'things of direct use in jobs' to the bottom two places. Examination achievement occupied the lowest place in teachers' objectives, with 'things of direct use in jobs' but three places higher. The educational objectives of headteachers and teachers centred rather upon 'personality and character', 'speaking well', 'independence', 'confidence', 'knowing right from wrong', 'getting on well with others'. These reactions were understandable. In 1966, early school-leavers had little opportunity of taking, let alone of succeeding, in external examinations. Their teachers thus often had little experience either of teaching for external examinations or of the jobs to which their pupils would be going. Significantly, however, the longer pupils intended to stay at school, or in the case of the 19–20-year olds, had stayed at school, the more interested they had been in history. This was true of most academic subjects. On the other hand, interest in the more practical subjects had declined. Thus boys in the older group who had left aged 17–18 thought that history had been more interesting than woodwork and carpentry. Girls in this category thought that history had been more interesting than housecraft, cookery and mothercraft (see Table 10.4).

There were similar discrepancies in attitudes towards the usefulness of history. For example, of the 19–20-year olds who had taken the subject in their fourth and fifth years, only 22 per cent of the girls who left at 15, but 58 per cent of the girls

Table 10.4 Percentages saying subject was interesting, by age of leaving school and sex (percentages are of those taking the subject)

Subjects	Age of leaving school	% saying subject is interesting (13–16-year olds)		% saying subject is interesting (19–20-year olds)	
		Boys	Girls	Boys	Girls
History	15	41	40	42	37
	16	58	53	46	53
	17/18	61	63	65	69
Maths	15	49	44	52	46
	16	60	49	59	47
	17/18	62	50	64	48
Woodwork	15	75	—	72	—
Carpentry	16	65	—	71	—
	17/18	50	—	63	—
Housecraft	15	—	87	—	80
Cookery	16	—	82	—	83
Mothercraft	17/18	—	76	—	66

Note: The bases were of 13–16-year olds who were taking the subject and of 19–20-year olds who took the subject in their fourth or fifth year at school.

Table 10.5 Percentages of those taking the subjects saying that various school subjects were interesting in excess of percentages saying they were useful (15-year olds among the 13–16-year olds)

15-year old leavers

%	Boys	%	Girls
+ 25	Art and handicraft	+ 28	Art and handicraft
+ 12	History	+ 20	Physical education and games
+ 11	Physical education and games	+ 12	Music
+ 7	Woodwork	+ 11	History
+ 6	Music	+ 4	Science
+ 5	Metalwork, engineering	− 1	Religious instruction
+ 3	Geography	− 4	Housecraft
=	Science	− 6	Geography
− 2	Technical drawing	− 11	Foreign languages
− 4	Religious instruction	− 12	Current affairs, social studies
− 9	Current affairs, social studies	− 13	Commercial subjects and typing
− 14	Foreign languages	− 14	Needlework
− 37	English	− 24	English
− 44	Mathematics	− 48	Mathematics

who left aged 17–18, subsequently thought it had been a useful subject to have learned at school. Table 10.5 shows that even the 15-year-old leavers among the 13–16-year olds gave history a much higher rating for interest than for usefulness.

Evidence from the 8,039 pupils and ex-pupils interviewed in 1966 for Schools Council Enquiry I suggests that the longer they had stayed at school, the more they had appreciated, both in terms of interest and value, the history studied in fourth- and fifth-form years. Since that date comprehensive re-organization, the growth of CSE, the raising of the school-leaving age and problems of unemployment have brought new dimensions to secondary schooling. These changes, in spite of the strong plea for vocationally oriented courses by the sample of 15-year-old leavers and their parents, and the low priority given to examination achievement by their teachers, have not so far ousted history from its traditional position as a major subject in the secondary school curriculum. Thus whereas in the summer of 1966 there were 136,893 passes in history at GCE and CSE levels, by the summer of 1976 there were 243,802. The vast bulk of this increase was accounted for by CSE passes which roughly quadrupled in this period.

Conclusion

Three brief conclusions may now be drawn. First, the historian of education can point to evidence from the early twentieth century onwards of a number of well-informed works on the aims and methods of history teaching in schools. Some of these works, in common with the advocates of today's new history such as R. Ben Jones, have laid 'less emphasis on content and more on the process of learning' and on 'what is popularly called the Enquiry Method'. In the second place the authors of these earlier works, whether university dons, teacher trainers, schoolteachers or inspectors, whether singly or in committee, whether motivated by a wish to inculcate historical skills, mental discipline, patriotism, peace or moral excellence, have, almost without exception, taken pains to condemn the practice of teaching history as a simple body of received fact. An official memorandum on the study of history produced by the Scottish Education Department in 1907 provides a typical example. Having outlined the value of interest in the life of the past, of training in the laws of evidence, of a philosophical understanding of the development of human civilization, and 'a clarified moral sense', it concluded that 'compared with these, the mere accumulation of a knowledge of historical facts is a matter of quite secondary importance'.[60]

Finally, it is clear that whatever the faults and failures of history teachers and history teaching in the distant and immediate past, and much attention has been drawn to them by advocates of today's new history, it cannot be denied that the subject has achieved considerable prominence in our society. History has flourished as an independent area of academic inquiry, as a key component in programmes of liberal and professional education, as a favourite examination subject at secondary school level, and as an essentially popular interest and activity. This has not been the product of pure chance. It reflects, in part, a number of general social and political factors. It also reflects the fact that the new history of today is but the most recent in a series of new histories which in the last 100 years have enriched and enlarged the teaching and study of the subject.

Notes

1 W.E. Marsden (ed.), *Post-war Curriculum Development: An Historical Appraisal*, Leicester: History of Education Society, 1979.
2 History of Education Society, *The Changing Curriculum*, London: Methuen, 1971. Individual papers from the 1975 conference were published in the journal, *History of Education*.
3 W.E. Marsden, 'Historical approaches to curriculum study', in Marsden, op.cit., p. 82. One notable exception is the introduction to M. Palmer and G.R. Batho, *The Source Method in History Teaching*, London: Historical Association, 1981, pp. 5–7.

4 R. Ben Jones, 'Introduction: the new history', in R. Ben Jones (ed.), *Practical Approaches to the New History*, London: Hutchinson Educational, 1973, p. 14.
5 M.W. Keatinge and N.L. Frazer, *A History of England for Schools with Documents, Problems and Exercises*, London: Black, 2nd edn 1920, p. iv.
6 M.W. Keatinge, *Studies in the Teaching of History*, London: Black, 1910, pp. 38–9.
7 H.A. Drummond, *History in Schools: A Study of Some of its Problems*, London: Harrap, 1929, pp. 140–1.
8 Ibid., p. 138.
9 C.B. Firth, *The Learning of History in Elementary Schools*, London: Kegan Paul, Trench, Trubner and Co., 1929, pp. 10–11.
10 Ibid., p. 12.
11 F.C. Happold, *The Study of History in Schools, as a Training in the Art of Thought*, London: Bell, 1927, p. 4.
12 F.C. Happold, *The Approach to History*, London: Christophers, 1928, p. xv.
13 Ibid.
14 J.W. Allen, *The Place of History in Education*, Edinburgh: Blackwood, 1909.
15 J.J. Findlay, *History and its Place in Education*, London: University of London Press, 1923.
16 E.L. Hasluck, *The Teaching of History*, Cambridge: Cambridge University Press, 1926.
17 C.H. Jarvis, *The Teaching of History*, Oxford: Oxford University Press, 1917.
18 A. Rogers, 'Why teach history? The answer of 50 years', *Educational Review*, 1961–2, 14(2): 153–4, 160. The latter comment in particular refers to Happold. For the nineteenth century see G.R. Batho, 'Sources for the history of history teaching in elementary schools 1833–1914', in T.G. Cook (ed.), *Local Studies and the History of Education*, London: Methuen, 1972; and J. Roach, 'History teaching and examining in secondary schools, 1850–1900', *History of Education*, 1976, 5(2): 127–40.
19 For a recent comment on the state of play on this issue, see A. Gard and P.J. Lee, 'Educational objectives for the study of history reconsidered', in A.K. Dickinson and P.J. Lee (eds), *History Teaching and Historical Understanding*, London: Heinemann Educational Books, 1978, pp. 21–38.
20 Figures quoted in IAAM, *The Teaching of History in Secondary Schools*, Cambridge: Cambridge University Press, 3rd edn 1965, p. 2.
21 F.W. Maitland *et al.*, *Essays on the Teaching of History*, Cambridge: Cambridge University Press, 1901.
22 Ibid., p. 2.
23 Ibid., p. 66.
24 LCC Education Committee, *Report of a Conference on the Teaching of History in London Elementary Schools*, 1911, p. 46.
25 Ibid., p. 63.
26 F.R. Worts, *The Teaching of History in Schools: A New Approach*, London: Heinemann, 1935.
27 Ibid., p. ix.
28 IAAM, *Memorandum on the Teaching of History*, Cambridge: Cambridge University Press, 1925, preface.
29 Ibid., p. 9.
30 Worts, op. cit., p. 10.
31 Ibid.
32 Ibid., p. 12.
33 Ibid., p. 3.
34 Ibid., p. 48.
35 F.C. Happold, *Citizens in the Making*, London: Christophers, 1935, p. 15.
36 Ibid., p. 14.
37 See, for example, H.M. Madeley, *History as a School of Citizenship*, Oxford: Oxford University Press, 1920; and P.B. Showan, *Citizenship and the School*, Cambridge: Cambridge University Press, 1923, especially Part II, 'A scheme of civic instruction based on history', pp. 39–141.
38 Firth, op. cit., pp. 159–75.
39 M.V.C. Jeffreys, *History in Schools: The Study of Development*, London: Pitman, 1939, pp. 91–4.
40 F. Clarke, *Foundations of History Teaching*, Oxford: Oxford University Press, 1929, p. 167.

41 B.J. Elliott, 'The League of Nations Union and history teaching in England: a study in benevolent bias', *History of Education*, 1977, 6(2): 131–41.

42 IAAM, *The Teaching of History*, Cambridge: Cambridge University Press, 2nd edn 1957, p. 3.

43 W.H. Burston and C.W. Green (eds), *Handbook for History Teachers*, London: Methuen, 1962, 1972.

44 I.J.D. Steele, 'The teaching of history in England: an historical perspective', *History Teaching Review*, 1980, 12(1): 6, 11.

45 P. George, 'New syllabus problems in the comprehensive school', in G. Jones and L. Ward (eds), *New History, Old Problems: Studies in History Teaching*, Swansea: University College of Swansea Faculty of Education, 1978, p. 8.

46 D.J. Steel and L. Taylor, *Family History in Schools*, London: Phillimore, 1973, p. 3.

47 D. Gunning, *The Teaching of History*, London: Croom Helm, 1978, p. 13.

48 Ibid., p. 17.

49 Ibid., p. 13.

50 Ibid.

51 For example, M.B. Booth, *History Betrayed?*, London: Longmans, Green, 1969; and J. Duckworth, 'The evolution of the history syllabus in English schools in the first quarter of the 20th century', *History of Education Society Bulletin*, 1975, 15: 44–51.

52 B.J. Elliott, 'An early failure of curriculum reform: history teaching in England, 1918–1940', *Journal of Educational Administration and History*, 1980, 12(2): 41.

53 Ibid., p. 45.

54 Duckworth, op. cit., p. 44.

55 Quoted in E.J.R. Eaglesham, *The Foundations of 20th Century Education in England*, London: Routledge & Kegan Paul, 1967, p. 59.

56 *Report of the Consultative Committee on Examinations in Secondary Schools* (Cd. 6004), HMSO, 1911, pp. 164–6, 177–80, 357–8.

57 IAAM, *The Teaching of History*, Cambridge: Cambridge University Press, 2nd edn 1957, p. 117, quoting results published in the national press in 1955–6. Of a total of 990 awards, 196 were made in history, 176 in Classics, 210 in science and 408 in all other subjects combined.

58 Even by Steele, op. cit., p. 3.

59 Schools Council Enquiry I, *Young School Leavers*, HMSO, 1968, p. 3. Tables 10.4 and 10.5 have been compiled from statistics supplied in chapter 2 of the report.

60 Scottish Education Department, *Memorandum on the Study of History in Schools* (Cd. 3843), HMSO, 1907, p. 18.

CHAPTER 11

IMPERIALISM IN THE STUDY AND TEACHING OF HISTORY

J.A. Mangan (ed.), 'Benefits Bestowed'? Education and British Imperialism, Manchester: Manchester University Press, 1988, pp. 23–38

Introduction

This chapter is set in a British[1] context and is divided into four unequal parts. Following this brief introduction the second section considers the relationship between imperialism and formal historical study in the 1880s and subsequent years. The third part revisits that relationship in the 1980s. Finally some brief conclusions are drawn. Regrettably, in a piece of this length which takes a broad historical span for the purpose of indicating both change and continuity over time, many key issues can only be indicated rather than developed.

The formal educational system of a society, especially as expressed in its formal curriculum, represents a selection from the activities which certain members of that society – politicians, benefactors, administrators, clerics, teachers, parents, employers, students, pupils – regard as being particularly worthwhile.[2] A hundred years ago, the place of history in the formal curriculum of England was becoming measurably stronger, and recognized as worthwhile, just as in the 1980s it has become measurably weaker.[3] In the 1870s, separate honours degrees in history were established in the universities of Oxford and Cambridge. The *English Historical Review* was founded in 1886. At Manchester from 1890 and London from 1903, Tout and Pollard respectively helped to develop important historical schools in the newer universities. From the 1870s, history also became an accepted subject of study among the upper standards of elementary schools – a grant-earning 'Class' subject, indeed, under the terms of the Code of 1875. In 1900, it was included in the list of subjects expected to be taught in elementary schools 'as a rule'. The Secondary School Regulations of 1904 made history a compulsory subject at secondary school level.[4] Thus history was to achieve an important, if not always a central, role in the formal curricula of the English education system.

What is history and why should it be studied and taught?[5] The word has been used in several ways, for example, to mean the past, the human past or the disciplined study of the human past. By the 1880s, the apparatus of such disciplined study – university courses, an academic journal, a 'scientific' rather than a 'literary' approach – were emerging. In 1906, the Historical Association was founded. Its first council, which included 11 university staff, 9 from secondary schools and 4 from training colleges, reflected the status which history had achieved throughout the educational system and provided a forum for collaboration amongst its practitioners.[6]

The 1880s

In the 1680s, John Locke had written that 'As nothing teaches, so nothing delights more than history.'[7] Two hundred years later the new breed of professional historians were less interested in delighting their audiences and readers, and more concerned to find and teach the lessons of history.

At their head stood John Robert Seeley,[8] Regius Professor of History at Cambridge from 1869 until his death in 1895. His lecture course on the British Empire, delivered in 1881–2 and published in 1883 as *The Expansion of England*, established imperialism as a central theme of modern British history and in the public mind. Within two years the book had sold 80,000 copies. It remained in print until 1956. Thus Seeley, in the words of one of his followers:

> threw a powerful searchlight on the development of the British empire, and brought home to thousands of readers, who have never before thought of it, the sense that, after all, our Colonies are only England beyond the seas – a greater England but England all the same...[9]

Seeley, who had previously been Professor of Latin at University College, London, and who had been appointed to the Cambridge chair by Gladstone, thus helped to popularize and legitimize British imperialism in an intellectual sense, although the term was used only twice in the book, and on both occasions with reference to despotic rule.[10] The irony of all this was not lost upon contemporaries. In 1895 Jacobs, writing in *The Athenaeum*, declared, 'our Imperialism of today is the combined work of Beaconsfield and Seeley, a curious couple of collaborators'.[11]

What then did Seeley contribute to imperialism, socialization and education? On imperialism itself Seeley had little to say that was new as a result of research and analysis. Neither his idea nor his term of 'Greater Britain' was novel. The lesson that he drew from the history of the United States, namely not that colonists would inevitably outgrow the mother country but that in North America a federal state had been created which in spite of vast territories and a civil war was a nation of the first rank, was widely appreciated. But in predicting the emergence of Russia and the United States as the two superpowers and in arguing that if Britain wished to join them she must become a federal empire, he offered Greater Britain an ideal, which he justified by reference to history.

Seeley's ideal of empire, which influenced politicians, administrators, the general public and students in universities and schools, both within Britain and within the empire as well, may be summed up as follows. The British Empire was unlike most previous empires. It represented, particularly in Australia, Canada and New Zealand, an extension of British people into lands that were so thinly populated that little conquest or domination took place. This was Britain's or England's natural destiny, achieved in unplanned fashion, 'in a fit of absence of mind'.[12] Seeley even extended some of this interpretation to India: 'for we are not really conquerors of India and we cannot rule her as conquerors'.[13] No specific racial superiority was claimed. Rather he argued that medieval societies needed to be transformed into modern ones – by peace, good government, railways, sanitation and Christianity – and that being part of the British Empire was a mutually beneficial way of achieving these ends. He recognized that 'great mischiefs' as well as 'vast benefits'[14] might occur in India, and acknowledged that a nationalist movement, as opposed to a mutiny, could not be resisted. He also acknowledged that Canada and the West Indies might prefer to join the United States rather than to stay with Britain.

Seeley's examples were drawn from the 'white' dominions, India and the West Indies, but the principle of mutual benefit was subsequently extended to all areas. Lord Lugard, for example, expounded the principle of the 'Dual Mandate' – that British rule benefited the colonized as much as the colonizers – in respect of central Africa.[15] In 1924 Lord Leverhulme, with complete disregard for historical accuracy, declared that 'organizing ability is the peculiar trait characteristic of the white man' which would make the 'African native... happier, produce the best, and live under the larger conditions of prosperity when his labour is directed and organized by his white brother who has all these million years' start ahead of him'.[16]

The flaws in Seeley's own analysis are easily seen. He failed sufficiently to examine the legitimate needs and aspirations of colonial populations or to suggest practical schemes for promoting mutual self-interest.[17] At the turn of the century, John Burns, John Morley and David Lloyd George were among the leading Liberal critics of empire as the defeats, incompetence and deaths of 20,000 Afrikaners (mainly women and children) in concentration camps during the second Boer War polarized imperial sentiment. In *Imperialism* (1902),[18] John A. Hobson, the journalist and economist, characterized the British Empire as an expression of exploitation and economic greed. By 1902, moreover, as Judd and Slinn have pointed out, barely 12 per cent of the people of the empire were of European let alone British origin, whilst Hinduism and Islam were the major religions.[19]

Seeley's contribution to the doctrine of imperialism, however, must be coupled, for the purposes of this study at least, with his concept of the historian as the educator, particularly the political educator, of the nation. His role in this respect may be compared with that of the historians of the so-called 'Prussian school' notably Droysen, Sybel and Treitschke, who used historical analysis to explain and justify the rise of Prussia into Germany.[20] The opening sentences of *The Expansion* indicate Seeley's personal commitment to the use of history for the purposes of socialization and of education:

> It is a favourite maxim of mine that history, while it should be scientific in its method, should pursue a practical object. That is, it should not merely gratify the reader's curiosity about the past, but modify his view of the present and his forecast of the future. Now if this maxim be sound, the history of England ought to end with something that might be called a moral.[21]

Seeley's history, indeed, was future-oriented. Whilst, however, his condemnation of the 'foppish kind of history which aims at literary display'[22] would be widely shared, statements such as 'We shall all no doubt be wise after the event; we study history that we may be wise before the event'[23] were more controversial. Seeley's emphasis was upon the usefulness of historical study and teaching – for the purpose of informing both the present and the future. He warned that a scientific approach to history, the mere collection of facts, would be of little value 'if they lead to no great truths having at the same time scientific generality and momentous practical bearings'.[24] In his concern to establish history as a social science and a means of socialization, Seeley argued that the training, equipment and purposes of historians would need to be radically revised. 'Each university will create a school of historians who will be as strong on the theoretical side as on the side of mere research. They will be sociologists, economists, jurists, as well as chroniclers and antiquarians.'[25] Such schools would be particularly concerned with history as 'the lesson book of politics... a record of truth not to be altered and not to be ended, written to correct our prejudices'.[26] Modern history would predominate. Let the historians of Holland and Sweden dwell in the sixteenth and seventeenth centuries. Their days of national greatness were past. England's development as 'a maritime, colonising and industrial country'[27] should be at the centre of the historical stage.

In the late-nineteenth and early-twentieth centuries, 'a succession of Seeleys'[28] developed these themes. Prominent among them were Hugh Egerton, appointed in 1905 as the first Beit Professor of Colonial History at Oxford, and A.P. Newton, the first Rhodes Professor of Imperial History at the University of London from 1919. Together with Sir Charles Lucas, Chairman of the Royal Colonial Institute from 1915, they not only promoted the study of imperial history at university level, but also sought, by means of an imperial studies campaign that included popular lectures, lantern slides and the promotion of Empire Day, to raise the imperial consciousness of the nation as a whole. In January 1916 at the height (or depth) of the First World War, the tenth annual meeting of the Historical Association began with a paper from Lucas on 'The teaching of imperial history'. This topic, coupled with naval history, dominated the whole meeting.[29]

Lucas's campaign for the teaching of imperial history was based upon his belief that the general public, and especially many elements of the working classes, had failed sufficiently to appreciate the benefits of empire. This was very serious in wartime when German propaganda might turn the empire into a source of weakness rather than of strength. Thus in 1915 in *The British Empire*, six lectures addressed to the members of the Working Men's College, Lucas sought specifically to counter 'a feeling among some, at any rate, of the working men of England, that the Empire was of no use to them, and that they had no use for the Empire',[30] with two main arguments. The first was the superiority of the British concept of empire over that of Germany. The Germans, he asserted, sought merely 'to remake men in their own image'.[31] The British approach, on the other hand, was 'to combine general supervision and control with toleration, and not toleration only, but encouragement of diverse customs and characteristics'.[32] Second, he argued that the success of this policy was shown by the support given by all members of the empire, even the recently defeated Boers, to the war effort.

Two years later, in an introduction to A.P. Newton's *The Old Empire and the New* (1917), itself based on a course of Rhodes lectures delivered at University College, London in the spring term of 1917, Lucas placed the responsibility for socializing the public further into the imperial ideal firmly upon history teachers in schools and universities:

> The citizens must be reached through the teachers: the teachers must be of the best quality: the universities, especially the younger universities in the great industrial centres must provide and equip the teachers...
>
> When Imperial Studies are mentioned, history naturally rises first to view, and none can doubt that greater prominence than at present ought to be given to our overseas history in courses of study, examinations and textbooks.[33]

After the war Lucas continued to press the message that teachers should educate pupils to accept the nation's and their own imperial destiny and responsibilities. For example, in 1921 he gave a series of lectures at the Royal Colonial Institute to a study circle of London County Council (LCC) teachers, lectures subsequently published as *The Partition and Colonization of Africa* (1922). Trusteeship was his theme. Given the historical fact that Africa had become 'a dependency of Europe',[34] he argued that Europeans should be 'trustees of the black men until in some distant future (if ever) the black men have become able to stand by themselves'.[35]

In his inaugural lecture as Beit Professor, delivered in April 1906, Hugh Egerton echoed Seeley in several ways. The study and teaching of colonial history would make for 'practical edification'[36] in respect of the present and the future. Modern history was stressed; the year 1837 at which the English history course at Oxford terminated 'marks the starting point of the self-governing British Empire of today',[37] and the time had come 'when the history of England should be identified with the history of the English Empire'.[38] Egerton went beyond Seeley, however, in his ideal of empire as 'a collection of allied nations under a common crown rather than a fusion of nationalities into a single type'.[39] This ideal also involved a greater awareness of other historical perspectives – an empathetic approach. 'It is for us to teach and learn history in such a way, as that the historical imagination may be cultivated, and we may recognize the point of view of those from whom we may fundamentally differ.'[40] Such a point of view included that of many Americans who, Egerton informed his audience, thought 'of our land as a played-out island, chiefly inhabited by the unemployed and by decaying industries'.[41]

With the outbreak of war in 1914, however, Egerton in common with other university dons put his pen to national service with his contributions to the series of Oxford Pamphlets.[42] C.R.L. Fletcher, fellow of Magdalen and co-author with Rudyard Kipling of the highly patriotic *A School History of England* (1911),[43] took the responsibility of explaining the German Empire to the British public. *The Germans, their Empire, and How They Made It* (no. 6) was an historical account of Prussian policy from the seventeenth century, whilst *The Germans, their Empire, and What They Covet* (no. 7) warned of the territorial ambitions aroused by the pan-German school. In *India and the War* (no. 22) Sir Ernest Trevelyan discussed 'the reasons which account for the striking manifestations of Indian loyalty', whilst Egerton contributed *The British Dominions and the War* (no. 21) and *Is the British Empire the Result of Wholesale Robbery?* (no. 23). In supplying a negative answer to this particular question, Egerton argued that overseas expansion was a natural development for powerful states, that much of the British Empire had been acquired before the creation of Germany, that in the acquisition the British had been no more unscrupulous than other colonizing powers, and that it was now the responsibility of the current generation to show themselves worthy, in battle, of the empire which their forefathers had committed to their care.

Egerton died in 1927, Lucas in 1931. Arthur Newton, some 20 years their junior, lived on until 1942. His *A Junior History of the British Empire Overseas*, published in 1933, was written at the suggestion and with the support of the Education Committee of the Federation of Chambers of Commerce of the British Empire, and of the Imperial Studies Committee of the Royal Empire Society, from whom teachers might borrow lantern slides and further pictures to supplement the several illustrations in the book itself. One distinctive feature of this work was its emphasis upon the co-prosperity of the empire. In the 1920s and 1930s, economic issues often outweighed political or military considerations, and the value of the empire to the hungry and unemployed of Britain needed to be reaffirmed. Thus emphasis was placed upon the role of Africa as a supplier of raw materials and a market for manufactured products. 'West Africa gives us the palm oil from which soap and margarine are largely made in British factories by British workmen', whilst 'A demand arises for manufactured goods that must be imported, and so trade flows both ways – raw materials out of Africa and manufactures in. So both sides benefit.'[44]

The general contribution of history textbooks to the socialization of British children, both in respect of imperialism and of other values, has been well charted in recent years and will not be further considered here. In 1970 Valerie Chancellor examined the nineteenth-century schooling process in *History for their Masters*,[45] while John MacKenzie showed that the message was not only conveyed through history textbooks but that geography, English and religion were also used as vehicles of imperial instruction.[46] F. Glendenning placed the racial attitudes contained in nineteenth- and twentieth-century history textbooks in a comparative perspective,[47] whilst a recent study by Kathryn Castle has distinguished British stereotypes of Africans, Chinese and Indians in school textbooks and children's periodicals in the period 1890–1914.[48]

Suffice it to say that by the early years of the twentieth century, although the formal teaching of imperial and colonial history as such was not dominant either at university or school levels in Britain, three basic tenets were widely accepted. First, that there was an empire with which Britain's immediate past, present and future were inextricably bound up, an empire whose bonds had been strengthened and bounds increased by a shared experience in the First World War. Second, that such an empire could be justified on the grounds of British constitutional, cultural, financial, legal, moral, religious and technological superiority, a superiority which though not predetermined was explicable in terms of her history and of her heroes. Third, that the peoples of the empire were largely contented with their increasing prosperity, and appreciative of British order, justice and fair play, and would in the fullness of time achieve dominion status within a federal system for which the term 'commonwealth' would be more appropriate than 'empire'.

The 1980s

In the 1980s in Britain the place of imperialism in the study and teaching of history is very different from what it was in Seeley's or even Newton's day. Radical changes have taken place within the last 25 years. Ronald Robinson, Beit Professor and thus a successor of Egerton, acknowledged these changes in the introduction to the second edition of *Africa and the Victorians* (1981), first published some 20 years earlier. Robinson stated that had he and the late John Gallacher been writing in the 1970s their 'gaze would have been fixed less on imperial decisions at the centre and more on African co-operation and resistance', but warned against simply replacing 'an empire of rulers almost without subjects' by another 'of subjects almost without rulers'.[49]

This section is divided into two broad areas. The first examines the general consequences for historical study of the ending of empire; the second focuses upon the specific implications for history teaching in schools in Britain today.

In the 1880s, Britain had a colonial empire whose existence impinged upon the histories of many other countries. Such an empire no longer exists. Thus imperialism as far as Britain is concerned would appear to have a past but not much of a present or a future. Britain's claims to superiority over other nations and peoples have been severely dented. The Commonwealth, a not-insignificant residue or achievement of empire, has no close federal structure. Britain herself is often isolated in Commonwealth discussions. She hovers uncertainly between the Commonwealth, Europe and an indeterminate 'special relationship' with a former colony – the United States.

Bernard Porter's widely acclaimed volume, *The Lion's Share* (2nd edn 1984), may be seen as rationalizing for British opinion in the 1980s the disappearance of empire, much as Seeley's *Expansion* had rationalized its appearance 100 years before. Porter's argument that imperialism was for Britain a symptom not of strength but of decline, a development that helped to obscure fundamental weaknesses in British society and economy which were becoming apparent by the 1870s, has been corroborated by studies from other historical perspectives.[50] His theory that Britain's freedom to pursue the true interests of her people was severely compromised by the need to maintain and defend the empire appears to have been confirmed, once again, by the decision to pursue the costly principle of 'fortress Falklands'. Porter, arguing within the broad concept of British decline, concluded that:

> The empire which she had accumulated...was an incident in the course of that decline. It was acquired originally as a result of that decline to stave it off. It was retained largely in spite of that decline and it was surrendered as a final confirmation of that decline.[51]

A second historical consequence of the disappearance of the visible British and other European colonial empires has been to focus attention on other types of imperialism, both pre- and post-colonial. International capitalism, multinational companies, communism, foreign-aid programmes, cultural programmes and the major military alliances dominated by the United States and USSR, may be counted as examples of post-colonial imperialism.[52] Such a development may allow a more detached view to be taken by historians of recent European imperialism. Indeed, David Fieldhouse has suggested that:

> The modern imperial historian, unlike Seeley, has no territorial base, or for that matter loyalties. He [*sic*] places himself in the interstices of his subject, poised above the 'area of interaction' like some satellite placed in space, looking, Janus-like, in two or more ways at the same time.[53]

One example of this overarching approach is to be found in R.O. Collins (ed.), *Problems in the History of Colonial Africa, 1860–1960* (1970)[54] which comprises 44 readings (including one from Fieldhouse headed 'The myth of economic exploitation') from a wide range of authors, grouped around seven key historical 'problems'. Such claims to detachment and objectivity, however, may be seen as an attempt to soften the full force of the legitimate reinterpretation of European colonization from the perspective of the colonized.[55]

Greater emphasis upon pre- and post-colonial periods of history, and a reconsideration of the profit and loss account of the colonial period itself, are two of the main themes in the recent historiography of formerly colonized countries, as of Britain. The cultural damage inflicted by imperialist powers who denied or diminished the history, religion, customs and language of those whom they conquered has been identified. Historians like Gopal have emphasized the harm rather than the benefit done by the British to the Indian economy in respect of agriculture, industry and commerce, and hence to Indian society as well.[56] Walter Rodney's influential volume, *How Europe Underdeveloped Africa* (1972),[57] has challenged the doctrine of dual mandate and mutual benefit. Much of this reinterpretation has taken place within a Marxist–Leninist historical framework.

There is no space here to consider in detail Lenin's theory of imperialism as the highest stage of capitalism – the oppression of nations on a new historical basis. In turning to consider the contemporary situation in British schools, however, instructive comparisons may be made with communist and colonial and post-colonial classrooms.

History lessons in all secondary schools in the USSR 'are conducted according to common programmes and textbooks' and are thoroughly grounded in Marxist–Leninist philosophy. In their study of the first 40 years of the twentieth century, ninth-grade pupils pay particular attention to Lenin's teaching on imperialism which is 'considered in the light of the economic, social and political development of foreign countries, including Britain. The programme covers the treatment of working-class and socialist movements, national-liberation struggles of peoples in Asia, Africa and Latin America.' In the following year, the culmination of these struggles is considered in a major topic entitled 'National liberation movements and the collapse of the imperialist colonial system'.[58]

More than 30 years ago in the pages of *History*, F. Musgrove reported on his experience of teaching School Certificate history to boys in Uganda. In an article entitled 'History teaching within a clash of cultures', he noted that his pupils had little interest in the history of the British Empire other than to criticize and to rejoice in its defeats. Given such an attitude, Musgrove found his attempts to promote the glory of belonging to the empire and the ideal of commonwealth falling upon deaf ears. 'If a pupil is already critical in his approach to the Empire, he will tend to read in its history only those things which discredit it: he looks for and sees, the way in which it has broken up rather than the way in which it has grown.'[59] In the 1950s the Ugandan boys' heroes were the newly liberated peoples of India and their leaders who had succeeded in throwing off British rule, not Warren Hastings or Robert Clive.

In India itself Jogindra Banerji, in a 1957 publication of the International Text-Book Institute at Brunswick in West Germany, confirmed this analysis but also described a progression to the neutralist position. As school children, Indians:

> were made to learn Indian history that sought to provide justification for the political relationship prevailing between Britain and India. Paradoxically, the reaction, at later stages of India's struggle, was to create blind spots in the young people's mind, encourage a black-and-white attitude to history that tended to make Britain the villain of the piece. Today, against the background of friendship between India and Britain, the entirely negative attitude of such history teaching has become evident.[60]

In British schools today, history teachers have the role of explaining the end of empire to their pupils. Within such schools, moreover, are many pupils who themselves, or whose parents or grandparents, were born in former colonies. The multicultural empire and its passing has produced, or rather re-emphasized and reproduced, the concept of multicultural Britain. Musgrove wrote of teaching history within a conflict of cultures. Today's history teachers face the daunting but important task of teaching their subject within a conciliation of cultures.

One strategy for achieving this end has been to emphasize Britain's earlier imperial or colonial past – as a part of the Roman empire, or as conquered by Angles, Saxons, Danes and Normans. For example, this longer historical perspective has been employed to good effect at Tulse Hill School in South London which poses the question to its second years of 'Who are the British?' Answers include not only Angles, Saxons, Danes and Normans, but also others from continental Europe, Irish and Jews who came to Britain in the early-modern and modern periods.[61] Similarly, a study of earlier black settlement in Britain provides a useful perspective on post-Second-World-War settlement by people from Afro-Caribbean countries.[62]

Another strategy has been to repeat the regular call for greater attention to be paid in school history courses to the histories and achievements of non-European civilizations and empires. Such a strategy may be justified by the very small proportion of the world's population who live on the European continent, by the increasing interdependence of today's world, and by the need to counter the doctrines, attitudes and assumptions of innate racial superiority and inferiority fostered, explicitly or implicitly, by some earlier teaching of imperial history.[63]

Further reference to the problems and successes of school history teaching (including imperial history) in contemporary Britain may be found in such publications as David Edgington's *The Role of History in Multicultural Education* (1982)[64] and *History in the Primary and Secondary Years: An HMI View* (1985).[65]

Conclusion

Two points many be made in conclusion – in respect of imperialism, socialization and the contribution of the study and teaching of history to education.

British imperialism rested ultimately upon a belief. By the end of the eighteenth century, as Marshall and Williams have shown:

> educated Englishmen and some wider sections of British society had come to believe that the workings of non-European societies were comprehensible to them, and that what was being revealed were societies inferior to their own and capable of being changed for the better by outside intervention.[66]

Socialization into acceptance of that belief became one of the purposes of the study and teaching of history. A collective historical consciousness or memory, based on a series of selected concerns and episodes, was established and handed down. The origins of empire were projected backwards to the Tudor period. Heroes, and less frequently heroines, were chosen to exemplify certain values and qualities, often exhibited in pursuit or defence of the cause of Greater Britain. Thus in the 1950s, in extolling the worth of imperial history as a vehicle for moral value and the improvement of character, an Historical Association pamphlet by C.R.N. Routh entitled *Notes on the Teaching of British Imperial History*, declared that 'Vision, courage, humanity and faith are qualities which shine out for all to see in such men as Raffles, Durham, Livingstone, Rhodes, therefore "Let the Great Story be Told." '[67]

Nevertheless, it is important to notice that Routh's starting point was the neglect of imperial history in schools and universities, coupled with pupils' and students' suspicions of imperialism. Socialization through history teaching in Britain has not been as closely controlled as in many other countries in which centrally prescribed syllabuses, textbooks and teaching methods have been employed. Whilst the themes of this chapter, and indeed of this book, have led to an emphasis on the highly visible manifestations of imperialism, socialization and education, important countercurrents have also flowed throughout the last 200 years. Opposition and indifference to imperialism has shown itself in Britain in all classes of society and on a variety of grounds – economic, moral, political and social. Such opposition and indifference have also been reflected in the study and teaching of history.

Notes

1 Although regrettably the use of the term 'British' in respect of the historical treatment of this topic is not consistent and is often equated with 'English'.

2 On this point see D. Lawton, *Class, Culture and the Curriculum*, London: Routledge and Kegan Paul, 1975, pp. 85–6.
3 See R. Aldrich, 'Interesting and useful', *Teaching History*, 1987, 47: 11–14; and A. Taylor Milne, 'History at the universities: then and now', *History*, 1974, 59(195): 33–46, with particular reference to Scotland.
4 P. Gordon and D. Lawton, *Curriculum Change in the Nineteenth and Twentieth Centuries*, London: Hodder and Stoughton, 1978, pp. 15–23.
5 See A. Rogers, 'Why teach history? The answer of fifty years', *Educational Review*, 1961–2, 14(1): 10–20 and 14(2): 152–62. For a recent international discussion see the *Journal of the International Society for History Didactics, Informations, Mitteilungen, Communications*, 1986, 7(2): 90–102.
6 *The Historical Association, 1906–1956*, London: Historical Association, 1955, p. 8.
7 J.L. Axtell (ed.), *The Educational Writings of John Locke*, Cambridge: Cambridge University Press, 1968, p. 293.
8 On Seeley see D. Wormell, *Sir John Seeley and the Uses of History*, Cambridge: Cambridge University Press, 1980, which has an extensive bibliography.
9 H.E. Egerton, *A Short History of British Colonial Policy*, London: Methuen, 1897, p. 6.
10 For the context see R. Koebner and H.D. Schmidt, *Imperialism: The Story and Significance of a Political Word, 1840–1960*, Cambridge: Cambridge University Press, 1964, pp. 173–4.
11 Quoted by P. Burroughs, 'John Robert Seeley and British imperial history', *Journal of Imperial and Commonwealth History* (hereafter *JICH*), 1973, 1(2): 207.
12 J.R. Seeley, *The Expansion of England*, London: Macmillan, 1883, p. 8.
13 Ibid., p. 234.
14 Ibid., p. 305.
15 F.D. Lugard, *The Dual Mandate in British Tropical Africa*, Edinburgh: W. Blackwood and Sons, 1922.
16 Quoted in A. Temu and B. Swai, *Historians and Africanist History: A Critique*, London: Zed, 1981, p. 153.
17 Though he supported the Imperial Federation League. See Koebner and Schmidt, op. cit., pp. 177–95.
18 J.A. Hobson, *Imperialism*, London: James Nisbet, 1902.
19 D. Judd and P. Slinn, *The Evolution of the Modern Commonwealth, 1902–80*, London: Macmillan, 1982, p. 4.
20 For an appreciation of the Prussian school see H. Flaig, 'The historian as pedagogue of the nation', *History*, 1974, 59(195): 18–32.
21 Seeley, op. cit., 1883, p. 1.
22 Ibid., p. 166.
23 Ibid., p. 169.
24 Ibid., p. 3.
25 J.R. Seeley, 'The teaching of history', in G.S. Hall (ed.), *Methods of Teaching History*, Boston, MA: Ginn, Heath and Company, 2nd edn 1902, p. 201.
26 Ibid., p. 202.
27 Seeley, op. cit., 1883, p. 80.
28 C.P. Lucas, *The British Empire*, London: Macmillan, 1915, p. 233. For a discussion of Seeley's successors see two articles by J.G. Greenlee, ' "A succession of Seeleys": the "Old School" re-examined', *JICH*, 1976, 4(3): 266–82 and 'Imperial studies and the unity of empire', *JICH*, 1979, 7(3): 321–35.
29 For an account of this meeting see K. Robbins, '*History*, the Historical Association and the "national past"', *History*, 1981, 66(218): 413–25. The Vere Harmsworth Professorship in Naval History was established at Cambridge in 1919, and converted into Imperial and Naval History in 1933.
30 Lucas, op. cit., 1915, p. 1.
31 Ibid., p. 197.
32 Ibid.
33 A.P. Newton, *The Old Empire and the New*, London: Dent, 1917, pp. vi–vii.
34 C.P. Lucas, *The Partition and Colonization of Africa*, Oxford: Clarendon, 1922, p. 196.
35 Ibid., p. 207.
36 H.E. Egerton, *The Claims of the Study of Colonial History upon the Attention of the University of Oxford*, Oxford: Clarendon, 1906, p. 8.

37 Ibid., p. 11.
38 Ibid., p. 21.
39 Ibid., p. 22.
40 Ibid., p. 32.
41 Ibid., p. 23.
42 The five Oxford pamphlets referred to in this paragraph were all published in 1914 by Oxford University Press. For a full discussion of Oxford's involvement with imperialism see R. Symonds, *Oxford and Empire: The Last Lost Cause?*, London: Macmillan, 1986.
43 C.R.L. Fletcher and R. Kipling, *A School History of England*, Oxford: Clarendon, 1911.
44 A.P. Newton, *A Junior History of the British Empire Overseas*, London: Blackie and Son, 1933, pp. 241–3.
45 V. Chancellor, *History for their Masters: Opinion in the History Textbook, 1800–1914*, Bath: Adams and Dart, 1970. The Historical Association's collection of textbooks is now housed in the School of Education at the University of Durham. A catalogue of the pre-1915 material was published as an appendix to the *History of Education Society Bulletin*, 1984, 33, whilst a separate handlist covering the period 1915–39, compiled by J.S. Thompson, was published by the Historical Association in 1985. Both lists have useful introductions by Gordon Batho.
46 J. MacKenzie, *Propaganda and Empire*, Manchester: Manchester University Press, 1984, especially ch. 7, 'Imperialism and the school textbook'.
47 F. Glendenning, 'School history textbooks and racial attitudes, 1804–1911', *Journal of Educational Administration and History*, 1973, 5(2): 33–44. F. Glendenning, 'The evolution of history teaching in British and French schools in the 19th and 20th centuries, with special reference to attitudes to race and colonialism in history textbooks', Keele, PhD, 1975.
48 K. Castle, 'An examination of the attitudes towards non-Europeans in British school history textbooks and children's periodicals, 1890–1914, with special reference to the Indian, the African and the Chinese', CNAA, PhD, 1986. Since published as K. Castle, *Britannia's Children: Reading Colonialism through Children's Books and Magazines*, Manchester: Manchester University Press, 1996.
49 R. Robinson, J. Gallacher and A. Denny, *Africa and the Victorians: The Official Mind of Imperialism*, London: Macmillan, 2nd edn 1981, pp. xxii–xxiii.
50 See, for example, M.J. Wiener, *English Culture and the Decline of the Industrial Spirit, 1850–1980*, Cambridge: Cambridge University Press, 1981.
51 B. Porter, *The Lion's Share: A Short History of British Imperialism, 1850–1983*, London: Longman, 2nd edn 1984, p. 364.
52 For a discussion of the paradoxes of imperialism after empire see R. Robinson, 'Imperial theory and the questions of imperialism after empire', *JICH*, 1984, 12(2): 42–54.
53 D. Fieldhouse, 'Can Humpty-Dumpty be put together again? Imperial history in the 1980s', *JICH*, 1984, 12(2): 18–19.
54 R.O. Collins (ed.), *Problems in the History of Colonial Africa, 1860–1960*, Englewood Cliffs, NJ: Prentice-Hall, 1970.
55 On this point see Temu and Swai, op. cit., especially pp. 115–20, 'The fallacy of objectivism'.
56 S. Gopal, *Modern India*, London: Historical Association, 1967.
57 W. Rodney, *How Europe Underdeveloped Africa*, London: Bogle-L'Ouverture, 1972.
58 A.G. Kiloskov, 'Teaching history in the Soviet secondary general education school', *Teaching History*, 1983, 37: 12–13.
59 F. Musgrove, 'History teaching within a conflict of cultures', *History*, 1955, 40(140): 301.
60 J.K. Banerji, *Laying the Foundation of 'One World'*, Brunswick: Albert Limbach, 1957, p. 3.
61 Tulse Hill School history syllabus. See also N. File, 'History at Tulse Hill School, London', *Teaching History*, 1982, 32: 14.
62 See N. File and C. Power, *Black Settlers in Britain, 1555–1958*, London: Heinemann Educational, 1981.
63 See I. Grosvenor, 'History and the multi-cultural curriculum, a case study', *Teaching History*, 1982, 32: 18–19; and the support materials produced by the Metropolitan Borough of Sandwell. Although A. Dyer, *History in a Multi-Cultural Society*, London: Historical Association, 1982, has suggested that the multicultural make-up of Britain makes the teaching of British history in schools more, not less, important.

64 D. Edgington, *The Role of History in Multicultural Education*, London: Extramural Division, School of Oriental and African Studies, 1982.
65 *History in the Primary and Secondary School Years: An HMI View*, London: HMSO, 1985.
66 P.J. Marshall and G. Williams, *The Great Map of Mankind: British Perceptions of the World in the Age of Enlightenment*, London: Dent, 1982, p. 303.
67 C.R.N. Routh, *Notes on the Teaching of British Imperial History*, London: Historical Association, 1952, p. 5.

PART 6

EDUCATION OTHERWISE

CHAPTER 12

LEARNING BY PLAYING

Education Today, MCB University Press, 1985, 35(2): 28–36

Understanding play

Playing is an activity generally, though by no means exclusively, connected with the young of higher mammals – for example, foals and lambs, kittens and puppies and children.[1] Play involves active participation by the player and is freely chosen. It appears to be essentially pleasurable, and apparently has no purpose outside itself. As such it can be considered to be the opposite of work, and even of learning. Playtime in school is the break between lessons, a chance to run and frolic, to let off steam before returning to the serious business of the classroom. Indeed, in 1855 in the *Principles of Psychology*[2] Herbert Spencer suggested the 'surplus energy' theory of play although, as he acknowledged, the idea had been foreshadowed some years before in the writings of the German poet, Friedrich von Schiller. This theory, which was reformulated in 1932 by E.C. Tolman,[3] maintained that animals expend a certain amount of energy on survival tasks – work, and that surplus energy is thus available for non-productive functions – play. In its cruder forms, however, the surplus energy theory of play takes inadequate account of other human needs. Playing, particularly by older children and adults, may draw deeply upon reserves rather than excesses of physical energy. For example, a game of squash at the end of a tiring day at school, home, office or factory may be physically exhausting but psychologically stimulating or relaxing – a genuine form of recreation. This alternative theory of play as recreation, restoration or relaxation seems particularly appropriate to the urban, industrialized and commercial world in which fatigue may be the result of excessive mental strain, and alleviation be provided by strenuous physical activity.

It will be convenient at this point to identify some other explanations of play, particularly in so far as they relate to learning.

The idea of play as preparation has a long history, and found a place in the writings of both Plato and Aristotle. It is in many respects the opposite of 'surplus energy' in so far as it maintains that play is an essential stage in survival. 'Lower' species often come into the world in a well-developed physical state, with instincts apparently so strongly implanted that they can almost immediately get on with the basic tasks of adult life – feeding and reproducing. On the other hand, human beings have a delayed start. They are born into the world in a particularly helpless and vulnerable condition, and require many years to gain full use and control of their several functions and faculties. Much of children's play involves obvious imitation of adult behaviour, for example, playing at mothers and fathers, teachers or doctors.

In 1901, the preparation theory of play found a particular expression in a book by Karl Groos entitled *The Play of Man*.[4] For Groos, play was the means whereby the young of this most complex organism in the animal kingdom could practise and perfect the wide range of instincts necessary for survival as adult human beings. Though the 'pre-exercise' theory of play, as it came to be called, may be criticized for the extent to which it is too strongly rooted in instincts and Darwinian notions of the survival of the fittest, its emphasis on the physical and sensual nature of early play – the scrabbling in sand, the pouring of water, running, swinging and jumping – is widely accepted today.

Charles Darwin's *Origin of Species* (1859),[5] which emphasized that human beings were essentially part of the animal kingdom, rather than part of a separate divine plan, has had important implications for theories of human play. For example, the 'recapitulation theory' was also grounded in evolutionary ideas, and in the first decade of the twentieth century came to prominence in the writings of the American psychologist, G.S. Hall. It differed from preparation and pre-exercise theories, however, in being essentially backward- rather than forward-looking.

Hall argued that, in playing, both children and adults recapitulate the earlier history of the species. In its more extreme forms this theory presents a simple developmental sequence. The toddler runs through a puddle in memory of her or his amphibious ancestors, soon progresses to climbing and swinging, the monkey stage, and at about the age of ten delights in group camping and outdoor pursuits in imitation of the activities of primeval men and women. Such recapitulation of encoded instincts, however, is for the purpose of their reforming or purging rather than for practising and completion.

Play as therapy is particularly linked with the name and work of Sigmund Freud and his followers. To the child the world is at times a confusing and disturbing place over which he or she has little control. Much play or fantasy gives children, and indeed many adults, the chance to re-order people, events and circumstances into patterns in which they can themselves feel secure and grown up, and assume an active rather than a passive role. Playing thus becomes therapeutic, a means of diminishing anxieties and pain and of increasing pleasure and wish fulfilment.

One of the closest connections between playing and learning appeared in the work of the Swiss developmental psychologist, Jean Piaget. For the first two years of life, the child engages in basic sensor-motor play, as for example, in the repetition of simple movements, waving a rattle, throwing it from the cot, playing pat-a-cake. From two to seven years the child enters the pre-operational stage of thinking. Play is now characterized by energy, creativity, imitation and imagination. There is much delight in climbing apparatus and tricycles, in dressing up and let's pretend. A doll becomes a baby brother or sister; a fallen tree, a spaceship. From 8 to 12 the concrete operational stage occurs. Play can now be subjected to rules and codes – team games become possible in the junior school. The development of motor skills has permitted the riding of bicycles, whilst greater understanding of the real world promotes a decline in make-believe play. The final stage of formal operational thinking allows the most sophisticated types of play, but also ushers in a period leading to adult life when playing as such may have a much lower priority than hitherto.

For Piaget, therefore, play is developmental, and essentially dependent upon the stage of thinking or cognitive processes of the child, who thus progresses from repetition and simple experimentation to elaborate playing. In terms of Piaget's general theory, early play has much in common with assimilation, the shaping of the world to fit the child's particularly limited cognitive state. Later on, however, accommodation of the self to the real world requires less play, or play for more utilitarian purposes, whether recreational or competitive. Nevertheless, play for Piaget is not simply a consequence of development, it is also a prime means of promoting development by providing a variety of pleasant and non-stressful learning situations. A developmental theory of play, however, must be sufficiently flexible to take account not only of variations in personalities and cognitive states, but also in environmental and cultural factors. For example, some children seldom experience rule-governed or team games. Others continue with symbolic play, albeit in more sophisticated forms, throughout their lives.

The theory of play as arousal or stimulus seeking, as a means of confirming one's existence, is widely held today and will doubtless gain increasing credibility in those societies or groups in which opportunities for work are in transition or decline. Its origins can be traced to German thinkers of the late eighteenth and early nineteenth centuries, including Friedrich Froebel, the founder of the kindergarten movement. He believed that the natural state of children, when not asleep, was to be in motion, to be active and to play. Human beings in general avoid boredom and monotony and seek stimulation and variety. Work carried out at the Motor Performance and Play Research Laboratory at the University of Illinois is but one example of modern research that confirms and substantiates this theory.[6]

Thus it appears that even in the first few months of life the human infant is playing an active role. The play between parent and baby – cooing, smiling, gurgling, laughing, gazing, tickling, bouncing – is a two-way process virtually from the start. The young child implores not only parents but also anyone and everyone to 'look at me' as he or she jumps down a step, splashes through a paddling pool, or throws a ball high into the air. Adult play, whether sporting, social or creative, whether principally characterized by effort or relaxation, may be interpreted as a means of seeking stimulus, approval and self-fulfilment in the perpetual human search for happiness.

In conclusion, although each of the given theories is useful in illuminating some of the dimensions of play, no satisfactory single, coherent explanation has yet been found. Indeed, the dividing line between games and work is frequently unclear. The games teacher writes on Susan's report (and on many others) 'she works well in this subject'. An adult sports team may include amateurs and part-time and full-time professionals in its ranks, yet all are players. The situation has been well summarized by Michael Ellis, himself a supporter of the arousal theory, in *Why People Play* (1973):

> Play is an artificial category. It is merely part of stimulus-seeking behaviour to which we cannot ascribe a prepotent motive. In trying to set it apart as a watertight category our understanding is clouded with the efforts necessary to seek the discriminants that differentiate work from play. We are led into an artificial dichotomization of the behaviour into work and play, when clearly some behaviour can be both. Any juxtaposition of work and play must be along a continuum with serious or critical behaviour at one pole and behaviour that serves only to maintain arousal and no other effect at the other.[7]

Playing the game

Johan Huizinga, Professor of History at the University of Leyden, spent many years reflecting upon the cultural significance of play. In his book, *Homo Ludens*, translated into English in 1949, he argued that play was older than culture, and had produced key utilitarian devices, including probably the sail and the wheel, as well as many of the fundamental forms of social life. He concluded, indeed, 'that civilization is, in its earliest phases, played. It does not come *from* play like a babe detaching itself from a womb: it arises *in* and *as* play and never leaves it'.[8] Huizinga believed that the play element in Western European culture had reached a peak in the eighteenth century, and declined thereafter in the face of revolution, romanticism and reform. Nevertheless, he did identify something of a rebirth in the second half of the nineteenth century in England, 'the cradle and focus of modern sporting life'.

Iona and Peter Opie's studies of children's games in streets and playgrounds are consistent with Huizinga's general thesis. They show that many games, for example, 'fivestones', 'finger or thumb', 'tug of war', 'hide and seek', 'blind man's buff', have been common across centuries and cultures. Many children's games, moreover, involve considerable social rituals. There is the picking of sides, the choice of roles and of starting, the repetition of rhymes and other established dialogues, the touching, releasing, turning round 3 times, the counting to 50. Such rituals obviated the need for umpires and scorers. There are winners, but games, once completed, have instant restarts in which all are equal once more. The Opies concluded that:

> If a present-day schoolchild was wafted back to any previous century he would probably find himself more at home with the games being played than any other social custom. If he met his counterparts in the Middle Ages he might enjoy games of Prisoners' Base, Twos and Threes, street-football, Fox and Chickens, Hunt the Hare, Pitch and Toss, and marbles, as well as any of the games from classical times; and judging by the illuminations in the margins of manuscripts, he would be a prince among his fellows if he was good at piggy-back fighting.[9]

Many factors contributed to the emergence of England as the 'cradle and focus of modern sporting life'. There were the eighteenth-century village cricketers of Hampshire who played upon Broad Halfpenny Down, and those of Kent who displayed their skills upon the picturesque Sevenoaks Vine. Football, in various forms, had existed for centuries, but the Football Association, established in 1863, drew up the modern rules that helped to transform this free activity into the most popular game in the world. The rules of rugby football, the handling game that originated in 1823 at Rugby School, were similarly codified. In the second half of the nineteenth century team games of this type provided increased opportunities for learning by playing and found particular expression and predominance in boys' public schools. Such schools were usually boarding in character and rurally located. Prior to the onset of this athleticism, boys in public as opposed to private schools had received little supervision outside the actual schoolroom. Exploring the countryside, trespassing, poaching, hunting, fishing, nesting were common pursuits. On occasion, however, school boys turned their sticks and stones upon local inhabitants, their domestic and working animals, livestock and other property, or even upon the school authorities themselves in open rebellion.

Organized games, as introduced by Cotton who became headmaster at Marlborough in 1852, or Vaughan at Harrow, where the famous Philathletic Club was established in 1853, became an essential, even *the* essential element in the life and curriculum of a school. Games were a powerful means of discipline and control, of canalizing excessive energy and exuberance and of keeping the boys within the bounds of the now greatly enlarged playing fields. Most boys, and many masters, doubtless found games infinitely preferable to an otherwise unrelieved diet of classical study. Sporting prowess, indeed, particularly as confirmed by the award of an Oxford or Cambridge 'blue', now became an important qualification for entry into a number of professions, including schoolmastering and the Anglican church.

It was widely believed that the playing fields of a public school were the most appropriate place for a boy to learn to play the game of life. Organized games taught boys to 'play the game': that is to play fair, to strive to win but to accept defeat with grace, to sacrifice personal interest for the good of the side, to respect and where necessary to assume leadership, to develop moral and physical strength and to face danger, whether in the shape of a pack of charging rugby forwards or a demon bowler, without flinching. There was a particular reverence for the spiritual beauty and holiness of cricket; its metaphors grace the published sermons of many a Victorian headmaster and cleric. The qualities so assiduously nurtured on the games field were tested in the acquisition and maintenance of a far-flung Empire, which also provided the perfect means whereby the British sporting gospel could be spread to all corners of the world.

The First World War provided the supreme test of this educational philosophy. In *War Letters of a Public Schoolboy* (1918) Paul Jones declared that:

> Nothing but athletics has succeeded in doing this sort of work [developing team spirit] in England. Religion has failed, intellect has failed, art has failed, science has failed. It is clear why: because each of these has laid emphasis on man's *selfish side*: the saving of his *own soul*, the cultivation of his *own mind*, the pleasing of his *own senses*. But your sportsman joins the Colours because in his games he feels the real spirit of unselfishness, and has become accustomed to give all for a body to whose service he is sworn. Besides this, he has acquired the physical fitness necessary for a campaign. These facts explain the great part played by sport in this War...we suggest that this War has shown the training of the playing-fields and the 'Varsities to be quite as good as that of the classroom; nay as good? Why far better, if training for the path of Duty is the ideal end of education.[10]

A quite different interpretation of playing the game appeared in *The Play Way*, published one year earlier in 1917. Its author, H. Caldwell Cook, a master at the Perse School, Cambridge, believed that the Great War, in spite of the sacrifices made, was essentially 'the biggest business deal on record'.[11] In his view a tragedy of this magnitude should not be seen as a confirmation and celebration of the educational system, but rather as a challenge and a condemnation. Cook's own wartime experiences only reinforced his abhorrence of the stuffiness of classrooms, the autocracy of pedants and the repugnance of learning by spoon feeding. His solutions, however, were arty rather than hearty. He saw the play way as a means and a method, as a journey rather than an arrival, and yet a perpetual journey which became an end in itself. The purpose of play was simply more and better playing. For Cook, the play way was not 'a bunch of contrivances for making scholarly pursuits pleasurable, but the active philosophy of making pleasurable pursuits valuable'.[12] He wanted schools to be replaced by play school commonwealths, bursting with 'freshness, zeal, happiness, enthusiasm'.[13]

The Play Way did not supply a blueprint for the play school commonwealth but centred upon a description of Cook's work at the Perse School. There was the junior republic of Form IIIB (average age 13 years) presided over by a prime monitor and cabinet and the general use of upgraded monitors called 'misters'. Self-discipline was the basic aim; from an early age boys should assume responsibility for their own learning and behaviour. Much of the book is concerned with the study of English and drama, the making of plays, miming and ballads, the giving of lectures. There were 'ilonds', picture maps of imaginary countries, about which boys would write ballads to be bound up in the form of chapbooks. Finally there was 'Playtown', constructed in a concrete back yard by some 60 boys of all ages from 9 to 19. It boasted farms, houses and roads, a river, a lock, a railway, a coal-mine, etc. Many boys played there, and so, too, did some of the masters.

The ideals of democracy and self-discipline, creativity and self-expression, albeit suffused in a warm glow of medieval romanticism, place Cook's concept of learning by playing firmly within the parameters of the modern progressive movement.

The right to play

The year 1961 saw the formation of two important organizations which sought to guarantee the right of children to play. In Britain the National Pre-School Playgroups Association sprang from the initiative of Belle Tutaev who, whilst petitioning the Ministry of Education for state-financed nursery school provision, also suggested that in the short-term mothers might establish their own playgroups. The idea caught on, not least in those more affluent areas where mothers had the confidence, time and expertise to make the necessary organizational and financial arrangements and to participate in supervising the children. In 1983 there were some 14,000 playgroups in England and Wales.[14]

The International Playground Association (IPA) was set up in the same year. Its concern was that children should have full opportunities for play, not only in formal playgrounds but also in the home environment, at school and in other institutions including clinics and hospitals, and in the community at large. In 1977, in preparation for the United Nations' International Year of the Child, the IPA formulated the 'Malta Declaration of the Child's Right to Play'.

> The Malta Consultation declares that play, along with the basic needs of nutrition, health, shelter and education, is vital for the development of the potential of all children.
>
> The child is the foundation for the world's future.
>
> Play is not the mere passing of time. Play is life.
>
> It is instinctive. It is voluntary. It is spontaneous. It is natural. It is exploratory. It is communication. It is expression. It combines action and thought. It gives satisfaction and a feeling of achievement.
>
> Play has occurred at all times throughout history and in all cultures. Play touches all aspects of life.
>
> Through play the child develops physically, mentally, emotionally and socially. Play is a means of learning to live.

The Consultation is extremely concerned by a number of alarming trends, such as:

1   Society's indifference to the importance of play.
2   The over-emphasis on academic studies at school.
3   The dehumanising scale of settlements, inappropriate housing forms; such as high-rise, inadequate environmental planning and bad traffic management.

4 The increasing commercial exploitation of children through mass communication, mass production, leading to the deterioration of individual values and cultural tradition.

5 The inadequate preparation of children to live in a rapidly changing society.[15]

Conclusion

In conclusion, therefore, playing is widely recognized as an essential, perhaps *the* essential, means of learning for young children, including those at home, in play-groups, nursery, infant and other primary schools. Nevertheless, attempts by professional educators and parents to urge this as a priority in relation to the modern urban environment, in such matters as housing, playgrounds and other leisure and traffic-free areas, have met with little response.

Huizinga's thesis that play as an element of culture declined from the eighteenth century may be related, in England and Wales at least, to the development of an urban and industrialized culture suffused with the seriousness of Evangelical Christianity. In the second half of the nineteenth-century play in prestigious boys' public schools and elsewhere found a particular expression in team games, a pheno-menon that today is virtually world wide. In the second half of the twentieth century this has been paralleled to some extent by the development of simulation and computer games.

The most significant area for the development of learning by playing, however, is surely at the adult level and especially in affluent societies. The removal of time-work discipline from those whose working roles have been relocated to a personal environment, downsized, suspended or ended may provide opportunities for restoring an element of play, fun and self-fulfilment to human civilization.[16] Such a change would doubtless enable learning by playing for the young to receive a much higher priority as well. Education for and through leisure and learning by playing are well connected.

Notes

1 P.K. Smith (ed.), *Play in Animals and Humans*, Oxford: Basil Blackwell, 1984, provides a useful introduction to this topic.
2 H. Spencer, *Principles of Psychology*, New York: Appleton, 3rd edn 1898.
3 E.C. Tolman, *Purposive Behavior in Animals and Men*, New York: Appleton, 1932.
4 K. Groos, *The Play of Man*, New York: Appleton, 1901.
5 C. Darwin, *The Origins of Species by Means of Natural Selection*, London: John Murray, 1859.
6 See M.J. Ellis and G.J.L. Scholtz, *Activity and Play of Children*, Englewood Cliffs, NJ: Prentice-Hall Inc., 1978, pp. 127–8.
7 M.J. Ellis, *Why People Play*, Englewood Cliffs, NJ: Prentice-Hall Inc., 1973, p. 109.
8 J. Huizinga, *Homo Ludens: A Study of the Play-element in Culture*, London: Routledge and Kegan Paul, 1949, p. 173.
9 I. Opie and P. Opie, *Children's Games in Street and Playground*, Oxford: Clarendon Press, 1969, p. 7.
10 Quoted in J.A. Mangan, *Athleticism in the Victorian and Edwardian Public School*, Cambridge: Cambridge University Press, 1981, p. 196.
11 H.C. Cook, *The Play Way*, London: Heinemann, 1917, p. ix.
12 Ibid., p. 8.
13 Ibid., p. 366.
14 Information kindly supplied by the National Pre-School Playgroups Association. For a recent assessment of the Association and its significance see H. Penn, 'Round and round

the mulberry bush; the balance of public and private in early education and childcare in the twentieth century', in R. Aldrich (ed.), *Public or Private Education? Lessons from History*, London: Woburn Press, 2004, pp. 89–90.

15 Reproduced in full in P.F. Wilkinson (ed.), *In Celebration of Play*, London: Croom Helm, 1980, pp. 14–17.

16 For a recent analysis of the changing nature of work see J. White, *Education and the End of Work: A New Philosophy of Work and Learning*, London: Cassell, 1997.

CHAPTER 13

APPRENTICESHIP IN ENGLAND

An historical perspective

A. Heikkinen and R. Sultana (eds), *Vocational Education and Apprenticeships in Europe – Challenges for Practice and Research*, Tampere: Tampereen Yliopisto, 1997, pp. 71–97

Introduction

Apprenticeship is one of those institutions, in common with the university and parliament, which has a history stretching back at least to medieval times. Such longevity immediately suggests a host of basic questions to the historian. Why has apprenticeship lasted so long? What basic human need or needs does it fulfil? Has it fulfilled the same function across the centuries or been subject to considerable changes? Has it, indeed, been a catch-all term to describe a variety of practices which have been, and remain, essentially different? These and other issues are considered in this chapter which is organized in four parts. The first provides a basic identification of the key elements of apprenticeship in medieval and early modern England. The second is concerned with the impact upon apprenticeship of the first industrial revolution, and highlights the pupil-teacher apprenticeship scheme of the second half of the nineteenth century. The third period focuses upon the twentieth century. Finally, some conclusions are drawn.[1] Such periodization, with its emphases upon the last two centuries, is somewhat at variance with traditional historical divisions. As a recent article has rightly suggested:

> When historians consider 'apprenticeship', they often generalize in terms of three extended periods. These may broadly be characterized as that of 'guild apprenticeship', let us say from about the twelfth century to 1563, with the state underpinning much practice; the period of statutory apprenticeship, from 1563 to 1814 (with guilds slowly attenuating); and finally a great diversity of forms which might be summarized as 'voluntary' apprenticeship, often agreements between employers and unions, from 1814 to the present day.[2]

Medieval and early modern

It would appear that the essential elements of apprenticeship in medieval England were consistent with those that existed in other European countries. Apprentices (who were usually male) were bound by indentures to a master for a term of years, commonly seven, and invariably between five and nine, while they were initiated into the theory and practice and other mysteries associated with a particular occupation. Parents (or other guardians) of the apprentice paid a premium and signed a contract of articles with the master which specified the conditions of service. While premiums varied considerably, those for entry to prestigious occupations might be very high indeed. Apprentices were provided with food, clothing, shelter and instruction by the master, and in return worked for him during the term of their apprenticeships. The system, which was enforced both by custom and by law, was certainly flourishing by the fourteenth century and was applied to a range of occupations. These included both manual and professional pursuits. Although the main emphasis, both historically and conceptually, has been upon the former, it is important to note here that many of the principles and practices of apprenticeship as applied to the university (with its master's degree), to medicine and to the law, were to continue into the modern period. In the England of the twentieth century the training of doctors and lawyers, and the status and roles of partially and newly qualified staff in these professions, have continued to exhibit apprenticeship characteristics.

Two pieces of legislation from the Elizabethan period, the Statute of Artificers of 1563 and the Poor Law Act of 1601, indicate the two main species of apprenticeship which had emerged by that time. On the one hand was the classic system inherited from the guilds of the medieval period, which indeed provided much of the administrative machinery for the former act. The Statute of Artificers prescribed that written indentures were to be drawn up for each apprentice, and that no person should exercise a craft or trade until at least a seven-year apprenticeship had been served and the age of 24 attained. Even entry to apprenticeship in certain occupations was to be denied to those who could not boast parents of the appropriate condition and status. This requirement was not necessarily as restrictive as might first appear, because in certain crafts the habit had grown up of apprenticeships being restricted to the sons or other relatives of masters. Such restrictions in respect of family membership, though enforced by custom rather than by law, continued in some occupations, for example, those of dockers and printers, until the twentieth century. A ratio was also established between the numbers of apprentices and journeymen, for example, each master with three apprentices was compelled to keep one journeyman. This stipulation was introduced both to guard against the possibility of apprentices simply being used as cheap labour and to furnish some role models and guidance in addition to that provided by the master. Justices of the Peace, who also had the authority to determine wages in many occupations, were required to ensure that the statute was being obeyed. These provisions of 1563 reflected the recognition by central government of the importance of apprenticeship and of the need to regulate it, both in the general interest of social, economic and political stability, and in the particular interests of consumers, producers and the very apprentices themselves.

The 1563 Act, however, also contained other clauses which were to be extended in 1597 and finally consolidated in the Poor Law Act of 1601. These set out a different model – that of parish apprenticeship. Parish apprenticeship was designed to transfer immediate responsibility for illegitimate and orphaned children, and those of vagrants, paupers or criminals, from the parish and local justices to local employers and residents. Thus the Act of 1601 empowered 'Churchwardens and Overseers ... by the assent of any Two Justices of the Peace ... to bind any such children ... to be Apprentices, where they shall see convenient.'[3] From 1662, when apprenticeship also afforded the right of settlement, it was sometimes in the interests of parish authorities to send their young charges as far away as possible.

In the medieval and early modern periods, therefore, apprenticeship was widely used. But while skilled crafts and trades, for example, those of cabinet makers and grocers, recruited almost entirely through indentures freely entered into by both parties, occupations of low status or some danger – farm labourers, menial household servants, brickmakers, chimney sweeps – were supplied from parish apprentices.

Industrial revolution

During the seventeenth and eighteenth centuries social and geographical mobility, population increases and the development of new occupations, made serious inroads into both the concept and the practice of apprenticeship. The details of eighteenth-century legislation have been well summarized by Joan Lane who has shown how parliamentary statutes of 1709, 1747, 1757, 1766, 1768, 1780, 1788, 1792 and 1793 reflected the continuing regulatory concerns of successive governments.[4] The purposes of this legislation ranged from the raising of governmental revenue by a tax on premiums, to combating some of the more common abuses of the system, both by masters and by apprentices themselves.

The Act of 1563 was finally repealed in 1814, and in her seminal study of 1912 Olive Dunlop[5] saw this event as marking the end of the true period and nature of apprenticeship. It is difficult to determine precisely what was lost at this point, for apprenticeship continued both in name and in a variety of practices throughout the nineteenth and twentieth centuries. Five elements may be suggested: the loss of a continuity with the medieval tradition provided by the legislation of 1563; the abandonment of the mutually binding nature of the indentures; a diminution in the breadth of the master's responsibilities, which had formerly extended both to occupational instruction and moral supervision, as well as to board and lodging in his own premises; an increase in the scale of operations which led to the withdrawal of the master from immediate supervision of the workshop and its trainees; an increase in the numbers of occupations for which little skill or training was required.

It is clear that the changes that took place in England at the turn of the eighteenth and nineteenth centuries, changes characterized by industrialization, urbanization and population explosion, were accompanied by considerable changes in apprenticeship. Nevertheless, the name and many of the original concepts and practices (albeit in modified context and form) survived into the new era. Traditional apprenticeships continued in many occupations and were added to and redefined in others. For example, Charles More has suggested that 'In the second half of the century, what I will call new-style apprenticeship was associated in particular with five growing industries: engineering, iron-shipbuilding, building, woodworking and printing.'[6] The complexity of the situation is shown by the fact that in some trades apprenticeships were still necessary for some sectors of the operation, for example, to ensure the production of good quality furniture and clothing, while goods for the mass market might be produced by unskilled labour by means of modern machinery.

The fate of parish, pauper or factory apprentices under the impact of the industrial revolution excited considerable, though belated, contemporary attention. The factories, mills, mines and workshops of early nineteenth-century England had an apparently insatiable appetite for child labour. Accordingly, cartloads of children were despatched from various parts of England to the industrial areas. There they were maintained, as apprentices had always been – fed, clothed and housed – but frequently worked very hard indeed and without either training or hope of advancement. Three features of this type of apprenticeship which proliferated during the early years of the industrial revolution may be noted. First, children were sent to industrial occupations by parishes whose principal motive was to be rid of them so that they would no longer be a charge on the rates. Second, although a premium might be paid by the parish, on occasion apprentices were virtually bought by employers who had no interest in teaching them skills and mastery of a trade, but simply wanted to use them as cheap labour. Third, there was no intention that these apprentices would become masters themselves. When their apprenticeships were ended, the young people, far from being equipped to find a job, might find themselves supplanted by the next batch of juveniles.

In 1802 the seriousness of this situation was recognized when an Act for the Preservation of the Health and Morals of Apprentices and Others employed in Cotton and other Mills and Cotton and other Factories was placed on the Statute Book. This legislation, which applied to cotton and wool mills with three or more apprentices, stated that:

> Every apprentice shall be instructed in some part of every working day for the first four years at least of his or her apprenticeship . . . in the usual hours of work in reading, writing and arithmetic or either of them according to the age and abilities of the apprentice, by some discreet and proper person to be provided and paid for by the master or mistress of such apprentice . . .[7]

Three elements in this legislation may be noted here. First, it placed the responsibility for instruction upon the mill owner; second, the instruction was to be of a general kind, rather than specifically devoted to the occupation; third, these provisions were rendered largely ineffective by the absence of any proper inspectorate. Not until 1833 were the first government factory inspectors appointed; not until the 1870s was legislation extended to cover all occupations; not until 1880 were all children in England required to attend school. Compulsory schooling, indeed, was to be another crucial factor in redefining the nature of apprenticeship.

Nevertheless, one important new link between the worlds of schooling and apprenticeship was created on the initiative of central government. This was the pupil-teacher system begun in 1846, under which boys and girls aged 13 were bound to a 5-year apprenticeship. These apprentices received a basic payment of some £10 per year, rising by increments of £2.10 shillings per year to a maximum of £20. During their five years of apprenticeship pupil teachers taught in schools, and received extra instruction from the master or mistress of the school at the beginning or end of the school day. On completion of their apprenticeships pupil teachers would either leave teaching altogether, proceed to a teaching post in a school, or go on to a training college in order to acquire a teaching certificate.

In the second half of the nineteenth-century pupil teachers, who were annually inspected by one of Her Majesty's Inspectors (HMIs), were essential to the staffing of elementary schools in England. At times, indeed, they constituted about a quarter of the whole teaching force. In the last 20 years of the nineteenth century the system underwent significant modification as the larger school boards established centres in which pupil teachers could receive structured education and training in groups, rather than at the hands of individual headteachers in separate schools. These pupil-teacher centres proved to be very effective means of instruction, as measured by the performance of their students in the highly competitive Queen's scholarship examinations.

From the beginning of the twentieth century, however, the numbers of pupil teachers rapidly declined. Several reasons may be adduced for this change. First, there was a growing belief that the education of a large percentage of the children of the country should not be directed by those who were little more than children themselves. Second, since from 1902 there were maintained grammar schools which offered free secondary education to able pupils, there was no need for the pupil-teacher apprenticeship to serve as a substitute for secondary schooling. Third, the decline in the birth rate reduced the numerical pressures on schools. Fourth, the development of teachers' unions and professional associations from

1870 and the establishment of local education authorities (LEAs) as employers from 1902, helped to make teaching a more stable career and one in which increasing numbers of people, both men and women, would be prepared to spend their whole lives.

Technical education provided a further extension of, and challenge to, apprenticeship. Pupil-teacher centres indicated that some elements in the apprenticeship of prospective teachers could be more effectively supplied outside the schools themselves. Similarly it became apparent that some elements, for example, basic scientific and technical knowledge necessary for other forms of apprenticeship, could be supplied more efficiently in the classroom than in the workplace. In England, however, provision of technical education was and remained poor. Writing of the situation in the second half of the nineteenth century, Andy Green has drawn attention to the failures of English apprentices, and shown how a commentator such as Silvanus Thompson, in his study *Technical Education: Apprenticeship Schools in France* (1879), contrasted the repetitive and unimaginative drudgery of an English apprenticeship with the combination of theoretical and practical training provided in the French trade schools. As Green has rightly maintained, in England 'apprenticeship was often of dubious efficacy and rarely sought to train beyond the level of basic practical skills'.[8] By contrast, students in French trade schools, as Thompson argued:

> are more methodical and intelligent in their work, steadier in general conduct, have a far better grasp of the whole subjects, and are pronounced to be more competent than the average workman at executing repairs, since they have learned the principles and have not been kept doing the same thing...all through the years of their apprenticeship.[9]

Explanations of this failure either to adapt the old apprenticeship system or to replace it with something better, have been many and various. Some have blamed the general anti-industrial ethos exemplified in the rural, classical culture of the landed elites and many of the intelligentsia. Others have placed the responsibility at the door of those industrial and commercial entrepreneurs whose successes in the first industrial revolution were secured without any scientific and technical training themselves or recourse to a highly skilled workforce. The triumphs of the Great Exhibition of 1851 produced a mood of confidence in British industrial and commercial might which stood firm against the warnings of such commentators as Thomas Huxley, Lyon Playfair and Bernhard Samuelson. In the third quarter of the nineteenth century, there were neither the incentives nor the mechanisms in place for employers to develop substantial technical and scientific schemes of training at local, regional or national levels. Others, again, would emphasize the reluctance of central governments to intervene in this sphere. Such reluctance stemmed from a general anxiety about interfering in economic matters for fear of upsetting the free operation of the market, an anxiety which affected not only the area of general economics, but also that of education itself. In consequence, the Department of Science and Art, established in 1853 at South Kensington in the wake of the Great Exhibition, remained separate from the Education Department until 1899, and had to proceed by a haphazard and supplementary system of examinations and grants.

Twentieth century

The last 20 years of the nineteenth century have been identified, in relative terms, as a 'golden age' for vocational education in England. This was manifested in a relaxation in hostility towards central intervention, the authorization of local authority expenditure on technical studies, and the development of institutes and polytechnics. In this situation apprenticeship was strengthened and sustained, and in a volume entitled *Skill and the English Working Class, 1870–1914* (1980) Charles More calculated that in any single year in the early twentieth century there were some 350–400,000 apprentices in the United Kingdom.[10] Apprenticeship still dominated recruitment to engineering fitting, and to many areas of building, ship-building and printing. In 1906 the largest groups of apprentices were in building (100, 200) and engineering (94, 100), and More suggests that in this year 21 per cent of all working males between the ages of 15 and 19 were serving apprenticeships.[11]

Nevertheless it was generally perceived, and the perception was to be heightened during two world wars, that in comparison with many of their European counterparts, British workers, including those who had undergone apprenticeships, were still less competent both in general theoretical, and in the more specifically practical, elements of their work. Although a national system of awards, the ordinary and higher national certificates and diplomas, backed both by government and professional bodies, was introduced in the 1920s, a part-time, evening approach still prevailed in the technical field. Product standards were frequently inferior in comparison to those of goods produced in other countries. Some luxury items apart, the label 'Made in Britain' began to acquire a negative connotation. In the second half of the twentieth century criticisms of, and explanations for, the failure of apprenticeship in England current in the third quarter of the nineteenth century, were still being repeated.

In 1948, a Central Youth Employment Executive was created under the terms of the Employment and Training Act of that year, while in 1958 an Industrial Training Council was established by the British Employers' Confederation, the Trades Union Congress and the boards of the nationalized industries. Apprenticeship places were increased by some 25 per cent and a number of useful training manuals produced, but vast areas of commercial and administrative work had no apprenticeship schemes.[12] Indeed, a survey carried out by the Acton Society Trust in the 1950s found that fewer than one in five managers had any professional qualification at all.[13] Some notable attempts were made to improve upon this situation. For example, Wednesbury College pioneered commercial apprenticeship programmes from 1946, while a Commercial Apprenticeship Scheme of the Chambers of Commerce provided a five-year course of vocational education combined with practical training.[14] Successive governments encouraged apprenticeship schemes by means of exhortations and grants, but in her classic study, *Apprenticeship in Europe: The Lesson for Britain*, published in 1963, Gertrude Williams, Professor of Social Economics in the University of London, was still able to write that 'there exists no legislation whatever governing industrial training. The apprenticeship schemes in operation derive from collective agreements between employers' organisations and trade unions and have no legal sanction or supervision'.[15]

The Industrial Training Act of 1964 sought to remedy this situation, and by 1970 29 boards had been established to oversee the industrial training and education of some 16 million employees. Different apprenticeship patterns emerged for different occupations. For example, in engineering the general pattern was of a one-year general training followed by specialist studies. Post Office engineers, however, underwent a three-year apprenticeship which had two years of general training followed by one of a specialist nature. Apprentices in motor mechanics eschewed general studies and worked towards a specific national craftsman's certificate. While it was argued that such diversity was a useful means of tailoring apprenticeships to the needs of specific occupations, many other traditional weaknesses, including those of age entry restrictions and time-serving, continued. Employers, such as the Post Office, complained that their apprentices, once trained, would secure jobs in private firms whose ability to pay higher wages depended in part upon their unwillingness to provide apprenticeships themselves. Criticisms of the 1964 Act mounted in the 1970s,[16] while comparative studies also continued to reinforce the view that the existing apprenticeship and other training arrangements were not working well. In 1975, some 16,000 mechanical and engineering qualifications were awarded at craft level in Britain, as opposed to 51,000 in France and 78,000 in West Germany. In 1987 the respective figures were 12,000, 68,000 and 89,000.[17]

New initiatives of the 1980s included those promoted by the Manpower Services Commission (MSC), a body established in 1973 but used by the Conservative governments of Margaret Thatcher to ensure that there should be no unemployed youngsters between the ages of 16 and 18. The basic principle of this agency was that all such young people who were neither in education nor employment 'should have the opportunity of training, or participation in a job creation programme, or work experience'.[18]

The Youth Opportunities Programme (YOP) was the first such scheme and in 1983 was replaced by the more ambitious Youth Training Scheme (YTS). This guaranteed a year's work experience, off-the-job training and a weekly allowance of £25 to all unemployed 16- and 17-year-old school-leavers. In 1986, a two-year programme was introduced, with greater emphasis upon educational achievement in vocational, core and personal areas.

YOP and YTS were national, centrally directed forms of modern apprenticeship which did much to combat juvenile unemployment in the short term. But the problems of these schemes were two-fold. The first was that some employers used YOP and YTS trainees as a form of cheap labour, in place of adult workers; the second that the great majority of participants in YOP and YTS ended their one or two years of training with no recognized or marketable qualifications. In some senses these schemes were the twentieth-century equivalents of parish apprenticeship. In the second half of the 1980s, an appreciation of their deficiencies led to a series of radical changes in organization and administration. The central body, the MSC, was replaced by a Training Agency (TA), while employer-led Training and Enterprise Councils (TECs) were established at the local level. In 1990 responsibility for the former YTS, now simply known as Youth Training (YT), was transferred to these bodies.

In 1986 the problem of vocational qualifications was tackled by the establishment of a National Council for Vocational Qualifications (NCVQ). Five levels of vocational qualifications were established, from basic to postgraduate. While some of these were specific to particular types of work (NVQs), others, General National Vocational Qualifications (GNVQs), covered broader areas of occupation.

By the early 1990s, both the terminology and practice of apprenticeship in England appeared to be largely a thing of the past, and confined to a single area of industry. An international survey of 1994 declared that:

> In Anglo-Saxon countries, apprenticeship of young people in companies has survived mainly in the building trade. In these countries education policies during the 1960s and 1970s concentrated on developments in general and academic education, while large numbers of young people continued to enter the labour market without recognised qualifications.[19]

The same survey, however, also concluded that in such countries no satisfactory substitute for apprenticeship had been produced. It was generally critical of efforts to develop partnership between employers and schools, commenting that 'due to the marked decentralisation, the absence – or weakness – of collective organisation by employers and relatively low commitment of unions...these efforts remain more isolated and less "systematic" than those in continental Europe'.[20]

One response to such criticisms was the Modern Apprenticeship initiative, begun in 1994. Modern Apprenticeships were industry-designed frameworks offering training in technician, craft and supervisory skills at least to NVQ 3 (equivalent to two GCE A levels) with progression to NVQ 4 (equivalent to a first degree). The original plans were drawn up by a consortium consisting of government, TECs and Industry Training Organizations (ITOs). By the end of 1996 some 40,000 young people had begun Modern Apprenticeships and although, during the prototype phase, only one in eight apprentices was female, by 1996 this had become one in four. Over 50 per cent of entrants to Modern Apprenticeships had achieved five or more GCSE passes at grade C or better.

In some ways Modern Apprenticeships represented a significant advance over previous initiatives such as YOP or YTS, not least in being tied into the new national system of vocational qualifications. Changes in employers' attitudes were demonstrated by the fact that almost two-thirds of those involved with Modern Apprenticeships had not been providing training to NVQ level 3 a year before, and that 90 per cent of apprentices now have employed status. Some problems, however, were also apparent. These included a difficulty in securing the participation of smaller firms, and a more general reluctance on the part of all firms in the general service sector, both large and small, to become involved. The term and concept of apprenticeship were still strongly identified in the minds of public, employers and potential apprentices themselves, with the notion of craft apprenticeship – with the making or servicing of durables such as domestic appliances or cars. By 1996 only 4 per cent of 21-year olds had achieved NVQ level 3 through a work-based route.[21]

Conclusion

Several conclusions may now be drawn.

The first, in answer to those questions raised in the opening paragraph, is that apprenticeship has survived in some form or forms across the centuries because it was originally composed of many elements that lay at the centre of human existence. Changes across the centuries have led to a concentration upon some of those original elements to the neglect of others. Apprenticeship as it existed as an ideal (though not always as a reality) from the twelfth to the seventeenth centuries was a most substantial phenomenon indeed, which encompassed social, occupational, educational, religious, familial, group and legal dimensions. It was a central core, both formal and informal, which impinged in a variety of ways upon individuals – males and females, young and old alike – and upon communities large and small. Centrality and variety were exemplified by the parish apprentices, whose lives were lived under similar but more stringent structures to those experienced by their more fortunate contemporaries. Informal apprenticeships seem to have operated particularly in respect of girls, for example in the case of handywomen. Informal apprenticeship in this area was ended by the Midwives Act of 1936 which restricted the right to deliver babies to qualified midwives. Even less formal and more secretive were the apprenticeships of those who trained to be abortionists.

The early years of the nineteenth century saw the legislation of 1563 finally overturned, the replacement or re-designation of many traditional occupations, and a new and even more stringent set of structures within which many parish or factory apprentices were located. Such legal and economic changes, however, were accompanied by social changes, including changes in traditional arrangements for social welfare which, in the long run, were to prove equally damaging to the traditional elements of apprenticeship. The relationship between apprenticeship and the right of settlement, that is to say the right to receive welfare at the hands of the parish, was particularly important in the period between 1662 and the introduction of the new poor law in 1834. Discussion of this topic has often focused upon the desire of parish authorities to offload their potential claimants (the parish apprentices) upon another area. But equally important was the positive side of that relationship. As Snell has argued:

> A parish... operated in the security that time expended in training young people within its parochial boundaries was likely to be of future benefit to itself. The close dependency between apprenticeship, settlement, employment, poor relief, rate-paying, access to local raw materials and means of production guaranteed this.[22]

A third point concerns a relatively neglected cause of the decline of apprenticeship in the nineteenth and twentieth centuries – that of a fundamental change in the nature and location of education. The integrated nature of education as expressed through apprenticeship, whereby the master was responsible for the total well-being of the apprentice's health, morals, religious observance, literacy, occupational skills, etc., was replaced by a division of labour. The nineteenth century witnessed industrialization, urbanization and population explosion, but it also saw the decline of the educative family and the rise of the schooled society. Education itself was subjected to a division of labour, so that it became accepted that some skills would be learned at home, others at school and others again in employment. Considerable benefits accrued from these developments, and universal schooling provided some guarantees against the evils of widespread ignorance and premature employment. In contrast apprenticeship, linked through settlement to the notion of small self-sufficient enclaves and the maintenance of the social, economic and political status quo, a system which required young people to reside in a master's household, and in that further enclosed environment to acquire all manner of skills, might well appear anachronistic and outdated. Not surprisingly those arch advocates of national and social efficiency, Sidney and Beatrice Webb, opposed it in the strongest terms, arguing in 1919 that:

> undemocratic in its scope, unscientific in its educational methods, and fundamentally unsound in its financial aspects, the apprenticeship system, in spite of all the practical arguments in its favour, is not likely to be deliberately revived by a modern democracy.[23]

Whereas the all-embracing nature of apprenticeship had its disadvantages, subsequent problems in respect of education and employment in England were frequently seen as stemming from fragmentation, coupled with poor standards of provision and performance. In the 1990s, there were some seven million people in the United Kingdom without any qualifications at all. The United Kingdom ranked 24th in the World Economic Forum league of workforce skills, while the overall performance of its education system was placed only 35th out of 48 countries.[24] The 1994 World Competitiveness Report on the availability of skilled labour put the United Kingdom only 18th out of 23 countries, while an IMF Competitiveness Report placed the United Kingdom 19th out of 22 countries for in-company training.[25]

The causes of such low standards of performance are many and complex, and these figures themselves, some of which are quoted from one side of the political spectrum, must be balanced by other perceptions that employment rates and economic prospects are better in the United Kingdom than in many other countries. Nevertheless, it is not difficult to point to uncoordinated and unfulfilled government policies in the areas of apprenticeship and broader vocational training. Indeed the reluctance of central governments to intervene in these areas, as opposed to frequent interventions in respect of mainstream schooling, is most noticeable. After 1945 there was an acute failure either to develop technical and vocational schools (the third element in a supposedly tripartite system) or to implement radical changes in respect of apprenticeship of the type which took place in West Germany. Even those clauses in the 1944 Education Act that required the establishment of county colleges and the implementation of compulsory continuation education to 18, were never put into effect.

While the pupil-teacher system rapidly declined in the first decade of the twentieth century, in the last decade apprenticeship methods of training – learning by doing on the job under the control of skilled practitioners – saw a remarkable resurgence. In contrast to changes in other occupations such as nursing where the apprenticeship model continued to decline, central government directives and initiatives strengthened the practice. The term 'teacher training' supplanted that of 'teacher education' and was enshrined in the very names of such bodies as the Teacher Training Agency. Students on one-year courses must spend two-thirds of their time in schools rather than in institutions of higher education. Indeed, those students enrolled under a School-Centred Initial Teacher Training scheme may spend all of their time in schools.

Finally, the potential of apprenticeship to reach and inspire across the ages must be acknowledged. In a speech to a conference entitled 'Modern Apprenticeships in Action', held in London in April 1994, Valerie Bayliss stated that:

> In Penzance in 1459 an apprenticeship was reckoned to last for eight years. We have made a great deal of progress since then, and time-serving will not be an element in Modern Apprenticeships. But, to aim (in the words of the fifteenth century) to 'teach, train and inform' strikes me as not a bad watchword for what we are now trying to do in not a twentieth-century but, I hope, a twenty-first-century way.[26]

Notes

1 I am most grateful to my colleagues, David Crook, Andy Green and Susan Williams for their comments on an earlier draft of this paper.
2 K. Snell, 'The apprenticeship system in British history: the fragmentation of a cultural institution', *History of Education*, 1996, 25(4): 303.
3 Quoted in J. Lane, *Apprenticeship in England, 1600–1914*, London: UCL Press, 1996, p. 3.
4 Ibid., pp. 4–5.
5 O.J. Dunlop, *English Apprenticeship and Child Labour: A History*, London: T. Fisher Unwin, 1912.

6 C. More, *Skill and the English Working Class, 1870–1914*, London: Croom Helm, 1980, p. 43.
7 Quoted in M. Sanderson, 'Education and the factory in industrial Lancashire, 1780–1840', *Economic History Review*, 1967, XX(2): 267.
8 A. Green, 'Technical education and state formation in nineteenth-century England and France', in A. Heikkinen (ed.), *Vocational Education and Culture: European Prospects from History and Life-history*, Hämeenlinna: Tampereen Yliopisto, 1994, p. 69.
9 S.P. Thompson, *Technical Education: Apprenticeship Schools in France*, London, 1879, p. 44, quoted in Green, op. cit., p. 87.
10 More, op. cit., p. 64.
11 Ibid., pp. 99, 103.
12 For a summary of the situation in this period see A. Beveridge, *Apprenticeship Now*, London: Chapman and Hall, 1963.
13 H. Harman, *Commercial Apprenticeship*, London: Pitman, 1958, p. 8.
14 Ibid., p. 46; E. Tonkinson *et al.*, *Commercial Apprenticeships*, London: University of London Press, 1962, pp. 18–25, 49–54.
15 G. Williams, *Apprenticeship in Europe: The Lesson for Britain*, London: Chapman and Hall, 1963, pp. 3–4.
16 E. Venables, *Apprentices Out of Their Time*, London: Faber and Faber, 1974, pp. 128–38.
17 H. Steedman and A. Green, *Educational Achievement in Britain, France, Germany and Japan: A Comparative Analysis*, London: Institute of Education, 1993, p. 44.
18 P. Ainley and M. Corney, *Training for the Future: The Rise and Fall of the Manpower Services Commission*, London: Cassell, 1990, p. 40.
19 OECD, *Apprenticeship: Which Way Forward?*, Paris: OECD, 1994, p. 9.
20 Ibid., p. 11.
21 G. Kinnock, *Could Do Better – Where is Britain in the European Education League Tables?*, London: National Union of Teachers, 1996, pp. 44–5.
22 Snell, op. cit., p. 311.
23 Quoted in Snell, op. cit., p. 318.
24 Kinnock, op. cit., p. 15.
25 Ibid., p. 25.
26 'Modern apprenticeships: a conference report', *Insight*, 1994, 30: 13.

CHAPTER 14

FAMILY HISTORY AND THE HISTORY OF THE FAMILY

R. Aldrich (ed.), *Public or Private Education? Lessons from History,* London: Woburn Press, 2004, pp. 127–43

Introduction

Family history is no doubt as old as human history itself. Indeed it has been argued that just as the family was the oldest and most basic unit in society, so family history was 'the ancestor and root of all other forms of historical enquiry'.[1] Nevertheless there has been no single historical model of the family. Indeed, a recent estimate identified 'as many as two hundred different arrangements that Europeans and Americans now regard as legitimate "family"'.[2] Nor should families be placed exclusively within the private sphere. In 1973 Barbara Laslett adduced a considerable amount of evidence in support of the hypothesis that in the United States the private family 'is a modern development which has only occurred within this century'.[3]

Families are not only concerned with history, the doings of their contemporaries and forbears, but with education and knowledge, both private and public. Over the centuries children have learned their first social and cultural skills, from toilet training to speech, within a family context. During the modern period, however, in England as in many other parts of the world, the concept of the educative family was complemented or replaced by the rise of the schooled society. This chapter locates family history, including its dimensions of knowledge and education, within a variety of contexts, both private and public.

It is divided into three sections. The first deals with the 'public' dimensions of what is here referred to as 'the history of the family'. The second examines the 'private' sphere – family history as represented by research undertaken by individuals into their own families. The next section provides a case study by means of an examination of an aspect of the author's family history. Finally some conclusions are drawn. These relate to the problems and possibilities of reconciling private and public knowledge in respect of family history and to its potential role in histories of education and of knowledge.

Public: the history of the family

Examples of family history in England can be traced from the later middle ages. The major era for the formation of hereditary English surnames has been placed between 1250 and 1450. This chronology has a general acceptance in the 'Western' world. Thus a conference on surnames that took place at Lyons in France in December 1998 was 'limited to those European and North American societies in which surnames were established, according to codified rules, before the sixteenth century; and which had records allowing for the study of the transmission of surnames over generations'.[4] In England in the fifteenth century John Rous made a collection of more than 50 genealogies, while William Worcester listed the pedigrees of ancient Norfolk families. Such lists of names and dates were soon complemented by more substantial studies. In the sixteenth century, the Elizabethan Society of Antiquaries, which included leading historians, William Lambarde and John Stow, provided an impetus to further work, for example the production of county histories.[5] Another famous Elizabethan scholar, the antiquary and historian, William Camden, best known for his survey, *Britannia*, first published in 1586, provided an important account of the formation and development of surnames. Motives were mixed. While some scholars sought to produce objective works of reference, other studies were conducted by, or on behalf of, family members for the specific purpose of legitimizing power and influence, enhancing their family status and of confirming (sometimes spurious) claims to land and property. In England during the later sixteenth century, a fashion arose not only of constructing elaborate family trees, but also of displaying them as works of art.[6]

The late nineteenth and early twentieth centuries saw significant advances in historical study in England. Amateur and antiquarian approaches to the study of the past came under attack. The recognition of history as a public discipline, conducted in accordance with generally recognized rules and conventions, was aided by such developments as the foundation of the *English Historical Review* in 1886 and the establishment of important schools of history at the newer universities, most notably London and Manchester. Some prospective schoolteachers received training in the teaching of history, which from the 1870s became an accepted subject in the higher classes of elementary schools. Government regulations of 1904 made it a compulsory subject at secondary level. The Historical Association, founded in 1906, provided a forum in which members from these different constituencies could pool their professional historical expertise. Its first council included 11 university staff, 9 from secondary schools and 4 from training colleges.

Prior to the 1960s, practitioners of the public discipline of history dealt mainly with public events and public figures. Biographical studies might encompass both the 'life and work' of such public figures and even, on occasion, as with Lytton Strachey's *Eminent Victorians* (1918), highlight some of their foibles. In general, however, the lives of ordinary people and of their families were not believed to be appropriate subjects of study for professional historians. Nor was the family itself. This was partly because such matters were considered to be essentially private, and of private interest. Concerns also existed about the nature and extent of possible sources. In 1960 the situation changed dramatically with the publication of Philippe Ariès, *L'Enfant et la vie familiale sous l'Ancien Régime*.[7] Henceforth childhood and the family, two of the most private dimensions of human existence, would become legitimate subjects of study for professional historians. They would also become part of the public discipline that is history. Thus following an international conference held at Clark University in November 1985, Tamara K. Hareven, editor of the *Journal of Family History*, could not only look back with some pride at the contributions made by the journal during the first ten years of its existence, but also declare that 'The time has come, therefore, to assess twenty years of research in this field, and to identify the main goals of future research.'[8]

Although on occasion the term, 'family history', was employed to describe the work of both amateur and professional historians, a division was also apparent between what came to be known as 'family history' on the one hand, and 'the history of the family', on the other. For example, in 1980 in a short work entitled, *Approaches to the History of the Western Family 1500–1914*, Michael Anderson, Professor of Economic History at the University of Edinburgh, noted that 'Over the past twenty years family history has been one of the main growth areas in the development of social history'.[9] As his title indicated, however, for Anderson family history did not mean the investigation of an individual family by one of its members, but rather research by university-based professionals into the family as an historical phenomenon. Other academic writers stressed the interdisciplinary nature of the history of the family. Thus in a contribution to an important collection of essays of 1973, all of which had originally appeared in the *Journal of Interdisciplinary History*, Hareven argued that 'the history of the family utilizes the tools of demography and the conceptual models of anthropology, psychology, and sociology'.[10]

Anderson identified four broad approaches to the history of the Western family in the modern era – psychohistory, 'the demographic, the sentiments and the household economics'.[11] He also associated each of these approaches with particular groups of professional historians and their publications.

Thus the work of the psychohistorians, to which Anderson gave very short shrift indeed, was exemplified by *The Journal of Psychohistory* and Lloyd de Mause's edited volume of 1974.[12] The demographic approach to the history of the family was traced to family reconstitution studies emanating from France from the mid-1950s. This approach, which was based upon the accumulation of data from such sources as parish registers and tax returns, was associated with the *Société de Demographie Historique*, established by Louis Henry in 1966. It was exemplified in the United Kingdom by the Cambridge Group for the History of Population and Social Structure. Peter Laslett and other professional historians associated with this group were not particularly interested in the details of individual families. Their prime aim was the collection and analysis of banks of data in order to pose and answer questions about the size and composition of households and families in general.[13]

As Anderson acknowledged in 1980, data collected by the demographers clearly provided a much sounder basis for the historical study of the family than previous unsystematic and impressionistic accounts that drew upon very limited evidence. Nevertheless, sophisticated interpretation of these statistics would require them to be located within appropriate socio-economic settings. Members of the household economics group sought to interpret data about households and families 'in the context of the economic behaviour of their families'.[14] Anderson used the themes of inheritance, peasant family economy and the proletarianization of labour to review the work of these scholars.[15]

The sentiments approach, which concentrated upon continuities and changes within the meaning of families, was not so readily identified with groups of historians or particular projects. Matters of sentiment such as modes of child-rearing, attitudes towards love, sex and illegitimacy, the very concept of privacy within the family itself, were less susceptible to statistical accumulation and analysis. Nevertheless, the key texts identified by Anderson as representative of this school, for example, Philippe Ariès, *Centuries of Childhood* (1962),[16] and Edward Shorter, *The Making of the Modern Family* (1975),[17] also emanated from professional historians.

Both books proved to be highly contentious and generated a series of responses. Ariès gained support from those who agreed that there was no real concept of childhood in the middle ages and that childhood was subsequently 'invented', for example, in the late eighteenth and early nineteenth centuries by writers such as Rousseau and Blake who replaced the concept of original sin with that of children's innocence. An alternative view was that there were many concepts of childhood across the centuries, while parents' attitudes towards their children were governed as much by individual circumstance and temperament as by general concepts.[18]

Shorter's work provoked even more controversy. Few doubted its importance. Ariès declared it to be 'truly excellent...a powerful synthesis presented with a logical rigor and grace rare among historians',[19] while Anderson referred to it as 'an immensely stimulating book'.[20] Nevertheless Anderson also declared *The Making of the Modern Family* to be 'marred by a distracting style, some grossly inflated generalisation on the basis of minimal data (sometimes used out of context) and an over-emphasis on vaguely conceptualised cultural causation'.[21] In the preface to the paperback edition Shorter, Professor of History at the University of Toronto, noted that he had expected his work, conceived in 'the frosted glass of my ivory tower', to have been read by 'a somnolent audience of historians picking away at minute quarrels in the remoter reaches of the library stacks'. Instead, to his surprise, he found that he had 'landed in a hornet's nest of feminists, Marxists and caretakers of academic prose'.[22]

Over the last 20 years, interest among professional historians in the history of the family and of childhood has continued. Further levels of sophistication have been introduced. For example, in an important volume published in 1989 Carol Dyhouse examined feminist thinking about the family during the period 1880 to 1939. In the introduction, she noted that historical studies of feminism in England in the late nineteenth and early twentieth centuries had tended to concentrate on public issues such as the suffrage movement and educational reform rather than on the private domain of the family. Her examination of women's experiences of family life, their economic independence within the family, domestic organization and marital relationships was based upon exhaustive research into a wide range of sources. Nevertheless, the private nature of family history or the history of the family continues to pose considerable challenges for professional historians. Dyhouse concluded that 'large areas of women's experience in the family remain shadowy'.[23] The relationship between women's history and the history of the family is an intriguing one and too substantial to be considered in detail here. Nevertheless, Dyhouse's analysis of the different historiographical trajectories of these two fields in respect of private and public has been confirmed by other studies. For example, Louise A. Tilly conducted a systematic analysis of the content of articles published in the period between 1976 and 1985 in the *Journal of Family History*, three 'self-defined feminist or women's studies journals' and four general historical journals. She concluded that 'women's history, unlike family history, is movement history: it is closer to more central historical fields'.[24]

The professional historian who contributes to the public discipline of history is also a private individual, a member of a family. For example, Edward Shorter dedicated his book to the memory of his grandparents. At first sight, *A World of Their Own Making: Myth, Ritual, and the Quest for Family Values* by John R. Gillis, although dedicated to his wife, sons and a daughter-in-law, is also a public piece, a history of the family rather than family history. The first of the book's three parts surveys the meanings of family and home 'before the modern age'; the second the 'Victorian origins of modern family cultures'. Part three is entitled 'mythic figures in the suburban landscape'; the conclusion is devoted to 'remaking our worlds' in the context of 'myths and rituals for a global era'. Yet, as Gillis explained in a prologue, as a professional historian he had no intention of writing such a book: 'I did not seek out the subject; it was something that found me.'[25] At Christmas 1991, the death of a son in a flying accident confronted the Gillis family, who had no religious affiliations, 'with the task of creating and performing a ritual entirely of our own making, a remembrance of Ben that would recall the dimensions of his life and spirit'.[26] It also left Gillis, himself, who belatedly recognized his lack of family involvement and many deficiencies as a parent, with an acute sense of guilt. *A World of Their Own Making* ranged widely over time and space, but it did so in order to examine the appropriateness or otherwise of current myths and rituals. The book was Gillis's 'way of contributing to a process of cultural reconstruction that I regard as vital to our future as families and to the creation of more caring communities'.[27]

No doubt the majority of scholarly publications in the field of the history of the family proceeded from the academic or personal interests of their authors. Others, however, were written in support of specific courses. For example, *From Family Tree to Family History* (1994), edited by Ruth Finnegan and Michael Drake, was produced as part of an Open University course (DA301) entitled 'Studying family and community history: 19th and 20th centuries'. This was an honours level undergraduate course designed for part-time adult distance learners. The prime purpose of this volume, which served both as academic text and 'active workbook', with short questions, exercises and questions for research, was to equip such students with the skills and understanding required to enable them to complete a project in family or community history.[28] With Finnegan and Drake's definition of family history as 'something wider than genealogy' the very title, *From Family Tree to Family History*, might usefully serve as an epitome of the history of family history in England across the centuries. In the context of this chapter and volume, however, its principal significance lies in the editors' attempt to bring private and public dimensions together by encouraging students to link 'work on a single family into findings about families in general'.[29]

Thus in England from the 1960s academic historians, principally located within institutions of higher education, were to the fore in historical studies of the family. By the 1970s, interest in the history of the family had been extended to schools and institutions for the training of teachers. Curriculum innovations flourished at this time, many of them under the auspices of the Schools Council, which between 1964 and 1978 funded 172 curriculum development projects. In the preface to their influential volume, *Family History in Schools* (1973), Don Steel and Lawrence Taylor acknowledged the contribution of several of these projects to studies of the contemporary family. Although less emphasis had been placed upon its history, on the basis of their research with teachers in six primary and five secondary schools in Berkshire and Hampshire, Steel and Taylor made substantial claims for the value of family history in schools, arguing that:

> Family history has important implications for interdisciplinary work and for the relationship of the school to parents and the community at large. History is about people and for the child we have found no better approach to the past than through the study of his own people, his family.[30]

Steel and Taylor acknowledged that developments in history in schools, as for example with social history, often followed a generation after they had achieved credence in academic circles. They were also aware of academic studies of the history of the family.[31] Nevertheless, their emphasis upon educational justifications for family history in schools led them to question whether the normal sequence of events would be reversed and that in this instance 'it will be the teachers who will show the historians the validity of the approach?'.[32] For many teachers in schools, family history was seen as being consistent with contemporary educational philosophy and psychology. Steel and Taylor argued that family history provided motivation and relevance for children, in that it proceeded from their own experience. It was also comprehensible, because it dealt with a small unit over a recognizable time span, or series of time spans, which began in the present. Educational and historical benefits would go hand in hand. Children would no longer be mere recipients of historical facts handed down by teachers and textbooks. Nor would they simply engage in projects of historical research into topics to which answers had already been provided. Family history would provide a curriculum element in which the pupil 'is not only an authority, but can be a unique authority, an idea which has great appeal for children'.[33] Thus, in addition to its general educational rationale and benefits, family history was advocated as the most appropriate means of introducing school pupils to the skills of the historian and to an appreciation of the relationships between historical evidence and historical facts.

Developments from the 1960s and 1970s in the history of the family in higher education and of family history in schools may be situated within two broad contexts. The first was a general democratization and liberation of British society. Traditional institutions and hierarchies were questioned as never before and family life was revolutionized by the contraceptive pill and divorce legislation. The second context was the establishment of new universities (including the Open University) polytechnics and comprehensive secondary schools. Many staff in these institutions were keen that the study of history should reflect contemporary social changes, both in terms of curriculum content and of teaching methods. In 1964 social and educational changes were complemented at the political level when, after 13 years of Conservative governments, the 'fourteenth Earl of Home' was replaced as Prime Minister by the 'fourteenth Mr Wilson'.[34]

Private: family history

The private dimensions of family history are to be found principally in the work of numerous individuals who engage in research into their own families. As indicated in the previous section, such amateur studies of family and local history can be traced back to the early modern period. They received a boost in the nineteenth century when historical societies flourished at county, town and other local levels, often producing their own journals or annual transactions. The Society of Genealogists was founded in 1911.

Writing in 1973, Steel and Taylor identified a post-Second World War surge in interest, with a sharp rise in the numbers of do-it-yourself genealogical manuals from 1953 and an increase in membership of the Society of Genealogists, from some 650 members in 1948 to more than 3,000 in 1972.[35] The main growth of family history in the United Kingdom, and elsewhere, however, occurred during the last quarter of the twentieth century, so that by 1987 David Hey could claim with some justification that 'family history has become England's fastest-growing hobby'.[36] He also noted that 'Genealogy used to be a rather snobbish pursuit but nowadays all that has changed.'[37] By the start of the twenty-first century the Federation of Family History Societies, formed in 1974 and granted charitable status in 1982, had a membership of some 200 societies throughout the world, including national, regional and one-name groups.[38]

Explanations for the growth of interest in family history and in the numbers of family historians may be divided into two broad categories. The first relates to interest and context; the second to means.

Why are we interested in our ancestors? In some cultures the veneration of ancestors is marked annually, as in Mexico on the Day of the Dead, or in Vietnam on the Day of Lost Souls. No doubt many people experience a natural human curiosity about their origins and forbears. There is a pioneering excitement in discovering information which no one has known before. The search for a family past may also be interpreted as a search for oneself. Whether such a concern about family identity, both past and present, has been increased or diminished by late-twentieth-century modern society is more difficult to determine. In our contemporary, highly mobile, globalized world people are less likely than in previous ages to live all their lives in traditional locations within an immediate family context. They may, therefore, research their family history for the particular purpose of securing an increased awareness of their own location both in time and space – 'roots within the unending cycle of the past, and something to hold on to in the confusions of the present'.[39] There is no conclusive evidence, however, that highly mobile, modern societies have a greater interest in family history than traditional populations. For example, those who occupied the same houses and tilled the same soil over the centuries might have had just as keen an interest, an interest expressed in a private and less visible way, by the recounting of family tales and the recording of names in the family bible.

Contextual features, therefore, must also be taken into account. The democratization of English society in the 1960s and 1970s, referred to in the previous section, was one factor. Genealogy and family history were no longer regarded as being the exclusive (or predominant) preserve of the nobility and gentry. A second was the decline in the influence of other institutions – religious, communal and national – which had supplied the myths and rituals which constrained and supported individuals in previous times. A third was the increased amount of leisure time enjoyed by some groups in society, including those retired from paid employment and others for whom the management of a house and/or household no longer occupied as much time as formerly.

As for means, a vast array of facilities, both public and private, has been generated in support of family history and family historians. As David Hey has argued, 'The sheer bulk of the archives in national and local repositories gives English people and those of English descent a decided advantage over the inhabitants of most other lands. These immense collections are now available for everyone to consult'.[40] For example, the Family Records Centre (FRC) in Myddelton Street, London, EC1, is a joint facility and service provided by the Office for National Statistics (ONS) and the Public Record Office (PRO). The plethora of PRO publications produced to assist family historians include a newsletter, *The Family Record*, and glossy magazine, *Ancestors*. These are supplemented by fact sheets, pocket guides, specialist works, for example William Spencer's, *Air Force Records for Family Historians* (2000), and general guides such as Amanda Bevan (ed.), *Tracing Your Ancestors in the Public Record Office*, which reached a sixth edition in 2002. Another indication of the numbers of family historians and the range of available support is provided by *The Family and Local History Handbook*, edited by Robert Blatchford. The 2002 edition listed more than 300 national, local, genealogical, specialist and one-name family history societies within the United Kingdom alone. Australia supplied a further 126, Canada 107 and New Zealand 29.[41] The *Handbook* also included more than 150 advertisements from individuals, companies and other organizations offering to assist family historians in their research.

Family historians have also benefited greatly from the more general developments in communications. Between them the computer and the internet have revolutionized the capacity to acquire and transmit information. The computer provides both access to archives and other sources, and the facility for the rapid reception and transmission of large amounts of information. Even the circular letters chronicling the family deeds of the past year which have increasingly come to accompany Christmas cards can now (like the cards themselves) be instantly transmitted to family and other members around the globe.

An indication of the potential value (and problems) of the internet for family historians occurred in 2002. On 2 January the 1901 Census, a complete list of the 32.5 million inhabitants of England, Wales, the Channel Islands and the Isle of Man who were at home on 31 March 1901, comprising 1.5 million pages of census enumerators' books, was placed on-line. Over a period of five days no fewer than 1.2 million users per hour attempted to access the census website.[42] Not surprisingly, the system crashed. No doubt numbers of visitors to the site were swollen as a result of major features about the 1901 Census which appeared in national newspapers. Many family historians were furious, and reacted angrily to the PRO's pleas for understanding and patience. Their anger was directed at prohibitive online costs, 'a tax on knowledge', 'just another tax on genealogy, something else for the family historian to pay for' and at the chronic underestimate of interest and demand. A British Telecom spokesman described the situation as 'selling 20 million tickets for a stadium with 20,000 seats'.[43] Correspondents to the *Family Tree Magazine* for February 2002 condemned 'a typical British cock-up which just about everybody except those offering the service foresaw', wondered at the failure to appreciate 'the keen interest that would be generated', and called on those responsible to be sacked or at least have the courage to resign.[44] This incident shows that, as yet, the fastest-growing hobby in the land continues to grow.

Personal: George Aldrich

This section examines a brief fragment of the work of an amateur family historian whose elder son is an historian by profession. Its purpose is to provide further perspectives on the relationships between private and public with reference to the construction of family history and the acquisition and ownership of knowledge and education.

My father, George Arthur Aldrich (hereafter George), was born in February 1910 and died in January 1999. The eldest of three boys, his second brother, Charles, died tragically in Guy's Hospital in 1922 at the age of nine following an accident while playing football. His youngest brother, Arthur, died from cancer in 1967 at the age of 52. George's wife, Kathleen, also born in 1910 whom he married in 1934, predeceased him in October 1995. George was a survivor in every sense. Supremely self-sufficient in mind and body until suffering a stroke a few months before his death, in his final years George took it upon himself to become the family historian. He compiled an elaborate family tree, listed family photographs and memorabilia and produced a short draft autobiography.[45]

George's father, also George, was born in 1886 and killed in action in Belgium in November 1917. The eldest of six brothers and a 'Saturday night soldier', as the members of the Territorial Army were popularly known, he joined up when war was declared. Three other brothers, Fred, Arthur and Benjamin, also served in the army during the First World War and another, Charles, in the navy. Jack, the youngest, was not of military age. George grew up with but hazy memories of his father. There was not much to remind him – a couple of faded photographs and a few cards sent home from the trenches. The last one, a 'Souvenir de Belgique' embroidered with the year 1917 composed of the flags of the allied nations, said simply 'To George from Dad 12/9/17 B.E.F.'. Enclosed in the card pocket was a smaller card printed with the words 'Forget me not'. On the reverse, the young soldier had written 'With my Best Love and Wishes to you all, George'. On an embroidered card to his wife, 'A Kiss from France', bearing the same date, he had written 'To Annie From George. With Best Love'.

Early in December 1917 Annie received official notification that her husband, Gunner G. Aldrich of 279 Siege Battery, Royal Garrison Artillery, had been killed in action on 12 November 1917.[46] A separate brief letter written by Major Allen, George's commanding officer, informed her that 'he was struck by a shell splinter and was rendered unconscious so he suffered no pain. We are all sorry to lose him. May he who protects the widow and orphan assist you in your great grief.'

Prior to her marriage in 1909 Annie Smith, like her mother before her, had been in service. The remainder of Annie's life would consist of a perpetual struggle against poverty and hardship, making ends meet on a war widow's pension supplemented by a mere 6d a week from her husband's former employers, the Civil Service Company, where George had worked in the grocery department. Her main stay in this struggle would be her eldest son, George, who at the age of seven became the 'man of the family' and an important breadwinner.

In 1917 Annie and her three young sons were living at 22G Peabody Buildings, in Southwark Street at the junction with Southwark Bridge Road.[47] The 12 Peabody blocks were four stories high. Each level comprised four or five flats, a large wash/drying room, two lavatories and two sinks with cold taps. The buildings were lit by gas, the mantles on the landings being turned on by the porter from a control on the ground floor. Two boys were employed to light the lamps from a taper, with each boy responsible for six blocks. For several years George, who was both agile and reliable, was one of these boys and bounded up and down stairs every evening. Fitness and speed were essential because by the time he reached the sixth block the residents would be complaining of the smell and fumes from the gas. Not surprisingly George attributed his subsequent prowess as an athlete and gymnast in large part to this daily 'training'. His lamplighting duties made him well known to the Peabody Buildings residents, many of whom needed immediate access to the City or West End at the beginnings or ends of the normal working day. These included market workers, office cleaners and entertainers, even music hall and opera singers, who were markedly unpopular with other tenants on account of their 'practising scales all day'. George's other money-making activities included helping the men with teams of tow horses who assisted drivers of heavy vehicles struggling to surmount the steep rise on the south side of London Bridge. His main Saturday job, however, when slightly older but still at school, was to deliver *The Handy Shipping Guide*, a publication showing the movement of ships for the coming week, to City of London offices concerned with imports and exports. This was hard physical work, staggering under a heavy kitbag loaded with books, but the job was well paid and generous tips could be expected at Christmas time.

George's early formal education was at Christ Church School in Blackfriars Road. In 1922, he passed entrance and scholarship examinations for St Olave's Grammar School, then at the south side of Tower Bridge, and for the Borough Polytechnic School in the Borough Road. He chose the latter, taking a three-year, full-time day course and obtaining a first-class diploma in electrical engineering with distinction in workshop practice.[48] He remembered the strict discipline at Christ Church School where the cane was liberally used, and the influence of a number of outstanding teachers at the Borough Polytechnic, including his form master and mathematics teacher, Dr W.N. Rose. The author of mathematical text books and a keen motor cyclist, Rose believed in setting practical exercises, for example, problems based on results in the annual Tourist Trophy motorcycle races in the Isle of Man. Practical activities in woodwork and metalwork included the making and maintenance of tools, some of which George retained throughout his long life. On leaving the Polytechnic George began work as an instrument maker for GEC at their factory in North Wembley. The expense of fares combined with the impossibility of travel during the General Strike of 1926, however, soon convinced George to seek employment nearer to home. Thus he became a telecommunications engineer, his first job being at the Royal Manual Telephone Exchange in Cheapside where he worked a 48 hour week exclusive of meal times. On finishing his full-time course at the Borough Polytechnic George had been awarded an 'Evening Exhibition', enabling him to continue his studies part-time. This he did, gaining Ordinary and Higher National Certificates in electrical engineering with first-class passes once more.[49] He was also an avid reader of technical periodicals and purchased components to make his first crystal set and radiogram. George retired from Post Office Telecommunications in 1972, having attained the rank of Area Engineer.

George's formal schooling and subsequent part-time studies were instrumental in providing qualifications which underpinned his highly successful career in telecommunications. But his initial interest and confidence in practical matters stemmed from the influence of a substitute father figure, the porter in Peabody Buildings for whom George daily lit the lamps. It was he who taught George a range of useful household and potentially money-making skills, for example, how to change a tap washer or repair a broken sash cord.

George's contributions to the family income, physical fitness and competence in practical matters were complemented by a confident manner and charitable approach. As he readily acknowledged, 'from an early age I became "bossy"'. Such bossiness, however, was frequently put to work in good causes. Thus George became senior sixer in the Wolf Cubs, troop leader in the Scouts and then a Rover 'Mate'. He was to the fore in organizing Scout camps under the patronage of the local MP for North Southwark, Edward Strauss. He also became a server at Southwark Cathedral, where he had previously attended Sunday School and been confirmed.[50] His mother was a devout member of the Church of England and in return for various housekeeping duties secured a move to a Church property in Victoria Place in connection with an order of nuns. This modest terraced property, approached by a paved entrance under an arch from Union Street, Southwark, represented a distinct advance over Peabody Buildings. There was the principal use of a front sitting room, which also doubled as a 'quiet place' for clergymen and a transit lounge for girls passing through London from one main line station to another. The family also had sole use of a kitchen with inside tap and sink, two upstairs bedrooms and an outside lavatory. George's commitment to those whom he considered less fortunate than himself increased, and he became a helper with the Church Army. One of his major duties was to collect men sleeping rough on the Victoria Embankment and direct them to the hostel for homeless men in Waterloo Road where they could obtain free bed and breakfast for a limited period.[51]

Three points may be made in concluding this section. The first is that a small part of George Aldrich's life history, hitherto a matter of private concern, has by its inclusion in this book entered into a more public sphere.[52] The second is that George's account of his early years provides an important insight not only into his education, both familial and formal, but also into his understanding of what knowledge was of most worth. It confirms many of the points raised by Susan Williams in the previous chapter about the mother's role in education in respect of basic literacy, domestic economy and attitudes and values.[53] Finally it is clear that the construction of George's life history, as represented in his autobiography, has been shaped by different conceptions of its historical significance. For George, the most memorable incidents in his life were the famous people whom he met, not least the fact that, 'During the war Mr Churchill spoke to me on a number of occasions, not always politely, about my work.' The final version of his autobiography, however, was modified by my comments about the importance and interest of more everyday matters – living conditions, money-making activities, the formal and informal acquisition of knowledge and of education.

Conclusion

Five brief conclusions may now be drawn.

The first is that family history is of long standing and has principally been part of private knowledge. Second, during the latter half of the twentieth century in England, as in many other countries, there was a veritable explosion in family history. This explosion had both public and private dimensions. In the public sphere the history of the family became a matter for professional historians, both in higher education and in schools. The private dimensions of family history, however, soon came to predominate once more. The greater numbers of family historians of a private nature led both to the creation of specialist public facilities such as the FRC, and to a variety of private and public commercial provision, including search services and family history fairs.

There were some common features between private and public spheres. For example, both family historians and historians of the family were soon served by specialist journals, and both had strongly international frames of reference. Nevertheless, considerable differences also existed. Some professional historians and archivists looked askance at family historians and shuddered at the perceived naivety of their questions and working practices. In a preface to the 1977 paperback edition of *The Making of the Modern Family* Edward Shorter recounted the criticisms of his book including the charge that 'I "pitch it low in the trough" in order to appeal to readers who aren't professional historians.'[54] Ten years later David Hey encouraged family historians to 'widen their interests', arguing that family history was 'in the same state of antiquarian development as local history was (with some outstanding exceptions) a generation or two ago'.[55]

In the twenty-first century, however, in family history, as in many other spheres of human activity, there is increasing evidence of a narrowing of the private and public divide. Archive projects such as AIM25 (Archives in London and the M25 Area) which offers networked access to the archives of some 50 institutions of higher education and other colleges and societies in the London area, provide the opportunity for a greater interaction between private and public approaches to knowledge and to education than ever before.[56] The Clergy of the Church of England Database 1540–1835 (CCED), a project also based at King's College, London, will be available by internet to all researchers, including family historians. One of the most unusual features of this project is its use of amateur researchers.[57]

Finally, as the account of George Aldrich's life indicates, family and individual life histories of a private nature can complement traditional public histories of education which concentrate upon such issues as educational legislation, finance and the provision of formal schooling. For George, as for countless other boys whose fathers were killed in the First World War, from the age of seven his education consisted primarily in the assumption and fulfilment of the role of 'man of the family'.

Notes

1 D.J. Steel and L. Taylor, *Family History in Schools*, London: Phillimore, 1973, p. 5.
2 Quoted in J. Gillis, *A World of Their Own Making: Myth, Ritual, and the Quest for Family Values*, Cambridge, MA: Harvard University Press, 1997, p. 238.
3 B. Laslett, 'The family as a public and private institution: an historical perspective', *Journal of Marriage and the Family*, 1973, 35(3): 480.
4 See the Introduction to *The History of the Family: An International Quarterly*, 2000, 5(2): 154, a special issue edited by Guy Brunet and Alain Bideau entitled 'Surnames – history of the family and history of populations'.
5 D. Hey, *Family History and Local History in England*, London: Longman, 1987, p. 5.
6 D. Hey, *The Oxford Guide to Family History*, Oxford: Oxford University Press, 1998, p. 3.
7 P. Ariès, *L'Enfant et la vie familiale sous l'Ancien Régime*, Paris: Plon, 1960.
8 See the Introduction to the *Journal of Family History*, 1987, 12(1–3): ix, a special tenth anniversary commemoration issue entitled 'Family history at the crossroads: linking familial and historical change'.
9 M. Anderson, *Approaches to the History of the Western Family 1500–1914*, London: Macmillan, 1980, p. 13.
10 T. Hareven, 'The history of the family as an interdisciplinary field', in T. Rabb and R. Rotberg (eds), *The Family In History: Interdisciplinary Essays*, New York: Harper & Row, 1973, p. 213.
11 Anderson, op. cit., 1980, p. 15.
12 L. de Mause (ed.), *The History of Childhood*, New York: Psychohistory Press, 1974. See also the *History of Childhood Quarterly: The Journal of Psychohistory*, founded in 1973, which in 1976 became *The Journal of Psychohistory*.
13 See, for example, P. Laslett (ed.), *Household and Family in Past Time*, Cambridge: Cambridge University Press, 1972, and E. Wrigley and R. Schofield, *The Population History of England 1541–1871*, London: Edward Arnold, 1981.
14 Anderson, op. cit., 1980, p. 65.
15 Examples cited included his own M. Anderson, *Family Structure in Nineteenth Century Lancashire*, London: Cambridge University Press, 1971; and J. Goody *et al.* (eds), *Family and Inheritance: Rural Society in Western Europe 1200–1800*, Cambridge: Cambridge University Press, 1976.
16 P. Ariès, *Centuries of Childhood: A Social History of Family Life*, Harmondsworth: Penguin, 1962, originally published as *L'Enfant et la vie familiale sous l'Ancien Régime*, Paris: Plon, 1960.
17 E. Shorter, *The Making of the Modern Family*, New York: Basic Books, 1975.
18 This is a gross over-simplification of what has become a very complex debate. See, for example, H. Cunningham, *The Children of the Poor: Representations of Childhood since the Seventeenth Century*, Oxford: Blackwell, 1991; H. Hendrick, *Children, Childhood and English Society 1880–1990*, Cambridge: Cambridge University Press, 1997; L. Pollock, *Forgotten Children: Parent–Child Relations from 1500 to 1900*, Cambridge: Cambridge University Press, 1983; S. Shahar, *Childhood in the Middle Ages*, London: Routledge, 1990.
19 Shorter, op. cit., paperback edn, 1977, book cover.
20 Anderson, op. cit., 1980, p. 85.
21 Ibid.
22 Shorter, op. cit., 1977 edn, p. xiii.
23 C. Dyhouse, *Feminism and the Family in England, 1880–1939*, Oxford: Basil Blackwell, 1989, p. 6.
24 L. Tilly, 'Women's history and family history: fruitful collaboration or missed connection?', *Journal of Family History*, 1987, 12(1–3): 303.

25 Gillis, op. cit., p. ix.
26 Ibid., p. x.
27 Ibid., p. xi.
28 R. Finnegan and M. Drake (eds), *From Family Tree to Family History*, Cambridge: Cambridge University Press in association with The Open University, p. x.
29 Ibid., p. 1.
30 Steel and Taylor, op. cit., p. 1.
31 Ibid., pp. 5–6.
32 Ibid., p. 175.
33 Ibid., p. 8.
34 In the 1960s, the Conservative Party leader, Sir Alexander Douglas-Home, who in 1951 succeeded to the title of the fourteenth Earl of Home, responded to a gibe from the Labour Party leader, Harold Wilson, by referring to him as the fourteenth Mr Wilson.
35 Steel and Taylor, op. cit., p. 20.
36 Hey, op. cit., 1987, p. xii.
37 Ibid.
38 For a useful introduction to the last category see D. Hey, *Family Names and Family History*, London: Hambledon and London, 2000.
39 Finnegan and Drake, op. cit., p. ix.
40 Hey, op. cit., 1998, p. 1.
41 R. Blatchford (ed.), *The Family and Local History Handbook*, York: The Genealogical Services Directory in collaboration with the British Association for Local History, 2002, pp. 260–72.
42 '1901 Census Online', *Ancestors*, 2002, 6: 4.
43 Quoted in M. Armstrong, '1901 Census online launch sunk on first day. Researchers demand availability in other formats', *Family Tree Magazine*, 2002, 18(4): 4. See also articles and commentaries on the 1901 Census in *Ancestors*, *Family History Monthly* and *Practical Family History*.
44 *Family Tree Magazine*, 2002, 18(4): 4–5.
45 Much of the information in this section is derived from discussions with George during his compilation of an unpublished manuscript, 'My Life as a Telecommunications Engineer'.
46 His body now lies in the Oxford Road Cemetery in Weltje, within the city boundaries of Ypres.
47 George Peabody (1795–1869) an American philanthropist established himself in London in 1837 and contributed more than a million and a half pounds to charitable works. The Peabody Trust was set up in 1862 to provide housing for the working classes of London.
48 George stated that his initial preference for the Borough Polytechnic was confirmed when at interview the Headmaster of St Olave's made fun of his surname. For the background to the Borough Polytechnic, see E. Bayley, *The Borough Polytechnic Institute: Its Origin and Development*, London: Elliot Stock, 1910.
49 For several years after the Second World War at the invitation of Dr Rose, by then head of the mathematics department, George taught mathematics part-time for City and Guild and National examinations at the Borough Polytechnic.
50 His father's name is included on the memorial to the fallen of the First World War at the East End of the Cathedral.
51 In the 1920s there were large numbers of unemployed men and women who travelled to London in search of work.
52 For a classic example of how the story of three generations of an 'ordinary' family became part of the public domain see M. Forster, *Hidden Lives: A Family Memoir*, London: Viking, 1995. For a recent discussion of many of the issues raised by autobiographical and biographical studies, life histories and oral history in the history of education, see *History of Education*, 2003, 32(2), especially the contributions by Philip Gardner and Jane Martin.
53 S. Williams, 'Domestic science: the education of girls at home', in R. Aldrich (ed.), *Public or Private Education? Lessons from History*, London: Woburn Press, 2004, pp. 116–26.
54 Shorter, op. cit., 1977 edn, p. xiv.
55 Hey, op. cit., 1987, p. 265.
56 For further information see the website, www.aim25.ac.uk (accessed on 10.5.2005).
57 For further information see the website, www.kcl.ac.uk/humanities/cch/cce/ (accessed on 10.5.2005).

LIST OF PUBLICATIONS

Books and monographs

Sir John Pakington and National Education, Leeds: University of Leeds, 1979.
An Introduction to the History of Education, Sevenoaks: Hodder and Stoughton, 1982 (Chinese edition, 1987).
Education: Time for a New Act?, London: Institute of Education, 1985 (with P. Leighton).
Dictionary of British Educationists, London: Woburn Press, 1989 (with P. Gordon).
Education and Policy in England in the Twentieth Century, London: Woburn Press, 1991 (with P. Gordon and D. Dean).
History in the National Curriculum, London: Kogan Page, 1991 (editor).
School and Society in Victorian Britain: Joseph Payne and the New World of Education, New York: Garland, 1995 (paperback edition, Theydon Bois: College of Preceptors, 1995).
Education and Cultural Transmission, Gent: CSHP, 1996 (*Paedagogica Historica* Supplementary Series II) (co-edited with J. Sturm, J. Dekker and F. Simon).
Education for the Nation, London: Cassell, 1996 (Japanese edition, 2001).
In History and in Education: Essays in Honour of Peter Gordon, London: Woburn Press, 1996 (editor).
Biographical Dictionary of North American and European Educationists, London: Woburn Press, 1997 (with P. Gordon).
The End of History and the Beginning of Education, London: Institute of Education, 1997.
The National Curriculum beyond 2000: The QCA and the Aims of Education, London: Institute of Education, 1998 (with J. White).
Faiths and Education, Gent: CSHP, 1999 (*Paedagogica Historica* Supplementary Series V) (co-edited with J. Coolahan and F. Simon).
Education and Employment: The DfEE and its Place in History, London: Institute of Education, 2000 (with D. Crook and D. Watson).
History of Education for the Twenty-First Century, London: Institute of Education, 2000 (co-edited with D. Crook).
A Century of Education, London: RoutledgeFalmer, 2002 (editor).
The Institute of Education 1902–2002: A Centenary History, London: Institute of Education, 2002.
Public or Private Education? Lessons from History, London: Woburn Press, 2004 (editor).

Chapters in books

'W.E. Hickson and the *Westminster Review*, 1840–51', in R. Lowe (ed.), *Biography and Education: Some Eighteenth- and Nineteenth-Century Studies*, Leicester: History of Education Society, 1980.
'New History: an historical perspective', in A.K. Dickinson, P.J. Lee and P.J. Rogers (eds), *Learning History*, London: Heinemann Educational Books, 1984.

'Imperialism in the study and teaching of history', in J.A. Mangan (ed.), *'Benefits Bestowed'? Education and British Imperialism*, Manchester: Manchester University Press, 1988.

'The National Curriculum: an historical perspective', in D. Lawton and C. Chitty (eds), *The National Curriculum*, London: Institute of Education, 1988.

'Elementary education, literacy and child employment in mid-nineteenth-century Bedfordshire: a statistical study', in G. Genovesi *et al.* (eds), *History of Elementary School Teaching and Curriculum*, Hildesheim: Lax, 1990.

'The evolution of teacher education', in N. Graves (ed.), *Initial Teacher Education: Policies and Progress*, London: Kogan Page, 1990.

'The historical dimension' (with D. Dean) in R. Aldrich (ed.), *History in the National Curriculum*, London: Kogan Page, 1991.

'History in the National Curriculum in England: an historical perspective', in A.K. Dickinson (ed.), *Perspectives on Change in History Education*, London: Institute of Education, 1992.

'Discipline, practice and policy: a personal view of history of education', in K. Salimova and E. Johanningmeier (eds), *Why Should We Teach History of Education?*, Moscow: Rusanov, 1993.

'The emerging culture of educational administration: a UK perspective', in Australian Council for Educational Administration, *The Emerging Culture of Educational Administration*, Darwin: ACEA, 1993.

'Vocational education in Britain: an historical and cultural analysis', in A. Heikkinen (ed.), *Vocational Education and Culture – European Prospects from History and Life History*, Tampere: Tampereen Yliopisto, 1994.

'Educational reform and curriculum implementation in England: an historical interpretation', in D.S.G. Carter and M.H. O'Neill (eds), *International Perspectives on Educational Reform and Policy Implementation*, London: Falmer Press, 1995.

'Education and cultural identity in the United Kingdom' (with A. Green) in B. Hildebrand and S. Sting (eds), *Erziehung und Kulturelle Identität*, Münster: Waxmann, 1995.

'Historical perspectives upon current educational policy in England', in A. Heikkinen (ed.), *Vocational Education and Culture – European Prospects from Theory and Practice*, Tampere: Tampereen Yliopisto, 1995.

'Joseph Payne: an international educationist', in C. Wulf (ed.), *Education in Europe: An Intercultural Task*, Münster: Waxmann, 1995.

'History in education', in J. Sturm, J. Dekker, R. Aldrich and F. Simon (eds), *Education and Cultural Transmission*, Gent: CSHP, 1996 (*Paedagogica Historica* Supplementary Series II).

'Apprenticeship in England: an historical perspective', in A. Heikkinen and R. Sultana (eds), *Vocational Education and Apprenticeships in Europe – Challenges for Practice and Research*, Tampere: Tampereen Yliopisto, 1997.

'Education as a university subject in England: an historical interpretation' (with D. Crook) in P. Drewek and C. Lüth (eds), *History of Educational Studies, Geschichte der Erziehungswissenschaft, Histoire des Sciences de l'Education*, Gent: CSHP, 1998 (*Paedagogica Historica* Supplementary Series III).

'Joseph Lancaster: an individual and institutional appreciation', in Núcleo de Análise e Intervenção Educacional (ed.), *Ensaios em homenagem a Joaquim Ferreira Gomes*, Coimbra: University of Coimbra, 1998.

'The role of the individual in educational reform', in C. Majorek, E. Johanningmeier, F. Simon and W. Bruneau (eds), *Schooling in Changing Societies: Historical and Comparative Perspectives*, Gent: CSHP, 1998 (*Paedagogica Historica* Supplementary Series IV).

'Teacher training in London', in R. Floud and S. Glynn (eds), *London Higher: The Establishment of Higher Education in London*, London: Athlone Press, 1998.

'The apprentice in history', in P. Ainley and H. Rainbird (eds), *Apprenticeship: Towards a New Paradigm of Learning*, London: Kogan Page, 1999.

'Education and employment in England: historical perspectives, research and teaching' (with D. Crook) in A. Heikkinen, T. Lien and L. Mjelde (eds), *Work of Hands and Work of Minds in Times of Change*, Jyväskylä: University of Jyväskylä, 1999.

'A contested and changing terrain: history of education in the twenty-first century', in D. Crook and R. Aldrich (eds), *History of Education for the Twenty-First Century*, London: Institute of Education, 2000.

'Educational standards in historical perspective', in H. Goldstein and A. Heath (eds), *Educational Standards*, Oxford: Oxford University Press, 2000 (*Proceedings of the British Academy*, 102).

'Mathematics, arithmetic and numeracy: an historical perspective' (with D. Crook) in S. Bramall and J. White (eds), *Why Learn Maths?*, London: Institute of Education, 2000.

'Education as nationbuilding: lessons from British history', in S. Vaage (ed.), *Education and Nationbuilding*, Volda: Volda University College, 2001.

'Family history and the history of the family', in R. Aldrich (ed.), *Public or Private Education? Lessons from History*, London: Woburn Press, 2004.

'Teacher training, teacher education and pedagogy', in D. Halpin and P. Walsh (eds), *Educational Commonplaces: Essays to Honour Denis Lawton*, London: Institute of Education, 2005.

Journal articles

'H.H. Milman and popular education, 1846', *British Journal of Educational Studies*, 1973, XXI(2): 172–9.

'Radicalism, national education and the grant of 1833', *Journal of Educational Administration and History*, 1973, 5(1): 1–6.

'Facts behind the figures, 1839–1859', *History of Education Society Bulletin*, 1974, 13: 25–9.

'Association of ideas: the National Association for the Promotion of Social Science', *History of Education Society Bulletin*, 1975, 16: 16–21.

'Uncertain vintage: the origins of the Church of England Education Society', *History of Education Society Bulletin*, 1976, 18: 41–3.

' "The growing intelligence and education of the people" ', *History of Education Society Bulletin*, 1978, 22: 48–50.

'Literacy, literacy, semi-literacy and marriage registers', *History of Education Society Bulletin*, 1978, 22: 2–6.

'Sir John Pakington and the Newcastle Commission', *History of Education*, 1979, 8(1): 21–31.

' "National education by rates or taxes…" ', *Journal of Educational Administration and History*, 1980, 12(1): 25–30.

'Sir John Pakington and the Select Committee of 1865–66', *History of Education Society Bulletin*, 1980, 25: 45–50.

'Peel, politics and education, 1839–1846', *Journal of Educational Administration and History*, 1981, 13(1): 11–21.

'Sir John Pakington and education in the West Midlands', *West Midlands Studies*, 1981, 14: 10–14.

'1870: a local government perspective', *Journal of Educational Administration and History*, 1983, 15(1): 22–6.

'Educating our mistresses', *History of Education*, 1983, 12(2): 93–102.

'History of education in schools', *Teaching History*, 1984, 39: 8–10.

'Learning by playing', *Education Today*, 1985, 35(2): 28–36.

'History (of education) at the crossroads', *The Historian*, 1986, 11: 10–14.

'Learning by faith', *Education Today*, 1986, 36(3): 4–14.

'Sunday schools: a research report', *History of Education Society Bulletin*, 1986, 38: 14–17.

'Central issues in history of education: an English perspective', *Canadian History of Education Association Bulletin*, 1987, 4(3): 17–25.

'Interesting and useful', *Teaching History*, 1987, 47: 11–14.

'Renewed school history: an Hungarian perspective', *Teaching History*, 1988, 52: 28–9.

'Student experiences of teaching practice, 1985–6: a study in professional education' (with P. Leighton) *Education Today*, 1988, 38(1): 53–65.

'Class and gender in the study and teaching of history in England in the twentieth century', *Historical Studies in Education/Revue d'Histoire de l'Education*, 1989, 1(1): 119–35.

'A common countenance: national curriculum and national testing in England and Wales', *Policy Explorations*, 1989, 4(1): 1–12. (Published by the University of British Columbia, Canada.)

'School inspection: a research report', *History of Education Society Bulletin*, 1989, 43: 10–12.

'History of education in initial teacher education in England and Wales', *History of Education Society Bulletin*, 1990, 45: 47–53.

'History working group: Final Report 1990', *History of Education Society Bulletin*, 1990, 46: 12–15.

'The National Curriculum: an historical analysis', *Education Today*, 1990, 40(3): 13–17.

'Always historicise? A reply to Keith Jenkins and Peter Brickley', *Teaching History*, 1991, 65: 8–12.

'Mechanics institutes in South-Eastern England: a research report', *History of Education Society Bulletin*, 1991, 48: 11–14.

'Questões de gênero na história da educação na Inglaterra', *Educação em Revista*, 1991, 13: 47–54. (Published by the Federal University of Minas Gerais, Brazil.)

'Educational legislation of the 1980s in England: an historical analysis', *History of Education*, 1992, 21(1): 57–69.

'ERASMUS', *Cambridge*, 1992, 29: 83–8.

'Joseph Payne and the Denmark Hill Grammar School', *Camberwell Quarterly*, 1992, 94: 8–11.

'Joseph Payne and the Mansion Grammar School, 1845–63', *Leatherhead and District Local History Society Proceedings*, 1992, 5(5): 133–7.

'Education in Britain: what went wrong?', *Parliamentary Brief*, 1993, 2(7): 58–60.

'Can schools teach teachers?', *Parliamentary Brief*, 1994, 3(3): 107–8.

'John Locke', *Prospects*, 1994, XXIV(1–2): 61–76.

'Pioneers of female education in Victorian Britain: a research report', *History of Education Society Bulletin*, 1994, 54: 56–61.

'The Real Simon Pure: Brian Simon's four-volume history of education in England', *History of Education Quarterly*, 1994, 34(1): 73–80.

'National and international in the history of education', *History of Education Society Bulletin*, 1995, 55: 7–10.

'Joseph Payne: the College of Preceptors Joseph Payne Memorial Lecture', *Education Today*, 1996, 36(3): 3–7.

'Past and present, private and public in the history of education', *Bulletin of the UK–Japan Education Forum*, 1997, 47–63.

'Teachers in England: their education, training and profession', *Bulletin of the UK–Japan Education Forum*, 1997, 5–22.

'From Board of Education to Department for Education and Employment', *Journal of Educational Administration and History*, 2000, 32(1): 8–22.

'Reflections on the recent innovation of the National Curriculum in England', *Chung Cheng Educational Studies*, 2002, 1(1): 65–89.

'The three duties of the historian of education', *History of Education*, 2003, 32(2): 133–43.

'The training of teachers and educational studies: the London Day Training College, 1902–1932', *Paedagogica Historica*, 2004, XL(5–6): 617–31.

INDEX